ELECT
IN THE
SON

ROBERT
SHANK

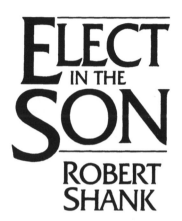

For the grace of God has appeared for the salvation of all men.

TITUS 2:11 RSV

Even so then at this present time also there is a remnant according to the election of grace.

ROMANS 11:5

ELECT
IN THE
SON

ROBERT
SHANK

Elect in the Son
Copyright © 1970, 1989
Robert Lee Shank

Published by Bethany House Publishers
11400 Hampshire Avenue South
Bloomington, Minnesota 55438
www.bethanyhouse.com

Bethany House Publishers is a Division of
Baker Book House Company, Grand Rapids, Michigan.

Printed in the United States of America

Library of Congress Cataloging-in-Publication Data
Shank, Robert, 1918–
    Elect in the Son.

    Reprint. Originally published: Springfield, Mo.: Westcott, 1970.
    Bibliography: p.
    Includes index.
    1. Election (Theology) I. Title.
BT810.2.S5   1989   234'.9   89–14991
ISBN 1–55661–092–0

---

*To Him who loved the Church
and gave Himself for it*

DR. ROBERT SHANK is known internationally among Bible scholars for his significant books in the field of biblical theology, which are used in seminaries and colleges of many denominations. He has been preaching and teaching in the pulpit, classroom, and visiting lectureships for over fifty years and his writings have been viewed as a major doctrinal contribution to the Church.

BOOKS BY THE AUTHOR

Life in the Son
Elect in the Son
God's Tomorrow: The Life Beyond Death
Sources of Power of the Apostolic Witness
Until: The Coming of Messiah and His Kingdom

PREFACE

TEN YEARS have passed since publication of my work *Life in the Son: A Study of the Doctrine of Perseverance.* The book was the outcome of a long, exhaustive study in a problem area of doctrine undertaken for my own satisfaction, with no thought of writing on the question. From the perspective of the years, I may now say that God, as I sincerely believed, was in the writing of the book and the years of study out of which it came.

The doctrine of perseverance is not finally defined until one defines also the doctrine of election. My study of the doctrine of perseverance laid the groundwork for a survey of the doctrine of election. In a footnote in *Life in the Son,* mention is made of a manuscript on the doctrine of election "now in preparation." Much time has been required for completion of the project, and the journey has been unduly lengthened by the disruptions and delays that attend the path of one who, wounded in the house of his friends, has the problem of establishing himself in exile. At long last the task is finished, and the book now goes forth to fulfill the purpose of Him who hitherto has helped.

In retrospect, a word of appreciation and gratitude is due the congregations of two village churches: my dear friends in the Baptist Church of Louisburg, Missouri, who stood by me so faithfully through four difficult years following publication of *Life in the Son* and are still my loyal friends, and my friends in the Christian Church of Billings, Missouri—equally dear—who graciously received me into their fellowship and their pulpit.

A word of profound appreciation is due Dr. William W. Adams, who wrote an introduction for *Life in the Son* (and for the present volume), whose concern for the stewardship of holy truth and for objectivity in the definition of the faith once delivered to the saints outweighed any concern for the comfort

7

of convenience. In the seminary classroom, on the lecture platform, in the pulpit, in private conversation, and in much correspondence, Dr. Adams has endeavored to secure for *Life in the Son* a careful, prayerful, objective reading by as many as possible. The object of much censure by men with closed minds (and some with closed hearts, for the two most often dwell together), Dr. Adams has faithfully endured. It is to the credit of men in responsible positions of administration and polity in Southern Baptist theological education that attacks against Dr. Adams were unsuccessful, and that he was able to continue his long and fruitful teaching career through several years until retirement. It was not without hazard and much cost to himself that Dr. Adams, on the strength of his own name and reputation, secured for *Life in the Son* such immediate and wide attention following publication. The attention the book commanded at the outset was due in no measure whatever to the name of the author, than whom nobody is more nobody.

Mention must also be made of Dr. Dale Moody, Chairman of the Department of Systematic Theology at Southern Baptist Theological Seminary. Despite the certain prospect of censure and witless vilification, Dr. Moody openly commended *Life in the Son,* endorsing the principal thesis of the book. Dr. Moody suffered much from the mouths of self-appointed defenders of what they imagined to be the faith, who, more generously endowed with emotions than with wisdom, conducted a vigorous effort to secure his dismissal from his professorship. Thanks be to God, their ill-advised efforts failed.

Thanks be to God, too, for the host of friends in the Baptist communion as well as in other communions who have contributed in important ways to the ministry *Life in the Son* has enjoyed in the past decade. And thanks be to God for the growing number in the Baptist fellowship, as well as in other communions of the Communion, who have found in *Life in the Son* help toward a better understanding of the doctrine of perseverance, a problem area of doctrine on which men and communions of the Household of Faith have been sorely divided for most of the generations of the Church.

A word of thanks is due my family for their long patience in these years past, and to my parishioners and to friends near and far for their patience in the face of neglect occasioned by the hard necessities imposed by such a task as writing *Elect in the Son.* A word of appreciation is due Mrs. James Weaver for her assistance and superb stenographic work in the preparation of the manuscript for the press.

Above all, thanks and praise are due God the Father, Son, and Holy Spirit, who alone know how unworthy am I to be given the task and the privilege of writing such a book as *Elect in the Son.* Together with *Life in the Son,* may it be blessed of God to bring to men a fuller understanding of profound truths at the heart of the holy faith we believe and confess. Praise be to Jesus Christ, who is Himself the final Word concerning the Election of Grace.

ROBERT SHANK

Mount Vernon, Missouri
January 22, 1970

CONTENTS

INTRODUCTION

THE UNUSUAL importance of Robert Shank's work *Life in the Son,* which I recognized when first I read the manuscript some ten years ago, has been confirmed in the decade now past. The wide distribution of the book, now in a sixth large printing, and the continuing demand for it ten years after publication reflect the significance of Mr. Shank's contribution to our understanding in an area of doctrine of critical importance and long debated.

From the pen of Mr. Shank now comes another of the most meaningful books of this generation. To those who have read *Life in the Son,* the singular significance of the new work will come as no surprise. After reading Mr. Shank's manuscript on the doctrine of election—not once, but several times—I must say that I find it a worthy companion of *Life in the Son* and, if anything, even more decisive. I have every confidence that time will prove *Elect in the Son* to be the definitive work on the difficult question of election, on which good men of contrary persuasions have differed from the days of Augustine, and more especially from the time of Calvin.

These observations I make from the background of a lifetime spent in the seminary classroom, beginning with my years at Southern Baptist Theological Seminary, first as a student, and then as a fellow and an associate professor of the mighty A. T. Robertson. No man can speak for another, but I can say that Dr. Robertson was profoundly concerned about the area of doctrine in which Mr. Shank has labored, feeling that consistent, Biblical definitions awaited new insights. Sharing Dr. Robertson's concern, through the years I have read carefully every serious work I could find on the question of election and perseverance. I found no work that addressed itself to the question in the thorough, objective, competent manner of Mr. Shank's volumes or afforded such satisfactory, obviously Biblical constructions.

Elect in the Son possesses several excellencies of which I must speak. First, it is Biblical all the way through. On page after page, the author brings to our attention Scriptures from both Testaments that bear on the question of election. It is to be doubted that many among us have been aware of the extent of the content of the Bible that bears on the doctrine of election. Just to go through the book and observe the Scriptures treated in the work is an enlightening experience.

Second, to all who are familiar with the Scriptures, especially in their original languages, the author's exegesis commends itself for its objectivity and its fidelity to the text. Here is exegesis that is consistently grammatical and contextual.

Third, the author's interpretations, founded as they are on solid exegesis, are never forced or ingenious, and his constructions are logical and consistent. One of the great strengths of the book is the consistently contextual interpretation of the Scriptures. As we know only too well, much error appears plausible and Biblical only because men have ignored context in their interpretations of the Scriptures. In *Elect in the Son,* Mr. Shank compels us to interpret the Scriptures contextually.

Fourth, it is evident that the author has read widely in the area of doctrine in which he labors and, drawing extensively on their writings, he interacts constructively both with Calvin and with leading contemporary Calvinists. In this, as well as in other respects, his treatise commends itself to all serious scholars.

Fifth, the book commends itself to laymen as well as to formal scholars, for it is written in a language and style that, though dignified and scholarly, can readily be understood by all earnest students of the Bible.

Sixth, the book exhibits an irenic spirit. Necessarily polemical, it obviously was written, not simply to differ or to attack or condemn, but to challenge and to enlighten. Though the author is compelled to demonstrate the errors of those with whom he differs, he does so in a kindly spirit. He respects his opponents and does not presume that they are neither gentlemen nor scholars, simply because he differs with them in certain areas of doctrine. Though he must reject the core of Calvin's system of theology, he does not reject Calvin, but honors him as a man and an important figure in the Reformation and acknowledges that we are indebted to him for many good things. He finds common ground on which Calvinists and non-Calvinists may and must unite, and though his book is designed to bring men to a common understanding of the doctrine of election, he asserts that love for God and our fellow men is "more important than understanding all mysteries and having all knowledge." Here is true Christian perspective along with exacting scholarship.

Seventh, the dynamic doctrine of election, at the heart of the holy faith and the total message of the Scriptures, is made clear and gloriously meaningful, as are all the relevant truths surrounding the election. Here are rich and practical insights into basic Bible truths—election, predestination, atonement, propitiation, ransom and redemption, vindication, reconciliation, justification, sin, judgment, condemnation, reprobation, the everlasting kingdom, and the role and agency of Jesus Christ, the Son of God and Son of Man, in the whole scheme of time and eternity. The cross is seen as the focal point of the election of grace and the event in which time and eternity find their true perspective. Here is a book that makes a major contribution to our total comprehension of the message of the Bible.

There will be those who will speak against Mr. Shank's new book, as they did against his earlier work. I venture to predict that nothing constructive will be offered against *Elect in the Son,* even as nothing of consequence has been offered against *Life in the Son* in the ten years since publication. If any propose to write a refutation of these two volumes, let them sit down first and count the cost to see whether they have sufficient to finish it. Let them make sure they have something more to offer in rebuttal than prejudice. If the product of their labor is to do more than confirm the prejudice of the unthinking, if it is to commend itself to the judgment of serious theologians and students of the Bible, it must be able to stand up under the minute examination of men capable of the same objectivity, exacting exegesis, and careful synthesis that Mr. Shank has exhibited in his two volumes.

It is ironic, and tragically so, that much of Mr. Shank's work had to be done under the stress of difficulties created by the ill-conceived actions of men in positions of authority in the ecclesiastical structure of his denomination. Happily, there are among Baptists many who recognize the enduring contribution Mr. Shank has made through his book *Life in the Son*. I predict that, with the publication of *Elect in the Son,* their number will increase more and more. Let it be remembered that, less than a hundred years ago, all five cardinal points of Calvin's system of theology generally prevailed among Baptists, as theological textbooks of the times will confirm. Today, only one point remains to any appreciable extent among Baptists, inevitable perseverance, and there is growing evidence that Baptists are increasingly questioning this last vestige of the central core of Calvin's system of theology. Our only legitimate concern in all of this is, What saith the Scripture?

As never in history, we are living in a dynamic age. In all areas of the human scene, change is the order of the day. Change for the sake of change is folly; but equally so is blind, unreasoning subservience to tradition. If the Church of Jesus Christ is to prove relevant in a fast changing world, it must fear neither new methods of ministry nor fuller, more comprehensive insights into holy truth. It would be a happy day for the Church at large if men should cast aside all prejudices and all concern for anything less than holy truth and honest and accurate definitions of it. Surely new direction, power, and success would attend our labors in the service of our God and our fellow men in the holy name of Jesus Christ our Lord.

It is my earnest prayer that, under God, the two volumes— *Life in the Son* and *Elect in the Son*—will help to bring men of all persuasions in all the Church to unity of understanding of two critically important doctrines, cardinal doctrines of the faith once delivered to the saints.

WILLIAM W. ADAMS

Kansas City, Missouri
January 10, 1970

FOREWORD TO THE EIGHTH PRINTING
OF *LIFE IN THE SON* AND THE
THIRD PRINTING OF *ELECT IN THE SON*

It is my considered judgment that Robert Shank's two books *Life in the Son* and *Elect in the Son* will stand against any attempt to refute them from the Scriptures, and that the passing of time can only prove them to be finally definitive on the long-debated theological questions of election and perseverance. I commend them to all students of the Scriptures and to every sincere steward of holy truth.

WILLIAM W. ADAMS

Kansas City, Missouri
May 7, 1971

Thy Kingdom Come

Thy kingdom come, thy will be done on earth as it is in heaven.

MATTHEW 6:10

Come, ye blessed of my Father, inherit the kingdom prepared for you from the foundation of the world.

MATTHEW 25:34

CHAPTER I

THY KINGDOM COME

IN A DAY when the foundations of society are crumbling, a day of gathering storm and deepening gloom, a day of unprecedented peril in which thoughtful men speak of the collapse of civilization and the possible annihilation of cities and nations—even of mankind, the sovereignty of God is an unfailing encouragement that lights the path of the just and affords assurance to all the faithful, who take great comfort in the words of James in the historic council of the church at Jerusalem: "Known unto God are all his works from the beginning of the world" (Acts 15:18).

God, who has "declared the end from the beginning and from ancient times things not yet done," has said, "My counsel shall stand, and I will do all my pleasure" (Isa. 46:10). He who "works all things after the counsel of his own will" is at work in the world in these momentous times, moving inexorably toward fulfillment of an eternal purpose that antedates creation and gives meaning to human history. History, by divine appointment, is teleological, and the sweep of human events, whatever the sound and the fury, moves toward the appointed end: "Thy kingdom come."

Nothing in the course of events can alter the appointed outcome. The unfolding of the days and years, whatever their number, ultimately will issue in all that was foretold by the prophets of old, by our Lord, and by His Apostles. The witness of history past, confirming "the prophetic word made more sure" (2 Pet. 1:19), attests that human events ever move toward

21

the inevitable denouement on which creation itself is predicated: the coming of "the kingdom prepared from the foundation of the world."

There is, of course, a sense in which the kingdom of God is eternally present rather than prospective, coexistent with Him who "before the mountains were brought forth or ever [He] had formed the earth and the world, even from everlasting to everlasting, [is] God" (Ps. 90:2). But the kingdom of God, as proclaimed and anticipated by both Jesus and the Apostles and prophets of old, is yet future and awaits its manifestation at the end of the age, to appear in a moment of spectacular divine intervention at the coming of Christ in power and judgment . . . but appearing also as the consummation of a long process, as implied by many of our Lord's parables.

Why a long process? Why not, instead, instant kingdom? Could not God, in the act of a moment, have created the everlasting kingdom He purposed from eternity? Are not all things possible for God?

All things indeed are possible for God, but only within the limitations of consistency with His own nature and being.[1] God cannot lie, for example, nor can He change, nor can He deny Himself. We may reverently assume that, for the kind of kingdom He intends, God is following the only possible course: the process of human history.

The process comprehends all that God has done, beginning even before His mighty acts of creation when He "laid the foundations of the earth [and] the morning stars sang together, and all the sons of God shouted for joy" (Job 38:4,7). It comprehends the creation of angels before earth itself and the origin of sin in the transgression of angels against the will of their Creator. It comprehends the creation of man in the image and likeness of God and the entrance of sin into human

---

[1]With respect to external factors, God is subject to no limitation. But He is subject to the limitations of His own inviolate character. All His actions are consistent with the nature of His being, a fact which is essential to His integrity and which does not in any way impinge on His sovereignty.

experience in the disobedience of man to the word and will of his Creator.

The process comprehends the moral self-discoveries and the redemptive revelations and encounters experienced by the patriarchs of old and all the faithful of their generations. It comprehends the experiences of Abraham, Isaac, Jacob, and a nation descended from them, and the judges and kings and prophets who appeared among them.

The process comprehends the redemptive mission of Jesus, unfolded in His incarnation, life, ministry, death, resurrection, ascension, and ultimate return in righteous judgment. It comprehends the labors of the Apostles and the witness of the Church to Christ and His saving Gospel in all generations until the coming of the King and the kingdom.

The process whereby God is creating the kingdom which He purposed before the world began comprehends "all nations of men . . . on all the face of the earth" (Acts 17:26) and involves every man. Human history in its totality is the milieu in which the everlasting kingdom is being wrought . . . and in which the election determined by God from before creation—an election wholly identified with the kingdom—is being realized.

"Thy kingdom come"—the kingdom which was the concern of Jesus in the days of His flesh, the burden of His preaching, the subject of splendid promises and solemn warnings, and the central theme of all His teaching from the beginning of His ministry to the time of His ascension (Acts 1:3). Thy kingdom come!

And blessed be his glorious name for ever: and let the whole earth be filled with his glory. Amen, and Amen.

PSALM 72:19

Elect in the Son

Blessed be the God and Father of our Lord Jesus Christ, who has blessed us with all spiritual blessings in heavenly places in Christ, according as he has chosen us in him before the foundation of the world, that we should be holy and without blame before him in love, having predestined us unto the adoption of children by Jesus Christ to himself, according to the good pleasure of his will, to the praise of the glory of his grace, wherein he has made us accepted in the Beloved; in whom we have redemption through his blood, the forgiveness of sins, according to the riches of his grace wherein he has abounded toward us in all wisdom and prudence, having made known to us the mystery of his will, according to his good pleasure which he has purposed in himself: that in the dispensation of the fulness of times he might gather together in one all things in Christ, both which are in heaven and which are on earth, even in him; in whom also we have obtained an inheritance, being predestined according to the purpose of him who works all things after the counsel of his own will, that we should be to the praise of his glory who first trusted in Christ; in whom you also trusted after you heard the word of truth, the gospel of your salvation; in whom also after you believed, you were sealed with the promised Holy Spirit, which is the earnest of our inheritance until the redemption of the purchased possession, to the praise of his glory.

EPHESIANS 1:3-14

CHAPTER II

ELECT IN THE SON

IN THE Epistle to the Ephesians, the Apostle Paul follows his brief salutation with a doxology praising God for the grace given to us in Christ, grace that spans the ages from before the foundation of the world to the dispensation of the fulness of times. The paramount importance of the passage rests in the fact that it contains the Bible's most definitive statement of a profound doctrine of the Holy Scriptures: God's gracious election of men in Christ before the foundation of the world and the predestination of the elect to holy privilege and everlasting felicity. Of all passages of Scripture touching the matter of election, Ephesians 1:3-14 is the foundation passage. Referring to Ephesians 1:4,9 and the cognate verse II Timothy 1:9, G. C. Berkouwer observes that "the history of the doctrine of election may be interpreted as an effort to understand the meaning of these words."[1]

I. Election Christocentric

In Paul's Ephesian doxology, as in certain other Scriptures, an essential aspect of election is explicit: the election is Christocentric. The first step toward a correct understanding of the Biblical doctrine of election is the recognition that the election of men is comprehended only in Christ; outside of Christ there is no election of any man. "There is election only

---

[1]G. C. Berkouwer, *Divine Election*, p. 135. Professor of Systematic Theology at Free University of Amsterdam, Berkouwer is among the foremost Calvinist theologians of today and representative of the Reformed tradition.

27

in Christ . . . God's election is election in Christ," as Berkouwer observes.[2] Westcott comments on the Ephesian doxology:

> The whole passage is a Psalm of praise for the redemption and consummation of created things, fulfilled in Christ through the Spirit according to the eternal purpose of God. This fulfillment is contemplated specially in the relation of believers to Christ, chosen in Him, redeemed, enlightened, sealed.
>
> . . . .
>
> From first to last, the fulness of the Divine blessing is shown to be realised 'in Christ' (v. 3). In Him God chose us (v.4). In the Beloved He graced us (v. 6). In Him we have our redemption (v. 7), even as God purposed in Him to sum up all things in the Christ (v. 10). In Him the faithful of Israel were made a Divine heritage (v. 11).[3] In Him the Gentiles found a place (v. 13). In Him they were sealed by the Spirit (v. 13), the pledge of a larger hope (v. 14).[4]

A. Christ, the Elect

The Canons of Dort, referring to Ephesians 1:4, affirm that election is in Christ, "whom [God] from eternity appointed the Mediator and Head of the elect and the foundation to salvation" (I:7). Calvin, following Augustine, observed that "in the very Head of the Church we have a bright mirror of free election" (3:22:1). That Christ assumed his Messianic office by the Father's appointment is clearly affirmed in the Scriptures. Matthew, whose Gospel abounds with applications of Old Testament passages, witnesses that in Jesus is fulfilled a prophecy of Isaiah concerning an elect Servant of Jehovah: "Behold my servant, whom I have chosen, my beloved, in whom I am well pleased: I will put my spirit upon him, and he shall show judgment to the Gentiles" (Matt. 12:18). Jehovah's election of the Servant-Messiah is declared in Isaiah 42:1-7:

---

[2]*Ibid.,* pp. 149,162.

[3]Westcott's exposition of vs. 11, 12 takes account of the fact that *eklērōthēmen* is passive rather than active (the converse is implied in AV), reflected in his rendering "were made a Divine heritage."

[4]B. F. Westcott, *Saint Paul's Epistle to the Ephesians: the Greek Text with Notes and Addenda,* pp. 4f.

Behold my servant, whom I uphold, mine elect in whom my soul delights. I have put my spirit upon him: he shall bring forth judgment to the Gentiles. . . . I, Jehovah, have called thee in righteousness and will hold thy hand and will keep thee and give thee for a covenant of the people, for a light of the Gentiles. (vs. 1,6)

The cognate passage Isaiah 49:1-13 makes the same affirmation of Jehovah's election of the Servant-Messiah:

Jehovah has called me from the womb; from the bowels of my mother has he made mention of my name. . . . [Thus] saith Jehovah that formed me from the womb to be his servant, to bring Jacob again to him . . . It is a light thing that thou shouldest be my servant to raise up the tribes of Jacob and to restore the preserved of Israel: I will also give thee for a light to the Gentiles, that thou mayest be my salvation unto the end of the earth. (vs. 1,5,6)

Delitzsch comments that, beginning with Isaiah 42:1, Jehovah

introduces His "servant." In ch. xli. 8 this epithet was applied to the nation, which had been chosen as the servant and for the service of Jehovah. But the servant of Jehovah who is presented to us here is distinct from Israel and has so strong an individuality and such marked personal features that the expression cannot possibly be merely a personified collective. Nor can the prophet himself be intended; for what is here affirmed of this servant of Jehovah goes infinitely beyond anything to which a prophet was ever called, or of which a man was ever capable. It must therefore be the future Christ; and this is the view taken in the Targum, where the translation of our prophecy commences thus: *"Hâ' 'abhdī Meshīchâ."* Still there must be a connection between the national sense, in which the expression "servant of Jehovah" was used in ch. xli. 8, and the personal sense in which it is used here. The coming Saviour . . . appears as the embodied idea of Israel, *i.e.* as its truth and reality embodied in one person. The idea of "the servant of Jehovah" assumed, to speak figuratively, the form of a pyramid. The base was Israel as a whole; the central section was that Israel which was not merely Israel according to the flesh, but according to the spirit also; the apex is the person of the Mediator of salvation springing out of Israel. And the last of the three is regarded (1) as the centre of the circle of the promised kingdom—the *second David;* (2) the centre of the circle of the people of salvation—the *second Israel;* (3) the centre of the circle of the human race—the *second Adam.*

. . . .

Israel's true nature as a servant of God, which had its roots in the election and calling of Jehovah and manifested itself in conduct and action in harmony with this calling, is all concentrated in Him, the One, as its ripest fruit. The gracious purposes of God towards the whole human race, which were manifested even in the election of Israel, are brought by Him to their full completion.

. . . .

"Behold my servant, whom I uphold; mine elect, whom my soul loveth: I have laid my Spirit upon him . . . "[5]

The elect Servant of Jehovah, "chosen of God and precious" (I Pet. 2:4), was "foreordained before the foundation of the world" (I Pet. 1:20). Throughout His ministry in the days of His flesh, Jesus moved always in the awareness of His appointment by the Father. He spoke of himself as "him whom the Father has sanctified and sent into the world" (John 10:36). Bengel comments, "This sanctification is mentioned in such a way as to be prior in time to His being sent into the world."[6] With respect to the sanctification declared by Jesus, Thayer asserts that in the use of the word *hagiazō* "God is said . . . to have selected [Christ] for his service . . . by having committed to him the office of Messiah. . . . "[7] There is good warrant for the rendering in *Today's English Version of the New Testament* "the Father chose me and sent me into the world." John 10:36 has numerous cognates which reflect Jesus' awareness of His election to His mediatorial office and His advent in His redemptive mission by the express design and will of the Father.[8]

---

[5]Franz Delitzsch, *Biblical Commentary on the Prophecies of Isaiah,* Vol. II, pp. 174f.

[6]John Albert Bengel, *Gnomon of the New Testament,* Vol. II, p. 387.

[7]Joseph Henry Thayer, *A Greek-English Lexicon of the New Testament,* p. 6.

[8]E.g., John 5:37; 6:27; 12:49; 16:28; ch. 17.

The Father's act of choosing, in which the Word and the Spirit concurred in the counsels of eternity, comprehended both the divine and the human aspects of the election: the Word made flesh to become the one Mediator between God and men (the divine), and the temporal circumstance of the Incarnation and the historical identity of the Messiah in the person of Jesus (the human).

B. Christ, the Foundation of Election

In Him who is *the* Elect from eternity is posited the gracious election of men. To refer again to the Canons of Dort: God from eternity appointed Christ "the Mediator and Head of the elect and the foundation to salvation" (I:7). In the realization of the kingdom purpose of God, the election is first of *Christ* and then of men *in Him*. Clement, first-century bishop at Rome who could speak of Peter and Paul as being of his own generation, wrote in his First Epistle to the Corinthians, "God . . . chose out the Lord Jesus Christ, and us through him for 'a peculiar people' "(64:1). Godet affirms that, in the election,

Christ Himself is its first object; and hence He is called *the Elect,* absolutely speaking, Isa. xlii. 1; Luke ix. 35 (most approved reading). His brethren are elect *in Him,* Eph. i. 4-6.[9]

Calvin insisted that the election to salvation is in Christ. Representative of numerous affirmations are the following:

[Christ] is the beloved Son, in whom the love of the Father dwells, and from whom it afterwards extends to us. Thus Paul says, "In whom he hath made us accepted in the Beloved" (Eph. i. 6). (3:2:32)

. . . .

Paul testifies indeed that we were chosen before the foundation of the world; but, he adds, in Christ (Eph. 1:4). (E.P.8:6)

. . . .

---

[9]Frederick L. Godet, *Commentary on the Epistle to the Romans,* p. 326, italics his.

... the whole sum of our salvation and every single part of it are comprehended in Christ. . . . (2:16:19)

1. Christ Instrumental in Election

Two aspects are intrinsic in the role of Christ in election: he is *instrumental* and *comprehensive.*

Important questions arise concerning the instrumentality of Christ in election, the first of which is, Was it necessary? Was the temporal career of Jesus essential to the realization of election, or was it actually extrinsic to the election? Was it the sole means, or at least *a* means, on which the election could be predicated, or was it optional? Was the redemptive career of Jesus in *time* actually decisive, or instead merely symbolic—only a temporal exhibit, the design of which was to reflect and delineate the dimensions of an election (and reprobation) already accomplished by fiat of God in the counsels of eternity?

Calvin's reference (following Augustine) to Christ as "the mirror of election" has been construed by some as indicative of his concept of the role of Christ in election as being merely to reflect what God already had accomplished in eternity by His decree. Thus Christ's "redemptive" career—the incarnation, His death and resurrection, His ascension and intercession—are seen as incidental and symbolic, divine pageantry rather than authentic saving acts. Election becomes predicated on God's decree in eternity *in abstractio* from all occurrences in time in the experience of Jesus.

It is true that Calvin sometimes argues from an *in abstractio* election, as may be observed in his writings. But in many passages he does affirm the real necessity of the redemptive mission of Christ.[10] Although he did not apprehend the full dimension of the agency of Christ in election,[11] in Calvin's concept Christ is instrumental rather than symbolic (though Calvin is not consistent on this point).

---

[10] E.g., *Inst.* 2:17.

[11] This matter will be treated in the following chapter.

Berkouwer, a leading exponent of Calvinism today, rejects any abstract decree of election deriving from mere determinism apart from God's love and grace operating in and through Christ. He asserts that when one reflects on the counsel of God in election,

... Ephesians 1:4 is always encountered ... for that text praises the election of God—not as an abstract act, as the counsel of a *potentia absoluta* [but] in such a manner that it can be immediately followed by these words: "having foreordained us unto adoption as sons through Jesus Christ" (Eph. 1:5). This makes impossible the idea of an abstract, merciless, and loveless sovereign decree.[12]

The real instrumentality of Christ in the election derives from the necessity of His ministry of mediation between God and man. The mediatorial office of Jesus Christ is among the greatest themes of Holy Scripture—a theme that, as a golden chain, binds together all the blessings for which Paul praises God in his doxology in the Epistle to the Ephesians: through Christ come gracious blessings to us now (1:3,7); through Christ will come to us gracious blessings in the fulness of times (1:10) when God will continue to show the exceeding riches of His grace in His kindness toward us through Christ Jesus (2:7). "There is one mediator between God and men," wrote Paul to Timothy, "the man Christ Jesus," whose gracious office—conceived in eternity past and wrought in time—reaches to eternity to come. And the heart of His ministry of mediation is the atonement.

But again, was it necessary? Even granting the necessity, or at least the expediency, of the incarnation and the life and ministry of Jesus among men, was His death actually necessary? Some think not. James Denney, in his classic on the doctrine of redemption, writes

Even in the eleventh century, Anselm met people who made the objections to the Christian faith which are current today. If God had to redeem men, why could He not redeem them *sola voluntate,* by the mere

---

[12]Berkouwer, *op. cit.,* p. 143.

exercise of His will? Why speak of redemption at all? Whose slaves are we from whom God cannot deliver us merely by putting forth His almighty power? If you speak of being redeemed from His anger, is not His anger simply His will to punish, and can He not change His will without more ado?[13]

Denney cites his own contemporary, the Catholic theologian M. Riviere, who wrote in a theological journal

If the Christ had not suffered, if He had not died upon the cross, would He nevertheless have redeemed us? To this question Catholic theologians unanimously answer in the affirmative. It follows with perfect clearness that neither the suffering, the death, nor the cross represents the essential, or, to use the language of the school, the formal element in redemption. They are so many contingent circumstances, the reason for which is to be sought [in the nature of the mystery, not in its absolute necessities].[14]

But contrary to Riviere's assumption (an assumption surely far from "unanimous" among Catholic theologians of his day or any other generation), the death of Christ was essential to His work of redemption. This was certain in the mind of Jesus, if we accept the witness of the Gospels to His words about His redemptive mission:

The Son of Man came to give his life a ransom for many . . . the bread that I will give is my flesh, which I will give for the life of the world . . . the Son of Man must suffer many things and be slain . . . even so must the Son of Man be lifted up . . . and I, if I be lifted up from the earth, will draw all men unto me . . . for this cause came I unto this hour.

The Gospels abound with these and other assertions of Jesus about the necessity of His death on the cross for the redemption of men. Appearing to His Apostles and other disciples in Jerusalem the evening of the day of His resurrection,

[Jesus] said to them, These are the words which I spake unto you while I was yet with you, that all things must be fulfilled which were written in

---

[13]James Denney, *The Christian Doctrine of Reconciliation*, p. 66.

[14]*Ibid.*, p. 265, bracketed material translated from the French text included in Denney's work.

the law of Moses, and in the prophets, and in the psalms concerning me. . . . Thus it is written, and thus it behoved Christ to suffer, and to rise from the dead the third day, that repentance and remission of sins should be preached in his name among all nations, beginning at Jerusalem. And you are witnesses of these things. (Lk. 24:44,46-48)

Turning again to Denney's great work, we read

The one thing that the apostles have to tell about Christ—what they deliver first of all to all men—is that Christ died for our sins. He suffered for them once, the just for the unjust, that He might bring us to God. We are reconciled to God by the death of His Son.[15]

Regardless of the relative merits and deficiencies of Anselm's doctrine of the atonement, he is correct in his construction of a rationale of the incarnation. Denney writes

The title of Anselm's famous work *Cur Deus Homo*?—Why did God become man?—intimates that what he is in quest of is the rationale of Christianity itself.

. . . .

Put briefly, the answer to the question is that God became man because only thus could sin be dealt with for man's salvation and God's end in the creation of man be secured. In other words, the rationale of the incarnation is the atonement.[16]

"Once in the consummation of the ages," as we read in the Epistle to the Hebrews, "has Christ appeared to put away sin by the sacrifice of himself" (9:26). Someone has said that an eternal past knew no other future, and an eternal future will know no other past, save Christ crucified.

A critical study of the atonement is beyond the province of this treatise, and an examination of the various theories and many facets of the atonement is not germane to our present purpose. But let us observe well the point of present concern in our study of the Biblical doctrine of election: there was a real necessity for the atonement, a necessity that derives from the character of God.

---

[15]*Ibid.*, p. 268.
[16]*Ibid.*, p. 65.

The problem of sin in God's universe relates not only to His finite creatures, but to God Himself. Anselm is correct in his thesis that it is God to whom the problem of sin must have ultimate reference. Can God forgive sin and remain consistent with His holiness and radical aversion to sin? The Scriptures affirm that He can—because of the atonement. Through the expiatory sacrifice of Christ, offered for the sins of the whole world, God can be both "just, and the justifier of him who believes in Jesus" (Rom. 3:26).

God is a moral being in a moral universe reflecting His own being, and the moral integrity of neither Himself nor His universe can be breached. Sin cannot be ignored or simply tolerated; ultimately it must be judged and final disposition must be made of it. But where sin abounded, grace did much more abound (Rom. 5:20), and Christ suffered for sins, the just for the unjust, that He might bring us to God (I Pet. 3:18), having offered Himself a ransom for all (I Tim. 2:6).

The atonement wrought by Christ was by no means symbolic. It was an authentic saving act made necessary by the holy character of God Himself, a saving act whereby God can adopt into sonship and into His kingdom men who have transgressed His righteous laws, outraged His holiness, and of themselves are sinners. The death of Jesus Christ was not pageantry. It was a decisive saving act in which Jesus Christ was truly instrumental in the election of men to salvation and the everlasting kingdom of God. Berkouwer writes

... in Christ there was a decisive happening in history, an act of God in which Christ "has earned for us the grace of God and salvation (*Inst.* II, xvii)." Although Calvin did not accept the concept of persuasion, and although he indicates that God the Father with His love precedes the historical reconciliation which He founded in Jesus Christ (*ibid.*, II, xvi, 3), this preceding does not imply a devaluation of the historical work of Christ, as if eternity would make any occurrence in time meaningless. It implies, rather, that God (as Calvin paradoxically puts it) reconciles Himself with us because He has loved us beforehand.[17]

---

[17]Berkouwer, *op. cit.*, p. 139.

The concept of persuasion mentioned by Berkouwer was rightly rejected by Calvin. God, who spared not His own Son but delivered Him up for us all (Rom. 8:32) and purposed the death of Christ from before the foundation of the world (I Pet. 1:20), needed no persuasion to elect men to salvation. The design of the atonement was not to furnish a ground on which God *would* save men, but rather on which he *could* save men (Rom. 3:25,26). God needed no persuasion: God was in Christ reconciling the world to Himself through the death of His holy Son, who was made sin for us that we might be made the righteousness of God in Him (II Cor. 5:19-21). For God so loved the world that He gave His only begotten Son, that the world through Him might be saved (Jn. 3:16,17). In this was manifested the love of God toward us: God sent His only begotten Son into the world to be the propitiation for our sins, that we might live through Him (I Jn. 4:9,10).

The love and grace of God, which received their supreme manifestation in the cross of Jesus, continue to be expressed and imparted to men through the priestly intercession of Christ who, as our Advocate with the Father, continues His gracious ministry of mediation founded on His eternal sacrifice in His death. Christ is truly instrumental in election.

An essential aspect of the real instrumentality of Christ in election is posited by Barth as a central thesis in his construction of a doctrine of election in his *Kirchliche Dogmatik.* Barth sees Christ, not only as the elect Man, but also as "the electing God," instrumental in the election—not only through the incarnation and His accomplishment of the atonement that is the basis of reconciliation and the foundation of the whole complex of mediation, but also in the *application* of the election to men:

> In its simplest and most comprehensive form, the dogma of predestination consists, then, in the assertion that the divine predestination is the election of Jesus Christ. But the concept of election has a double reference—to the election and to the elected. And so, too, the name of Jesus Christ has within itself the double reference: the One called by this name is both very God and very man. Thus the simplest form of the

dogma may be divided at once into the two assertions that Jesus Christ is the electing God, and that He is also elected man.

. . . .

[Christ] is not only the Elected. He is also Himself the Elector, and His election must be understood as active. It is true that as the Son of God given by the Father to be one with man and to take to Himself the form of man, He is elected. It is also true that He does not elect alone, but in company with the electing of the Father and the Holy Spirit. But He does elect.[18]

Thus Christ becomes the electing God as truly as the Father, and the personal election of individual men becomes disclosed in Christ—not symbolically, as the reflection of a fiat election determined in the counsels of eternity before the foundation of the world, but as historical, knowable reality in the personal experience of men.

Berkouwer rejects Barth's thesis:

Barth's appeal to Scripture for his doctrine of Christ as subject of election is limited almost wholly to a few passages in the Gospel of John which speak of Christ's calling and election to the apostolate.

. . . .

When Barth poses as main thesis for his doctrine of election that Christ Himself is the electing God, the question must be asked whether his appeal to John's words indeed warrants this thesis.[19]

In the judgment of Berkouwer, Barth's thesis is not substantiated.

It is interesting to note that Calvin writes that "Christ makes himself the author of election [and] claims the right of electing in common with the Father" (3:22:7). Calvin rests his thesis on the same passages to which Barth appeals. Berkouwer does not quote Calvin, though he devotes ten lines to an admission that "Calvin pondered this problem" of the relation of the Johannine passages to the question of the instrumentality of Christ in

---

[18]Karl Barth, *Church Dogmatics, Volume II: The Doctrine of God*, pp. 103, 105.
[19]Berkouwer, *op cit.*, pp. 157-160.

election to salvation and saw a "direct connection" between the election to the Apostolate in John 15:16 and the election to salvation:

In this call to discipleship there is a clear similarity to the structure of the election of God, namely, in the emphasis on Christ's full initiative. . . . This is not surprising, says Calvin, for the Father acts through Christ and Christ with the Father.[20]

Berkouwer appends a footnote, "See Calvin on John 15:16,[21] where he says that this election cannot be detached from eternal salvation." Especially pertinent in the passage cited by Berkouwer are Calvin's words

That Christ declares himself to be the Author of both [election to salvation and ordination to the Apostolate] is not wonderful; since it is only by him that God acts, and he acts along with the Father. So then, both election and ordination belong equally to both.[22]

Calvin's thesis that Christ is "the author of election" and "elects in common with the Father" has something in common with Barth's thesis that Christ is "the electing God." But Barth's definition of the implications of his central thesis differs radically from any possible implications of Calvin's thesis, which in his theology is subordinate rather than central. Rejecting Barth's thesis, Berkouwer continues

Without minimizing at all the unique significance of this act of Christ in electing his apostles, we ought to note that the Bible also directs our attention to Christ as the Chosen One of God.

. . . .

We see then that Christ is presented to us, not only in His activity, but also in His passivity, as the Chosen One of God, in whom God has His good pleasure. . . . In the New Testament we hear of the counsel of God that is

---

[20]*Ibid.*, p. 158.

[21]The text reads John 15:18, a typographical error.

[22]Calvin, *Commentary on the Gospel According to John,* Vol. II, p. 120.

fulfilled in and through Christ, all that the counsel and hand of God had foreordained beforehand to come to pass (Acts 4:28).

. . . .

Precisely the same Gospel, which gives such a clear account of Christ's calling the apostles, gives us also the testimony of Christ's submissiveness to the Father. "For I spake not from myself; but the Father that sent me, he hath given me commandment, what I should say and what I should speak" (John 12:49). Here all our attention is directed to that relationship and hence to the Messiah, to the Servant of the Lord, to the Mediator between God and man.[23]

Berkouwer implies that we must choose whether Christ is the *subject* or the *agent* of election, the elect or the elector, the chosen or the chooser. Here is a fallacy so often encountered in theological readings: an assumed *either . . . or.* Berkouwer opts for the former category and rejects the latter. But both are equally Biblical and represent valid aspects of the instrumentality of Christ in election. It is only as the Elect that He becomes the Elector, and neither aspect of His role takes anything away from the other.

Because John 13:18 and 15:16 clearly have reference to election to the Apostolate rather than to salvation and must (along with 6:70) be equated only with Luke 6:13 and Acts 1:2,24-26, they support Barth's thesis only by an assumed inference. However, John 15:19 is quite another matter: "I have chosen you out of the world." These words substantiate Barth's thesis, for here the election is to salvation rather than to the Apostolate. Godet comments

Exelexamēn, I have chosen, indicates here the call to faith, not to the apostleship; by this word *to choose* Jesus would designate the act by which He has drawn them to Himself and detached them from the world; the thought of divine predestination is not found here, any more than in ver. 16.[24]

---

[23]Berkouwer, *op. cit.,* pp. 158f.

[24]Frederick Louis Godet, *Commentary on the Gospel of John,* Vol. II, p. 302.

Godet is correct in his assertion that the thought of divine predestination is not found in John 15:19 (especially in the sense of Calvin's definition of predestination, which he erroneously confused with election, as we shall observe). The election here, however, comprehends salvation, and the immediate executor of the election is Christ.[25]

Barth is correct in his rejection of any limitation of the role of Christ in election to a passive relationship to the Father. Such a relationship indeed exists: Christ came not to do His own will, but the will of the Father who sent Him (John 6:38, etc.). But the will of the Father is that the Son should be as truly the executor of election as the Father Himself, and indeed the more *immediate* executor—the Son to whom the Father committed all authority and judgment (Jn. 5:22,27; Matt. 28:18), who has authority on earth to forgive sins (Matt. 9:6), who draws all men to Himself (John 12:32), who by grant of the Father has life in Himself equally with the Father (Jn. 5:26), and who quickens whom He will (Jn. 5:21). Christ's solemn words "He that overcometh . . . I will not blot out his name out of the book of life" (Rev. 3:5) reflect His role as the immediate executor of election.[26]

A consideration of the relation between the decree of election in the eternal counsel of God and Christ's saving act of atonement in history establishes the real instrumentality of Christ as "the electing God." Berkouwer writes

---

[25]Let it be observed that Christ's election of the Apostles "out of the world" does not constitute a reprobation of the rest of the world, for whom He was even then about to offer Himself as a "propitiation for the sins of the whole world" and to whom He would soon send His disciples to "preach the gospel to every creature." "Out of the world" is the ethical circumstance of the election to salvation.

[26]Certain passages may seem to some to suggest that Christ is only passive in election, merely the receptor and depository of those whom the Father gives to Him, (e.g., "all that the Father gives me . . . as many as thou hast given him"–Jn. 6:37,39; 17:2). These passages only reflect the fact that all believers are the Father's gift to the Son to be the heritage of Him who died for them, those in whom He rejoices as ones whose iniquities He has borne and by whom He is satisfied for the travail of His soul (Isa. 53:11). For a consideration of the question, Whom does the Father give to Jesus? see Appendix B of my work *Life in the Son: A Study of the Doctrine of Perseverence.*

It is clear that for Paul there is no discrepancy to be bridged between what happened in eternity and what happened in time. And he finds it impossible to think of the plan of God without thinking of Jesus Christ; as Van Leeuwen remarks, with reference to Ephesians 1:4, "the counsel of God is not an immutable and fixed decree." This fixedness and immutability are foreign to Paul's hymn on the love of God. The power and evidence of Paul's testimony have safeguarded the Church and theology at decisive moments against a devaluation of God's election to such a fixedness of decree, which is only later realized in the work of Christ. Scripture does say "through Christ" with respect to salvation, and there is no need at all to balk at the word "instrumental"—as when Paul writes that we are reconciled with God through (*dia*) the death of His Son (Rom. 5:10)—provided that the word "instrumental" is stripped of all impersonal connotations, and that we think of God's act as being in Christ who is the author of our salvation (Heb. 2:10). . . . There is no discrepancy for Paul between "in Christ" and "through Christ."[27]

Berkouwer here affirms that the decree of election in eternity becomes *fixed* only when it becomes realized in the redemptive work of Christ in time. This is true (but certainly not consonant with Calvin's definition of election, which will be cited later in this chapter). Writing from the context of Paul's Ephesian doxology, Berkouwer declares

. . . God elects us in Christ and because of Christ . . . Paul often speaks of "through Christ." "In" and "through" are not meant as two different aspects of one and the same situation. They both indicate the one electing act of God which in history becomes revealed as His act in Christ [the atonement, as context makes clear].[28]

Berkouwer is correct: Christ's saving act of atonement in *time* is the historical event in which the eternal decree of election becomes fixed. The atonement is a reflection of the decree of election in the counsels of eternity; but it is infinitely more: it is itself "the one electing act of God."

The decree in eternity was only of the intention of the temporal act. In the counsels of eternity, in the decree of the

---

[27]Berkouwer, *op. cit.*, pp. 148f.
[28]*Ibid.*, p. 148.

intention to elect, God the Father was the primary elector, who chose us in Christ before the foundation of the world. In history, in the realization of the intention of election in "the one electing act of God" in the atonement, God the Son was the immediate elector, who draws all men to Himself.

Calvary looks to eternity; but even more does eternity look to Calvary. The real agency of Christ as "the electing God" is established by the fact that, in His saving act of offering Himself up to the Father for the sins of the whole world, He was wholly voluntary.[29]

2. Christ Comprehensive in Election

Instrumental in election, both by the Father's appointment and by His own initiative, Christ is also *comprehensive* in election. The comprehensiveness is circumstantial, deriving from His instrumentality.

In the Ephesian doxology, Paul is emphatic in his affirmation that the gracious election is "in Christ . . . in him . . . in the Beloved." That the election to salvation is in Christ is a truth so obvious in the Scriptures that the point need not be labored. Representative of many pertinent exegetical comments that might be cited is the comment of Lightfoot on Ephesians 1:4:

en Christō] i.e. 'by virtue of our incorporation in, our union with, Christ.' As God seated us in heaven 'in Christ' (ii. 6), so also He bestowed His blessings upon us there in Him.

. . . .

en autō] i.e. en Christō. In God's eternal purpose the believers are contemplated as existing in Christ, as the Head, the Summary, of the race. The eklogē [the election] has no separate existence independently of the eklektos (Luke ix. 35, xxiii. 35) [the chosen One, Christ]. The election of Christ involves implicitly the election of the Church.[30]

---

[29]The voluntary character of Christ's act of atonement will be treated in the following chapter.

[30]J. B. Lightfoot, *Notes on the Epistles of St. Paul,* p. 312.

Lightfoot speaks of "our union with Christ." The election to salvation is only in union with Christ. Thus Christ is the *locus standi* of election, apart from whom no man is elect. As Berkouwer has well said, "There is election only in Christ."[31] The *locus standi* aspect of election is clearly apparent in the following quotations from Calvin, which were cited earlier in the chapter:

[Christ] is the beloved Son, in whom the love of the Father dwells, and from whom it afterwards extends to us. Thus Paul says, "In whom he hath made us accepted in the Beloved" (Eph. i. 6). (3:2:32)

. . . .

Paul testifies indeed that we were chosen before the foundation of the world; but, he adds, in Christ (Eph. 1:4). (E.P. 8:6)

Consider again Christ in His role as the elect Servant of Jehovah, as portrayed in Isaiah 42:

Behold my servant . . . mine elect. . . . I, Jehovah, have called thee in righteousness and will hold thine hand and will keep thee and give thee for a covenant of the people, for a light of the Gentiles, to open the blind eyes, to bring out the prisoners from the prison and them that sit in darkness out of the prison house. (vs. 1,6f.)

Here is one of the most beautiful concepts in the Holy Scriptures concerning the instrumentality of Christ in election. Jehovah says of the Servant-Messiah, "[I will] give *thee* for a covenant of the people." The Messiah is *Himself* the Living Covenant of reconciliation and election, through whom the grace of God flows to the people and in whom the people, Israel and the Gentiles together, are accepted.

Christ is *the* Elect, the one Mediator between God and men, the Living Covenant of reconciliation and election, the electing God, the *locus standi* in whom alone men are elect and outside whom no man is elect. In the face of many affirmations of Holy Scripture, it may in truth be said that Christ, who is our Life

---

[31]Berkouwer, *op. cit.*, p. 149.

(Col. 3:4), is Himself the Election. Instrumentally and comprehensively, the election is Christocentric.

II. Election Corporate

A second aspect of election is implicit in Paul's Ephesian doxology: the election to salvation is *corporate* as well as Christocentric. The corporate nature of election has been noted by many. In his comment on Ephesians 1:4, previously cited, Lightfoot writes, "The election of Christ involves implicitly the election of the Church."[32] Westcott comments on Ephesians 1:4, *"exelexato*] He chose us (*i.e.* Christians as a body *v. 3*) for Himself out of the world."[33] Bloomfield comments on Ephesians 1:5, "... the Apostle has here no reference to the *personal* election of *individuals.* ... "[34] Lange comments on Ephesians 1:3

... "us" should be taken in its wider meaning ... and should not be limited to the Apostle ... nor to the Jewish Christians, but applies to his people, all men, who have become or will become Christians.[35]

The corporate inference of Lange's words above is substantiated by his comment on Romans 8:28-30, "... Christ is the elect in God's real kingdom in the absolute sense, so that all His followers are chosen with Him as organic members, according to their organic relations (Eph. i)."[36]

Obviously, the corporate body of the elect is comprised of individuals. But the election is primarily corporate and only secondarily particular. The thesis that the election is corporate, as Paul understood it and viewed it in the Ephesian doxology, is supported by the whole context of his epistle:

---

[32]Lightfoot, *op. cit.,* p. 312.

[33]Westcott, *op. cit.,* p. 8.

[34]S. T. Bloomfield, *The Greek Testament, with English Notes,* Vol. II, p. 299, italics his.

[35]John Peter Lange, *Commentary on the Holy Scriptures: Ephesians,* p. 28.

[36]Lange, *Commentary on the Holy Scriptures: Romans,* p. 290.

... gather together in one all things in Christ ... the redemption of the purchased possession ... his inheritance in the saints ... the church, which is his body ... who has made both one ... to make in himself of twain one new man ... that he might reconcile both unto God in one body ... the household of God ... all the building fitly framed together ... an holy temple ... builded together for an habitation of God ... of the same body ... the mystery from the beginning of the world [now disclosed in] the church [as the fulfillment of] the eternal purpose which he purposed in Christ Jesus our Lord ... of whom the whole family in heaven and earth is named ... glory in the church by Christ Jesus throughout all ages ... one body ... the body of Christ ... the whole body fitly joined together ... increase of the body ... we are members one of another ... Christ is the head of the church ... the saviour of the body ... Christ loved the church and gave himself for it, that he might sanctify and cleanse it with the washing of water by the word, that he might present it to himself a glorious church ... they two shall be one flesh [but] I speak concerning Christ and the church.

The concept of the corporate body of the elect is intrinsic in all the above excerpts. Consider 2:12, "you were without Christ, being aliens from the commonwealth of Israel and strangers from the covenants of promise. . . . " The concept of the corporate election of Israel, a concept derived from many Scriptures, is clearly apparent. The concept of corporate election is equally apparent in Paul's assertion that Jews and Gentiles together are "reconciled to God in one body on the cross" (v. 16). The New Testament comprehends believers, not in isolation, but as members of the body of the elect. The election of individual men cannot be isolated from "the church, which is his body" any more than it can be isolated from Christ Himself.

Calvin recognized the corporate aspect of election. He writes, for example, "Do we not here [in election] find the very origin of the Church?" (3:21:1) Again, "All the elect of God are so joined together in Christ that, as they depend on one head, so they are as it were compacted into one body, being knit together like its different members" (4:1:2). But it is evident from his definitions that Calvin viewed election as *particular,* as well as unconditional, which makes the corporate aspect of election consequential and secondary rather than primary.[37] Consider the following definitions:

> By predestination we mean the eternal decree of God by which he determined with himself whatever he wished to happen with regard to every man. All are not created on equal terms, but some are preordained to eternal life, others to eternal damnation; and, accordingly as each has been created for one or other of these ends, we say that he has been predestinated to life or to death. (3:21:5)

> We say, then, that Scripture clearly proves this much, that God by his eternal and immutable counsel determined once for all those whom it was his pleasure one day to admit to salvation, and those whom, on the other hand, it was his pleasure to doom to destruction. We maintain that this counsel, as regards the elect, is founded on his free mercy, without any respect to human worth, while those whom he dooms to destruction are excluded from access to life by a just and blameless, but at the same time incomprehensible judgment. (3:21:7)

> When God prefers some to others, choosing some and passing others by, the difference does not depend on human dignity or indignity. . . . If what I teach is true, that those who perish are destined to death by the eternal good pleasure of God, though the reason does not appear, then they are not *found* but *made* worthy of destruction. . . . the eternal predestination of God, by which before the fall of Adam He decreed what should take place concerning the whole human race and every individual, was fixed and determined. . . . God chose out of the condemned race of Adam those whom He pleased and reprobated whom He willed. . . . (E.P. 8:5)

It is evident from his definitions of election (and reprobation) that Calvin viewed election as both specifically individual

---

[37]Barth points out (p. 307) that in the first edition of the *Institutes* and in the Catechism of 1542, Calvin "referred election primarily to the Church," but changed decisively through the years, so that in the final edition of the *Institutes,* the whole concept of election revolves about the unconditional election and reprobation of particular men. This became the concept of Reformed theology.

and unconditional. A central thesis of Calvin's doctrine of election may be stated thus:

> The election to salvation is of particular men unconditionally, who comprise the corporate body incidentally.

A central thesis of the Biblical doctrine of election may be stated thus:

> The election to salvation is corporate and comprehends individual men only in identification and association with the elect body.

With this thesis before us, let us cite again Lange's comment on Romans 8:28-30: ". . . Christ is the elect in God's real kingdom in the absolute sense, so that all His followers are chosen with Him as organic members, *according to their organic relations* (Eph. i)."[38] Lange cites Hoffmann (*Schriftbeweis*, vol. i, p. 227) to the effect that "election relates not merely to individuals, but to the entire body, and, accordingly, to individuals as members of the body."[39] Barth writes

> . . . an elect man is in any case elect in and with the community of Jesus Christ. . . . Thus every election of individuals is an election in the sphere of the [elect] community—on the basis of the fact that this sphere is both established and marked out in the election of Jesus Christ."[40]

Unlike Calvin's thesis that particular men are unconditionally elect from eternity and other particular men are unconditionally reprobate, the thesis that the election to salvation is corporate and comprehends individuals only in identification and association with the elect body does not require for its defense ingenious interpretations of simple, explicit categorical statements of Scripture. Furthermore, the thesis of corporate election is substantiated by the fact that, in certain passages of Scripture, the matter of the salvation of individuals within the

---

[38]Lange, *Commentary on the Holy Scriptures: Romans,* p. 290, italics mine.
[39]*Ibid.*
[40]Barth, *op. cit.,* p. 410.

body is abstracted from the matter of the salvation of the corporate body and is viewed as contingent. The possibility of apostasy posits the corporate nature of the election.

The Scriptures bear witness to actual instances of apostasy and abound with solemn warnings against the peril, which (contrary to the assumptions of some) is real rather than hypothetical.[41] For our present purpose, we shall cite only a few of the passages that clearly posit the peril of apostasy within the context of the elect body. First, consider the following excerpt from *Life in the Son: A Study of the Doctrine of Perseverance,* page 366:

* * *

The certainty of election and perseverance is with respect, not to particular individual men unconditionally, but rather with respect to the *ekklēsia,* the corporate body of all who, through living faith, are in union with Christ, the true Elect and the Living Covenant between God and all who trust in His righteous Servant (Isa. 42:1-7; 40:1-12; 52:13–53:12; 61:1,2). Consider the following:

God's eternal purpose in grace:
>   Eph. 1:4, He chose us in Christ that we should be *hagious kai amōmous* before Him.
>   Col. 1:22, He reconciled us to Himself in Christ, through His death, to present us *hagious kai amōmous* before Him.

Fulfillment corporately (certain):
>   Eph. 5:27, Christ will present the *ekklēsia* to Himself *hagia kai amōmos.*

Fulfillment individually (contingent):
>   Col. 1:23, He will present us *hagious kai amōmous* before Him—if we continue in the faith grounded and settled and be not moved away from the hope of the Gospel.

* * *

---

[41]For a critical consideration of the question of perseverance and apostasy, see my work *Life in the Son: A Study of the Doctrine of Perseverance.*

The fact that the election is corporate and comprehends individuals only in association with the elect body is reflected in many passages of Scripture. For example, in Romans 11 Paul declares that the corporate election of the *Israel* within Israel remained unimpaired, though some of the branches were broken off because of unbelief. Observe that the "breaking off" was from the elect *Israel* within the national Israel; the Jews who refused the Messiah were not thereby severed from the national Israel. Gentile believers, grafted into the corporate body, are warned that they face the same contingency (vs. 19-22). Therefore, let them be diligent to continue in faith in humility and fear (vs. 20-22). Hope is held out for the branches broken off: they may be grafted in again if they do not continue in unbelief. Thus the election is of *Israel*, and individuals are elect only in identification and organic union with the body through faith.

Paul addresses his letter to the Colossians "to the saints and faithful brethren in Christ" (1:2), whom he speaks of as "the elect of God"[42] (3:12) who have been "delivered from the power of darkness and translated into the kingdom of God's dear Son" (1:13) and who formerly were "alienated" from God but now are reconciled in the body of Christ's flesh through His death, ultimately to be presented holy and unreproveable in his presence (1:21f.). But he warns them that the ultimate purpose and goal will be realized in them only if they "continue in the faith grounded and settled and be not moved away from the hope of the gospel which they have heard" (1:23). The warning has no application to outsiders, but rather to the members of the elect body alone.

Paul addresses "the saints at Ephesus and the faithful in Christ Jesus" as men comprehended in the body of those chosen in Christ before the foundation of the world, predes-

---

[42]Referral of election to specific individuals or groups (e.g., Phil. 4:3, II Thess. 1:4, II Thess. 2:13) in no way militates against the fact of corporate election, for the election obviously comprehends individuals, in whom Paul can rejoice as "the elect of God."

tined to adoption as children of God through Jesus Christ (1:4,5) and who, having heard and believed the Gospel and having placed their faith and trust in Christ, have been sealed[43] by the Holy Spirit (1:13), having been quickened together with Christ, with the prospect of sharing the bounties of the riches of the grace of God in the ages to come (2:5-7). But he warns them against becoming participants in the wickedness of the world around them, thus becoming partakers of the wrath of God against the disobedient (5:1-7). Within the larger warning is a specific warning against allowing themselves to be deceived by the vain words and specious arguments of any who might seek to persuade them that such an eventuality could not happen (v. 6).

The Epistle to the Hebrews, which its author conceived of as primarily a "word of exhortation" (13:22), is filled with solemn warnings addressed, not to men who have only approached Christ in the confrontation of the Gospel but have halted short of actual saving faith (as some have assumed), but to believers confronted with the temptation to repudiate Christ and return to Judaism.[44] In the third chapter, he addresses his readers as "holy brethren, partakers of the heavenly calling," for whom Jesus is "the Apostle and High Priest of our confession" (3:1). He affirms that, as Moses was faithful as a servant in the house of Israel, so is Christ as a Son over His own house, "whose house are we–if we hold fast our confidence and our rejoicing in the hope firm to the end" (v. 6). He warns his "holy brethren" against departing from the living God through the subtle influence of sin and thus failing to be made the everlasting companions and fellows of Christ (vs. 12-14).

Writing to "them that have obtained like precious faith with us through the righteousness of God and our Saviour Jesus

---

[43]*Sphragizein,* to mark with a seal for identification, the seal here being the Holy Spirit present in the believers.

[44]For a brief analysis of the Epistle to the Hebrews, see *Life in the Son,* Chapter XV.

Christ" (II Pet. 1:1), Peter warns them to "give diligence to
make your calling and election sure" (v. 10) by earnestly
pursuing the things that will prevent them from becoming
"barren and unfruitful in the knowledge of our Lord Jesus
Christ" (vs. 5-8).[45]
Writing to "my little children" in the holy faith, the aged
John warns them against "them that would seduce you" (I Jn.
2:26) by persuading them to disown Christ, as they themselves
have done (vs. 18-23). Some expositors have assumed from
verse 19 that those who withdrew were reprobates from the
beginning. This may, or may not, have been the case; the
question is impossible to determine from the text.[46] In any
event, there is nothing about the actions of the Christ-disowners
and the circumstance of their withdrawal that in any manner or
degree qualifies the solemn warning John addresses to his little
children in the faith in the immediate context of his epistle:

"Let that therefore remain in you which you have heard from the
beginning [the true Gospel, in contrast to the arguments of the
Christ-disowners]. If that which you have heard from the beginning shall
remain in you, you also shall continue in the Son and in the Father. And
this is the promise that he has promised us, even eternal life" (vs. 24f.)

The "us" from whom the Christ-disowners withdrew is the elect
body, and the withdrawal was spiritual before it was physical.
John's warning to his little children follows immediately his
assertion that whoever disowns the Son no longer has the
Father (v. 23). The little children face the peril of succumbing
to the seductive persuasions of the Christ-disowners and
following the same tragic course, a peril against which they
must be on their guard.

In their interpretation of our Lord's Parable of the Ten
Virgins (Matt. 25:1-13), some expositors, influenced by the
necessities of their theology, have made the five foolish virgins
whose lamps went out representative of "false professors"

---

[45]Cf. John 15:1-6 for the peril of unfruitfulness in the knowledge of Christ.
[46]For a discussion of I John 2:19, cf. *Life in the Son*, pp. 361f.

whose lamps never burned from the beginning (an assumption which is contrary to the literary structure of the parable), hypocrites who never had arrived at true faith. But they are in radical opposition to our Lord, whose only application of His parable was not at all to outsiders, but to his auditors, his own Apostles: "Watch therefore, for you know neither the day nor the hour wherein the Son of Man cometh" (v. 13).[47]

In all these passages and others which could be cited, the warnings are directed to men who obviously are conceived of as being members of the elect body, the true *ekklēsia.* Unless the words of Christ and His Apostles are to be dismissed as mere rhetorical hypothesis, without foundation in fact, or unless we accept Calvin's assumption (3:2:11,12) of "an inferior operation of the Spirit" by which He enlightens some with a present sense of grace which afterwards proves "evanescent" and "sheds some rays of grace on the reprobate, afterwards allowing these to be extinguished" so that by the express design of God they perish—all because "the will of God is immutable" and His eternal counsel for them was reprobation rather than salvation, so that "when God shows himself propitious to them, it is not as if he had truly rescued them from death and taken them under his protection," despite the fact that they "believe God to be propitious to them, inasmuch as they accept the gift of reconciliation" . . . ad infinitum, ad nauseam (God plays games with the souls of men? The death of Christ for the sins of the whole world was all in fun?) . . . unless we can accept such horrible assumptions, we must recognize that the Bible affirms the reality of the apostasy of members of the elect body. With respect to the Apostles of our Lord, who can posit such fantastic assumptions as Calvin's? Who will say that our Lord entertained such fantastic assumptions as He addressed His solemn words to His Apostles? Who will say that Paul and other Apostles entertained such horrible assumptions as they ad-

---

[47]Cf. Luke 21:34-36, also addressed by Christ to His own Apostles, and Luke 12:35-46, a warning Christ addressed to all disciples.

dressed their warnings to the Ephesians, the Colossians, the "little children" in the faith, and all the "holy brethren"?

The certainty of election and perseverance is with respect to the corporate body, the *ekklēsia,* rather than with respect to particular men unconditionally. The election is corporate and comprehends individuals only in identification and association with the elect body. With equal truth, Paul can assure us that God has "chosen us [corporately] in Christ before the foundation of the world" and Peter can admonish us to "give diligence to make your calling and election [individually and personally] sure."

Westcott comments on Ephesians 1:1

> The three characteristics *saints, faithful, in Christ Jesus* give a complete and harmonious view of those to whom St. Paul writes. He addresses men who are consecrated to God in a Divine Society (*saints*), who are inspired by a personal devotion towards Him (*faithful*), who are in Him in Whom the Church finds its unity and life (*c.*iv.16). Thus the order *saints, faithful,* is seen to be perfectly natural. The two thoughts are complementary: God's will, man's answer. So the thought of the social consecration to God precedes the thought of the continuous individual faith by which the members of the body keep their place in it.[48]

Reflecting on our considerations in this chapter, it becomes easier to understand our Lord's severity in his solemn warning that to be drowned in the depth of the sea with a millstone hanged about one's neck would be preferable to offending "one of these little ones which believe in me" (Matt. 18:6). Clement's comment, in which he presents a paraphrase combining Mark 14:21 and Luke 17:2, is enlightening as reflecting the understanding of a contemporary of Peter, Paul, John, and others of the Apostles:

> Why do we divide and tear asunder the members of Christ, and raise up strife against our own body, and reach such a pitch of madness as to forget that we are members one of another? Remember the words of the Lord Jesus; for he said, "Woe unto that man: it were better for him if he had

---

[48]Westcott, *op. cit.,* p. 4.

not been born than that he should offend one of my elect; it were better for him that a millstone be hung on him, and he be cast into the sea, than that he should turn aside one of my elect."[49]

The thesis that the election is corporate and comprehends individual men only in identification and association with the elect body is completely consonant with John's thesis:

This is the record, that God has given to us eternal life, and this life is in his Son. He who has the Son has life, and he who has not the Son of God has not the life. (I John 5:11,12)

As there is life only in the Son, so the election is only in the Son, who is our Life (Col. 3:4)—the Way, the Truth, and the Life, apart from whom no man comes to the Father (John 14:6)—the Son who is the one Mediator between God and men, the Living Covenant of Grace and Reconciliation, the Elect, the electing God, and Himself the Election, who said, "Abide in me, and I in you."

Elect in the Son . . .

---

[49]Clement, *op. cit.*, 46:7f.

A Ransom for All

There is one God, and one mediator between God and men, the man Christ Jesus, who gave himself a ransom for all.

I TIMOTHY 2:5,6

We see Jesus, who was made for a little while lower than the angels for the suffering of death . . . that he by the grace of God should taste death for every man.

HEBREWS 2:9

CHAPTER III

A RANSOM FOR ALL

IN A WORLD in which the problems of man are many and multiplying, it remains true that in a profound sense the problems of man are but one: man's problem is sin.

Estranged from his Creator and alienated from Life, man lives in enmity against his Ancestor, at odds with his brothers, and in contradiction with himself. The election finds men, not holy and without blame (Eph. 1:4), but in the circumstance of the Fall—sinners and blameworthy.

Theologians long have pondered the problem of the Fall and the relation of Adam's transgression to all mankind.[1] We need not toil long over the sins of Adam, for we have sins of our own, and more than enough, for which to weep with David and with Peter. Who of us is not the prodigal son? Who of us needs not be on his guard lest, worse still, he be the elder brother as well? We know about sin.

The profoundest aspect of the tragedy of sin lies in the alienation from God which it imposes. Paul reminded the Ephesians that in time past they were "without Christ, being aliens from the commonwealth of Israel, and strangers from the covenants of promise, having no hope, and without God in the world" (2:12). Men without Christ, outside the elect body, are "alienated from the life of God" (4:18) and "dead in trespasses and sins" (2:1). In the tragic circumstance of alienation from God and the life of God, man is without strength to save

---

[1]This question will be taken up in the following chapter.

himself (Rom. 5:6). Sin is his problem, his burden, and—left to himself—his everlasting undoing.

But the good news of the Gospel is that man is not left to himself. One has come from God to men to put away sin by the sacrifice of Himself, that He might reconcile us to God.

I. One Mediator, the Man Christ Jesus

"There is one God, and one mediator between God and men," wrote Paul, "the man Christ Jesus." Profound meaning beyond all we can fathom attaches to the word *man*.

The incarnation is among the most sublime mysteries of holy truth. The Word was made flesh (Jn. 1:14). Here is the complete identification of God with man: the Word, from the unbegun beginning face-to-face with God as an equal (*pros ton theon,* Jn. 1:1) and very God, becomes very man and is found in fashion as a man (Phil. 2:8). In this act of complete identification, the Word divested Himself of His divine majesty and took on Him the likeness of men (2:7).

In the incarnation the Word, becoming Son of Man, became also Son of God. From the eternal "beginning," the Word was the *Son* only in prospect—a prospect realized in time in the incarnation: "Thou art my Son; this day have I begotten thee" (Heb. 1:5).[2] In the incarnation the Word became Son of God

---

[2]The words "Thou art my Son, this day have I begotten thee" do not have reference (as some have assumed) to some occasion in eternity past when God created a Son. In such case it would not be true that the Word was *with* God and *God* in the beginning (Jn. 1:1,2)—the "beginning" of eternal infinitude. It is nowhere said that the Word was begotten of God except with reference to the incarnation (Jn. 1:14).

The word of Gabriel to Mary, "That holy one who shall be born of you shall be called the Son of God" (Lk. 1:35), associates the God-Sonship with the incarnation and birth of the Word as Son of Man. Psalm 2:7, the prophetic original declaration of the words "Thou art my Son, this day Have I begotten thee," places the declaration within the context of the temporal career of the Messiah rather than in eternity past. Likewise the reference in Heb. 5:5 relates the declaration to the priestly career of Christ—obviously not prior to the incarnation. Phil. 2:6 posits parity for Christ in His pre-incarnate state rather than subordination, as in the relation of a son to his father.

In the opinion of many excellent commentators, Col. 1:15—"the firstborn of all creation"—militates against my contention, pointing to a generation by God of the

and Son of Man–a circumstance from which He can never withdraw in all eternity to come; a circumstance in which He is forever Emmanual, God-With-Us, having entered into the life-stream of humanity and the total corpus and community of mankind in complete identification with man and all that man is by creation. He who with Father and Spirit created man in His own image took upon Him once and for ever the image of man.

But the incarnation, wonderful as it is, was not an end in itself, despite the opinions of some who have felt that at least it *might* have been. Denney observes that

> There are those who hold that the incarnation is too great a thing to be contingent upon anything else, and especially upon such an unhappy chance as the appearance of sin in the world. It would have taken place in any case: the Son of God would have become man even if man had never fallen; He would have come in flesh to consummate creation and give the human race its true head and a true unity. There is an ideal or metaphysical necessity for the incarnation which is independent of sin.[3]

It is perhaps true to say that there were necessities for the incarnation other than for the atonement. At least it is true to

---

[3] James Denney, *The Christian Doctrine of Reconciliation*, p. 181.

Son at some time prior to creation. However, many equally excellent commentators reject that interpretation, and I think rightly so. I believe Eadie is correct (*Commentary on the Epistle of Paul to the Colossians*) in his assertion that prōtotokos is ethical and has reference, not to priority of time (which in any case He has toward creation, being "before all things," v. 17), but to prerogative, which is primarily emphatic in the passage: "all things created *for* him . . . that in all things he might have the pre-eminence." Eadie makes the interesting observation that "traces of the same idiom are found in the Jewish Kabbala–in which Jehovah himself is called the 'first-born of the world' "–which could have only an ethical sense. I sincerely believe that the concept that the Word is a creature–a created being brought into existence at some time prior to the material creation–is not intended by Paul in Col. 1:15 and is to be rejected, and that instead, *pros ton theon* and truly *theos* (Jn. 1:1) was an eternal circumstance of the Word who became flesh, to dwell among us full of grace and truth. An essential part of His voluntary humiliation in taking upon Him the role of Sonship was the assumption of the attendant circumstance of subordination, supplanting the status of parity which He had known from eternity (Phil. 2:6-8).

say that the incarnation served more than a single purpose and was indeed in order to the consummation of creation and the federal unity of humanity in the Creator Himself. Some, however, have even regarded the incarnation as redemptive in nature, sufficiently so to be fully efficacious:

Writers of the school of Ritschl [emulate] the speculative character of Greek Christology and soteriology. It is a Logos Christology, determined fundamentally by the idea that the eternal Logos takes human nature into union with Himself in the womb of the Virgin, and by doing so achieves the redemption of the race. In Christ's person humanity is actually redeemed and made one with the divine. The logic of this conception would entitle us to say that the incarnation—not in an ethical sense, as including the whole manifestation of the divine in the human throughout the life and death of Jesus, but in a physical or sacramental sense—was everything, and that the work of man's salvation was accomplished when the Word assumed flesh.[4]

But the election finds men in the circumstance of the Fall, under the condemnation of sin, and for man's redemption something more than the incarnation was required. The Scriptures emphatically affirm that the incarnation was essentially a prerequisite for the atonement:

Being found in fashion as a man, he humbled himself and became obedient unto death, even the death of the cross. (Phil. 2:8)

But we see Jesus, who was made for a little while lower than the angels for the suffering of death . . . that he by the grace of God should taste death for every man. (Heb. 2:9)

Once in the consummation of the age has he appeared to put away sin by the sacrifice of himself. (Heb. 9:26)

The incarnation was redemptive, but not per se; it was redemptive only in a subordinate sense as prerequisite to the central redemptive act of Christ in the atonement. As Denney has well said,

---

[4]*Ibid.*, p. 33f.

The New Testament knows nothing of an incarnation which can be defined apart from its relation to atonement; it is to put away sin and to destroy the works of the devil that even in the evangelist of the Incarnation the Son of God is made manifest. It is not in His being here, but in His being here as a propitiation for the sins of the world that the love of God is revealed. Not Bethlehem, but Calvary is the focus of revelation, and any construction of Christianity which ignores or denies this distorts Christianity by putting it out of focus.[5]

The Word was made flesh and became Man for the suffering of death for every man, that He might reconcile men to God. "There is one mediator between God and men, the man Christ Jesus." It was as *man* that Jesus accomplished the atonement.

The vocation of Jesus is represented in the gospels in two ways. On the one hand, He came to reveal the Father, and by doing so to enable men to become children of God. In this relation He is spoken of *simpliciter* as the Son, to whom alone all others must owe it that they have the knowledge of the Father and a place among the children (Matt. xi. 27 ff.). On the other hand, He came to bring in the Kingdom of God and to secure for men their citizenship in this divine commonwealth. In this relation He is spoken of as the Son of Man. . . . Whenever He speaks of [His] sufferings, as He does again and again, they are the sufferings of the Son of Man.[6]

"Since by man came death," wrote Paul to the Corinthians, "by man came also the resurrection of the dead" (I:15:21). Since by man came the Fall, by Man came also the Reconciliation. It does not lie within the province of *God* to be made sin for the sinful nor to die. These things Jesus did as *man*. In the same arena in which man was defeated by sin, Man, tempted in all points as all men are tempted, conquered sin in His own right, and having conquered it, accepted it as His own, died under its just penalty, and vanquished it forever for men. Having conquered sin for men, having vindicated God's just condemnation of sin by accepting the appointed penalty of death, Christ became Himself the ground on which God can be just and the justifier of all who believe in Jesus.

---

[5]Denney, *The Death of Christ*, p. 325.
[6]Denney, *The Christian Doctrine of Reconciliation*, p. 138f.

There is one God, and one Mediator between God and men,
the man Christ Jesus,

II. Who Gave Himself.

Reference has been made to those who have assumed that the
incarnation itself was sufficiently redemptive to obviate the
necessity of the death of Christ for atonement. As representative of this assumption, Denney cites Riviere (to whom
reference was made in Chapter II):

"What was necessary," asks M. Riviere, "that the Word incarnate might
achieve this work of reparation?"—that is, the work of moral reparation in
which, as he properly insists, a due satisfaction is made to God for sin. His
answer is, "In principle, nothing but His presence in humanity; the least of
His actions had a sufficient value . . . a single act of the incarnate Word
would have sufficed for this end. . . ."[7]

Quite to the contrary, Jesus recognized the necessity of His
death. Early in His ministry, to Nicodemus at Jerusalem He
said, "As Moses lifted up the serpent in the wilderness, even so
must the Son of Man be lifted up" (John 3:14). Matthew tells
us that, following Peter's great confession of Jesus as the
Messiah, the Son of the living God, "From that time forth
began Jesus to show to his disciples how that he must go to
Jerusalem and suffer many things of the elders and chief priests
and scribes, and be killed and be raised again the third day"
(16:21). At the time, Jesus still was popular with the
multitudes. But He knew what awaited Him at Jerusalem, and
He spoke of it often to His disciples. At Jerusalem in the final
week, facing the cross—now so near at hand, Jesus said, "For
this cause came I to this hour" (Jn. 12:27). The cross came as
no surprise to Jesus, no unforeseen contingency; He had
anticipated it from the beginning of His ministry. He had come,
He said, to give His life a ransom for many. There was necessity
for His death, necessity which Jesus recognized and declared.

---

[7]*Ibid.*, p. 240f.

The death of Jesus was a necessity with respect to both God and man. With respect to God, it was a *moral* necessity: only on the ground of the atonement wrought by Jesus, who accepted the just penalty for sin, could God retain His integrity and be both just and the justifier of him who believes in Jesus. With respect to men, the death of Jesus was a *mediatorial* necessity: when we were without strength, powerless to escape the condemnation of sin, Christ died for the ungodly, that we might be saved from wrath through Him.

But the death of Jesus, a *moral* and a *mediatorial* necessity, was not an absolute necessity per se, but rather an *instrumental* necessity. It was a necessity only on the predication of the election. This becomes clear to us as we reflect on the words of Jesus to Peter in Gethsemane:

Put away thy sword . . . Thinkest thou that I cannot now pray to my Father and he shall immediately give me more than twelve legions of angels? But how then shall the scriptures be fulfilled, that thus it must be? (Matt. 26:52-54)

Thus Jesus was completely voluntary in His death and laid down His life of Himself, by His own free choice. The voluntary character of His death made it the precise moment and the authentic act of election for time and eternity.

The Father chose that the Son should die and gave Him up to death . . . but *only* on condition that the Son should choose to die. The decision for death was made, not only in the counsels of eternity before creation; in the *final* deliberation, it was made by Jesus in Gethsemane. In His decision in Gethsemane, Jesus was completely free and faced real options. The Father would have concurred immediately and unquestionably in His decision for either option. Thus the decision of Jesus was finally decisive. And because He was completely free in the final decision, His decision in Gethsemane to drink the cup, and the death that followed, became the authentic decision and act of election, irrevocable and eternal.

It is impossible to appreciate all that was involved in the decision of Jesus. But it is evident from His words that even the authenticity of the Scriptures was involved: had He summoned legions of angels from the Father, "how then shall the scriptures be fulfilled, that thus it must be?" The integrity of the Scriptures depended on the decision of Jesus, and in that decision He was free. He had not to die, simply because He was Jesus or under the inescapable constraint of the prophetic Scriptures. He was to die only if He chose to die. Thus the Scriptures which foretold His death were not given somehow to "make it happen," and He was free to give them substance through His own free decision to ratify and confirm them, thus making them "a more sure word of prophecy" (I Pet. 1:19).

For any other man to suggest that, by his own decision, he would give substance and authenticity to the Holy Scriptures would be gross blasphemy. But no other man is who Jesus is and what He is, and no one else ever stood where He stood "once in the consummation of the ages." For Him to say such a thing was neither blasphemy nor presumption, but holy truth.[8]

We have said (Chapter II) that, while Calvin recognized the instrumentality of Christ in election, he did not apprehend its full dimension and was not consistent on this point. This is evident from many passages in his works. Consider the following:

I not only freely confess but emphasise everywhere in my writings both that the salvation of men is bound to faith, and that Christ is the only door by which all must enter into the heavenly kingdom.

· ·

[Christ] is the manner in which [God] discharges His work of grace in them. But *why* He takes them by the hand has another *superior cause,* that eternal purpose, namely, by which He destined them to life. (E.P. 8:4, italics mine)

Here the election (which for Calvin is the unconditional election of particular men) proceeds exclusively from a determinant decree prior to creation, in which case the "decision" of Jesus

---

[8]For a more extensive consideration of the implications of Matt. 26:52ff. and the voluntary character of the sacrifice of Jesus, see my work *Life in the Son: A Study of the Doctrine of Perseverance,* pp. 243-251.

in Gethsemane was *not* a decision and the whole redemptive career of Christ becomes symbolic rather than authentic.

The same defect appears in the Canons of Dort: " . . . it was the will of God that Christ by the blood of the cross should effectually redeem . . . all those, and those only, who were from eternity chosen to salvation" (C.D. 2:8). Here Christ is not the ground of the election, and the election becomes *in abstractio*, for the choosing stands as a thing apart and prior to the Cross, with Christ and His act of atonement merely an accessory after the fact. For the Synod of Dort, the atonement was *not* the act of election, but only an echo of the decree of election announced before the foundation of the world.

In such a view as Calvin's and Dort's, Christ is not the *fundamentum* of election that the Scriptures declare Him to be. Such a view is to be rejected, for it denies the proper and rightful place to the one Mediator between God and men, the man Christ Jesus, who gave himself

III. A Ransom.

The atonement is a holy fact of many facets, and it does not lie within the province of the present study to explore the doctrine of the atonement in depth. Only let us observe that, as Anselm rightly insisted, it is God to whom the problem of sin must have ultimate reference, since there are moral necessities in His own Person (and therefore in the divine economy) which must be vindicated. The New Testament concept of atonement is that it is indeed *atonement,* involving ransom, redemption, and propitiation—all of which is concerned primarily with God and His holiness rather than with man. The atonement for sin is indeed *for* man, but it looks toward God and the vindication of His holiness, that He might be just and the justifier of him who believes in Jesus (Rom. 3:26).[9]

---

[9]The propitiation wrought by Christ is *toward* God, *for* man. It was offered, not merely to satisfy God for the sake of God Himself, but more especially to satisfy the necessities of His moral economy and the kingdom He purposed from eternity and to

The sacrifice of Jesus as a ransom for men was acceptable to God, not merely because of *who* Jesus was, but more especially because of *what* He was—a Lamb without blemish and without spot. And Jesus came to the Cross as what He was—the just, offering Himself for the unjust—not as the inevitable and automatic consequence of the circumstance of His birth, but in virtue of His own righteousness, patiently perfected in the experiences of His lifetime.

It is too easy to assume that, because Jesus was the Son of God, He was somehow isolated from sin and automatically and impregnably righteous. Scripture knows of no such thing. Quite to the contrary, it knows only a Word who came into humanity in the circumstance of the *kenosis*—who, very God from the eternal beginning, laid aside His majesty to be conceived in the womb of virgin Mary of Nazareth, to become what He had not been before—Son of God and Son of Man: to become Son of God in the act of taking on Him the seed of Abraham, and as very *man* (not pseudo "man") to suffer, being tempted in all points like as we are tempted . . . and having met sin at its worst and having conquered it in His own right, He accepted in Himself both the *sin* and the sins of mankind and suffered the just penalty, offering up in death His body, His blood, and His soul[10]—all that He was—as a sacrifice and ransom for all men.

---

[10]Isa. 53:10. Clement of Rome wrote (Epist. to Corinth. I), "Jesus Christ our Lord gave his blood for us, and his flesh for our flesh, and his soul for our souls"—beautifully expressed, and an awesome truth.

---

provide the only circumstance in which men, having sinned, could become part of the kingdom.

The Bible clearly affirms that God's wrath is toward the impenitent, concurrently with His love. (There is no difficulty here; this dual attitude is found in parents toward their children, as well as in God toward men, His creatures.) Propitiation is required, not to vindicate the righteous indignation of God for His sake, so that He can be secure in His own person; judgment and condemnation serve this purpose. Rather, propitiation is required so that the moral economy and the kingdom of God may remain inviolate as what they necessarily must be—for man's sake, as well as for God's. It is essential for men themselves that God remain *just* while being at the same

Jesus came to the cross "without spot," not as the consequence of having lived 33 years in sterile isolation from sin—immune to temptation and impregnable in righteousness, but because He had met every temptation common to man—and temptations beyond those of all other men—with unwavering commitment to righteousness (Heb. 1:9), striving mightily against sin (12:4) and learning obedience to the Father's will through the things He suffered (5:8). Fully perfected, He became through His sacrificial death the author of eternal salvation to all who obey Him (5:9).

Christ "gave himself a ransom for all." To whom was the ransom paid? Some have suggested that the ransom was paid to Satan. No so. Although "the whole world is in the power of the evil one" (I Jn. 5:19 RSV, cf. Lk. 4:6) during the present moral probation, yet Satan is a usurper; what he has is not rightfully his, and a single word from God would destroy him. God owes Satan nothing but judgment, and no ransom was or ever will be paid to him.

Others have suggested that Christ paid a ransom to God to procure the release of men from their just condemnation. Hebrews 9:12 has been cited: Christ "by his own blood entered in once into the holy place, having obtained eternal redemption for us." It is true that Christ "offered himself without spot to God" for our redemption (v. 14). But His offering was in no sense a payment of ransom to a reluctant God. God needed no persuasion to be gracious toward men, for He so loved the world that He gave His only begotten Son and delivered Him up for us all. What ransom could be paid to God that He would value more than His own Son? In reality, the Father by proxy concurred with the Son in the payment of the ransom. Christ "by his own blood entered in once into the holy place," not to

time the justifier of all who believe in Jesus. The integrity of the kingdom requires it, and man's good equally requires it, that God may be for man the point of absolute moral reference man's own being requires, and that the kingdom may afford for man the eternal moral fulfillment predicated in his creation in the image of God.

procure salvation for us from God, but already "having obtained eternal redemption for us" (Heb. 9:12).

But having obtained eternal redemption from whom? We believe that He obtained it—not from *whom,* but from *what,* and that He obtained redemption in the sense of creating it, as the Author of eternal salvation, by the merits of His once-for-all-for-ever act of atonement whereby He vindicated and satisfied the inexorable necessities of the moral economy ordained of God, in behalf of sinners justly condemned in the face of those necessities and utterly unable to save themselves (Rom. 5:6-11; 3:24-26).

In a sense, the holy life of Jesus was redemptive—not per se, but as prerequisite to His sacrificial offering in the atonement. The validity of His death as a sacrifice and ransom for men derived from the virtue of His life as in Himself righteousness—tested, proved, and perfected. In the life He lived and the death He died, Jesus was the Elector, electing men to salvation and the kingdom of God.

> There was no other good enough
> To pay the price of sin;
> He only could unlock the gate
> Of Heaven and let us in.

There is one God, and one Mediator between God and men, the man Christ Jesus, who gave himself

IV. A Ransom for All.

An integral part of Calvinism's system of theology is the doctrine of limited atonement. Advocates of limited atonement, however, are divided into two schools: those who hold the position of Calvin, and those who hold the position posited in the Westminster Confession of Faith. Representative of those who hold the Westminster position is John Murray, Professor of Systematic Theology at Westminster Theological Seminary, Philadelphia. In his book *Redemption—Accomplished and Applied,* Murray writes

This doctrine has been called the doctrine of limited atonement.

. . . .

Whether the expression "limited atonement" is good or not, we must reckon with the fact that unless we believe in the final restoration of all men we cannot have an unlimited atonement. If we universalise the extent we limit the efficacy. If some of those for whom atonement was made and redemption wrought perish eternally, then the atonement is not itself efficacious. It is this alternative that the proponents of universal atonement must face. They have a "limited" atonement, and limited in respect of that which impinges upon its essential character. We shall have none of it. The doctrine of "limited atonement" which we maintain is the doctrine which limits the atonement to those who are heirs of eternal life, to the elect. That limitation insures its efficacy and conserves its essential character as efficient and effective redemption.[11]

Murray assumes that we are confronted with the necessity of choosing between an atonement unlimited in extent but limited in efficacy and an atonement limited in extent but unlimited in efficacy. But there is a third alternative—one acceptable alike to "Calvin" Calvinists and to non-Calvinists: an objective atonement sufficient for all men, efficient for the elect.

It is evident from careful reading of Murray's chapter "The Extent of the Atonement" that in the development of his material, Murray's perspective was almost exclusively anthropocentric. As we have already observed, while the atonement is *for* man, it is essentially Godward rather than manward. Its authenticity and value in no way depend on the response of any man, but depend instead on its satisfaction of God and the demands of His righteousness. Denney has well said

Even if no man should ever say, "Thou, O Christ, art all I want; more than all in Thee I find," God says it. Christ and His work have this absolute value for the Father, whatever this or that individual may think of them. And as it is only on the basis of Christ and His work that reconciliation becomes an accomplished fact, it is strict truth to say that reconciliation—in the sense of man's return to God and acceptance with Him—is

---

[11]John Murray, *Redemption—Accomplished and Applied*, p. 74.

based on an objective atonement. It is because divine necessities have had homage done to them by Christ that the way is open for sinners to return to God through Him.[12]

But Murray will have none of any objective atonement primarily Godward rather than manward and potentially efficacious for all men. As argument against unlimited atonement, he asserts (*supra*), "If some of those for whom atonement was made and redemption wrought perish eternally, then the atonement is not itself efficacious." But this is no more true than that the preaching of the Gospel, addressed to all, is a failure because some refuse . . . or that Jesus failed because He longed to gather to Himself all the children of Jerusalem, but they would not have it so . . . or that God fails because all day long He stretches forth His hands to rebellious Israel, but they refuse. Murray's argument is without foundation.

Murray raises the question, "Did Christ come to make the salvation of all men possible, to remove obstacles that stood in the way of salvation, and merely to make provision for salvation? Or did he come to save his people?"[13] Here is that ubiquitous theological bugbear, an assumed *either . . . or.* Christ came to do both: to make the salvation of all men possible (which is by no means a "merely") and to save His people from their sins. The former purpose is in order to the latter, and the fact that the atonement is universally sufficient in no way impinges on the fact that it is particularly efficient.

Again, Murray asks, "Did [Christ] come to put all men in a salvable state? Or did he come to secure the salvation of all those who are ordained to eternal life?"[14] Here is the crux of the whole matter for Murray: his definition of the atonement is dictated by the necessities of his doctrine of election—Calvin's doctrine of the unconditional election and reprobation of particular men effected by determinant decree before creation. Such an assumption requires a limited atonement.

---

[12]Denney, *op. cit.,* p. 235.
[13]Murray, *op. cit.,* p. 73.
[14]*Ibid.*

Murray will have none of any objective atonement. Or will he? Consider his words in connection with II Corinthians 5:18-21 in his chapter "The Nature of the Atonement":

Reconciliation is a finished work. The tenses in verses 18, 19, 21 put this beyond doubt. It is not a work being continuously wrought by God; it is something accomplished in the past.

. . . .

The exhortation "be ye reconciled to God" (vs. 20) . . . means: be no longer in a state of alienation from God but enter rather into the relation of favour and peace established by the reconciliatory work of Christ. Take advantage of the grace of God and enter into this status of peace with God through our Lord Jesus Christ.[15]

Murray's words read precisely as an objective reconciliation, a work of Christ "finished, accomplished in the past" into which men enter in a personal "be-ye-reconciled" experience as they "enter into this state of peace with God through our Lord Jesus Christ" and become "no longer in a state of alienation from God." But the thing that, for Murray, keeps the reconciliation from being objective (despite his apt description of it as an objective reconciliation) is the fact that, for him, "world" (v. 19) does not mean *world*. In his chapter "The Extent of the Atonement," Murray asserts

Such words as "world" and "all" and such expressions as "every one" and "all men" do not always in Scripture mean every member of the human race. For example, when Paul says with reference to the unbelief of Israel, "For if their trespass is the riches of the world . . . how much more their fulness" (Rom. 11:12), are we to suppose that he meant that the trespass of Israel brought the riches of which he is speaking to every person who had been, is now, and ever will be in the world? Such an interpretation would make nonsense. The word "world" would then have to include Israel, which is here contrasted with the world. And it is not true that every member of the human race was enriched by the fall of Israel. When Paul used the word "world" here he meant the Gentile world as contrasted

---

[15]*Ibid.,* p. 47f.

with Israel. The context makes this abundantly plain. So we have an example of the word "world" used in a restricted sense and does not mean all men distributively [sic].[16]

Murray reasons that, since Paul's use of the word "world" is restricted by the exclusion of Israel from its comprehension, we are at liberty to assume that not all Gentiles are comprehended, despite his acknowledgment that "when Paul used the word 'world' here he meant the Gentile world as contrasted with Israel." His assertion that "it is not true that every member of the human race was enriched by the fall of Israel" reflects his failure to reckon with the distinction between what is *potential* and what becomes *realized*. His contention collapses in the face of the fact that precisely the same collective, universal mode of procedure indicated here in God's dealings with the Gentiles obtains with respect to His dealings with Israel: the corporate election of the descendants of Abraham-Isaac-Jacob, with its potential privilege and blessing, did not profit many in Israel; but that fact in no way abrogated the covenant or vitiated the election or altered its corporate nature as embracing all descendants.

A serious fallacy in Murray's reasoning is his implicit assumption that if he can establish the frame of reference he wishes for *world* in Romans 11:12, he is at liberty to impose it on the word and its cognates in other passages whenever and however he may wish. Implementing his assumption, Murray cites Romans 5:18 ("As through one trespass judgment came upon all men unto condemnation, even so through one righteous act [acquital] came upon all men unto justification of life") and asserts that "though Paul uses the expression 'all men' in the first part of the verse in the sense of all men universally, yet he must be using the same expression in the second part of the verse in a much more restricted sense"[17] . . . to which we can only reply, Why so subtle, Paul? Murray assumes that Paul "must be . . . "—for Murray's theology requires it.

---

[16]*Ibid.*, p. 69f.
[17]*Ibid.*, p. 70.

"To take another example," Murray continues, "when Paul says that 'all things were lawful' for him (I Cor. 6:12; 10:23), he did not mean that every conceivable thing was lawful for him. It was not lawful for him to transgress the commandments of God."[18] Surely we can only agree with Murray that "all things" in these instances does not mean *all things,* just as it is equally true that the assertion that "with God nothing is impossible" does not mean that with God *nothing is impossible* (e.g., He cannot lie, fail, die, or be ignorant, deceived, or defeated). But to offer these passages as somehow pertinent to the "all men" passages concerning the atonement seems to us to be tongue-in-cheek proof-texting of the strangest sort. One does not read long from the apologists for Calvinism before finding them resorting to all manner of ingenious interpretations and applications in an effort to bolster their tottering theology.

To furnish "direct evidence provided by the Scripture to show the definite or limited extent of the atonement,"[19] Murray offers two "biblical arguments." First he cites Romans 8:31-39. Since the passage contains two references to the death of Christ (vs. 32,34), Murray asserts that "any indication given in this passage respecting extent would be pertinent to the question of the extent of the atonement."[20] Reasoning that the "for us" of verse 31 must be limited to the elect of verses 28-30, Murray proceeds to verse 32 where

. . . we find that Paul again uses this expression "for us" and adds the word "all"—"he that spared not his own Son but delivered him up *for us all.*" Here he is dealing expressly with those on whose behalf the Father delivered up the Son. And the question is: what is the scope of the expression "for us all"? It would be absurd to insist that the presence of the word "all" has the effect of universalizing the scope. The "all" is not broader than the "us." Paul is saying that the action of the Father in view was on behalf of "all of us" and the question is simply the scope of the

---

[18]*Ibid.*
[19]*Ibid.,* p. 75.
[20]*Ibid.,* p. 76.

"us." The only proper answer to this question is that the "us" in view in verse 32 is the "us" in view in verse 31. It would be doing violence to the most elementary rules of interpretation to suppose that at verse 32 Paul had broadened the scope of those to whom he is speaking and included many more than he included in the protestation of verse 31.[21]

Thus Murray concludes that the "us all" for whom Christ was delivered up can be only the elect. He finds his conclusion confirmed by Paul's mention of "the elect of God" (v. 33), by the reference to the resurrection and intercession of Christ "for us" (v. 34), and by the security posited in verses 35-39. From all of these considerations, Murray concludes

We see, therefore, that the security of which Paul here speaks is a security restricted to those who are the objects of the love which was exhibited on Calvary's accursed tree, and therefore the love exhibited on Calvary is itself a distinguishing love and not a love that is indiscriminately universal. It is a love that insures the eternal security of those who are its objects and Calvary itself is that which secures for them the justifying righteousness through which eternal life reigns. And this is just saying that the atonement which Calvary accomplished is not itself universal.[22]

To all of this, we can only reply that we must agree with Murray that, in the mind of Paul as he wrote the passage, the "us all" in verse 32 surely were the elect comprehended throughout the passage from verse 28 through verse 39. However, we must add a further consideration. The frame of reference of *all* in verse 32 is established by context, as Murray has done. It also remains true that the frame of reference of *all* (or any other noun or pronoun) in every other passage of Scripture must likewise be defined by context. And, contrary to Murray's implicit assumption, we are not at liberty to commandeer the frame of reference of *all* in Romans 8:32 and apply it indiscriminately as we may wish to the word or cognates in other passages of Scripture. This fact is one of "the most elementary rules of interpretation" (to borrow Murray's phrase).

[21]*Ibid.*
[22]*Ibid.*, p. 79.

Contrary to Murray's assumptions, Romans 8:31-39 establishes nothing about the universality of the atonement. Instead, it serves only to posit benefits of the atonement to the elect, "those to whom [Paul] is speaking" (again, to use Murray's phrase).

"The second biblical argument that we may adduce in support of the doctrine of definite atonement," asserts Murray, "is that drawn from the fact that those for whom Christ died have themselves also died in Christ."[23] Reasoning from affirmations of Scripture that Christians are "dead with Christ" to the old life, sharing a new life with Christ, as affirmed in Romans 6:3-11, II Corinthians 5:14,15, Ephesians 2:4-7, and Colossians 3:3, Murray concludes that

The inference is inevitable that those for whom Christ died are those and those only who die to sin and live to righteousness. Now it is a plain fact that not all die to sin and live in newness of life. And neither can we say that Christ died for all men, for the simple reason that all for whom Christ died also died in Christ. If we cannot say that Christ died for all men, neither can we say that the atonement is universal—it is the death of Christ for men that specifically constitutes the atonement. The conclusion is apparent—the death of Christ in its specific character as atonement was for those and those only who are in due time the partakers of that new life of which Christ's resurrection is the pledge and pattern.[24]

Again we must insist that the frame of reference for the pronouns in the passages cited by Murray posits nothing concerning the frame of reference of pronouns or cognates in other passages, which in all cases must be defined by context.

As we have observed, it is evident throughout his chapter that Murray thinks of the atonement as essentially manward rather than Godward. Because his perspective is anthropocentric rather than theocentric, the objective character of the atonement escapes him. Consequently there is no place in his thinking for the first clause of the proposition accepted by Calvin—"Christ suffered sufficiently for the whole world, but efficiently only

---

[23]*Ibid.*
[24]*Ibid.*, p. 80.

for the elect." Rejecting the first clause, Murray labors only to establish the second clause ... which indeed is where we ultimately must arrive with respect to the efficacy of the atonement, but which is not at all the starting point, as is clearly delineated throughout the Scriptures. "God so loved the *world* that he gave his only begotten Son" (here is the starting point), "that *whoever believes in him* should not perish, but have everlasting life" (here is the point of ultimate efficiency of the atonement). But Murray and his Westminster brethren refuse to begin where God begins, and labor instead to begin where God concludes.

The Westminster doctrine of the atonement, advocated by Murray, limits the atonement provisionally, which automatically limits its application to the elect (considered to be particular men unconditionally foreordained of God). The doctrine of the atonement as held by Calvin is somewhat different, though the end result is the same. Calvin acknowledges the provisional universality of the atonement but limits its application to the elect (considered to be particular men unconditionally foreordained of God). Calvin writes

It is incontestable that Christ came for the expiation of the sins of the whole world. But the solution lies close at hand, that whosoever believes in Him should not perish but should have eternal life (Jn. 3:15). For the present question is not how great the power of Christ is or what efficacy it has in itself, but to whom He gives Himself to be enjoyed.

. . . .

Hence, we conclude that, though reconciliation is offered to all through Him, yet the benefit is peculiar to the elect, that they may be gathered into the society of life.[25]

It is of interest to note that Calvin's acknowledgment that "Christ came for the expiation of the sins of the whole world" follows his censure of Georgius for appealing to I John 2:2 in support of the doctrine of an atonement unlimited in sufficiency. Although Calvin accepted the doctrine, he rejects

---

[25]E.P. 9:5.

Georgius's appeal and writes, "For this cause, the common solution does not avail, that Christ suffered sufficiently for all, but efficiently only for the elect."[26] This solution of the problem of the extent of the atonement, offered by Georgius (as by many others), Calvin dismisses as a "great absurdity [which] has no weight with me." But any difference between Georgius's "great absurdity" and the proposition Calvin himself offered is purely imaginary. Affirming that "it is incontestable that Christ came for the expiation of the sins of the whole world," Calvin obviously affirms that *Christ suffered sufficiently for all* (to use words to which Calvin objects in his censure of Georgius). Obviously, there is no difference whatever in the import of the proposition as offered by Georgius and as stated by Calvin.

"Christ is the propitiation for our sins," wrote John, "and not for ours only, but also for the sins of the whole world." Although Calvin accepted the doctrine of an atonement unlimited in sufficiency, he apparently felt that John's affirmation bears implications too cogent to allow him to accept its obvious import, implications that militate too strongly against the limitation on the atonement which the defense of his theology requires. Therefore, John's simple categorical affirmation required "interpretation" in his commentary on the passage:

Here a question may be raised, how have the sins of the whole world been expiated?

. . . .

[It has been] said that Christ suffered sufficiently for the whole world, but efficiently only for the elect. This solution has commonly prevailed in the schools. Though I allow that what has been said is true,[27] yet I deny

---

[26]*Ibid.*

[27]Here Calvin accepts the proposition stated in precisely the same words offered by Georgius which Calvin dismissed as a "great absurdity." His statement appears in his *Commentary on the Catholic Epistles,* published in 1551, one year earlier than his *Concerning the Eternal Predestination of God,* in which he rejects Georgius's identical statement of the proposition.

that it is suitable to this passage; for the design of John was no other than to make this benefit common to the whole Church. Then under the word *all* or whole, he does not include the reprobate, but designates those who should believe as well as those who were then scattered through various parts of the world. For then is really made evident, as it is meet, the grace of Christ, when it is declared to be the only true salvation of the world.[28]

Thus, according to Calvin, by his affirmation that Christ is the propitiation "for the sins of the whole world," John meant only that Christ died for the elect at Corinth and Rome quite as much as for the elect at Ephesus, and for the elect of generations to come quite as much as for the elect of his own generation. The artificiality of such an interpretation of John's sublime affirmation is readily apparent, except perhaps to those who bring to the Scriptures the same unfounded assumptions under which Calvin labored.

Murray's treatment of I John 2:2 is similar to Calvin's:

Perhaps no text in Scripture presents more plausible support to the doctrine of universal atonement than I John 2:2: "And he is the propitiation for our sins, and not for ours only but also for the whole world." The extension of the propitiation to "the whole world" would appear to allow for no other construction than that the propitiation for sins embraces the sins of the whole world. It must be said that the language John uses here would fit in perfectly with the doctrine of universal atonement if Scripture elsewhere demonstrated that to be the biblical doctrine. And it must also be said that this expression *of itself* would not offer any proof of or support to a doctrine of limited atonement. The question however is: does this text prove that the atonement is universal? In other words, is the case such that canons of interpretation are violated if we interpret it in a way that is compatible with the doctrine of limited atonement?[29]

Having posed the problem, Murray presents his argument:

1. It was necessary for John to set forth the *scope* of Jesus' propitiation—it was not limited in its virtue and efficacy to the immediate circle of disciples who had actually seen and heard and handled the Lord

---

[28]Calvin, *Commentary on the Catholic Epistles, ad loc.*

[29]Murray, *op. cit.*, p. 82.

in the days of his sojourn upon earth (cf. I John 1:1-3), nor to the circle of believers who came directly under the influence of the apostolic witness (cf. I John 1:3,4). The propitiation which Jesus himself is extends in its virtue, efficacy, and intent to all in every nation who through the apostolic witness came to have fellowship with the Father and the Son (cf. I John 1:5-7). Every nation and kindred and tongue is in this sense embraced in the propitiation. It was highly necessary that John, like the other writers of the New Testament and like the Lord himself, should stress the ethnic universalism of the gospel and therefore of Jesus' propitiation as the central message of that gospel. John needed to say, in order to proclaim this universalism of gospel grace, "not for ours only but also for the whole world."

2. It was necessary for John to emphasize the exclusiveness of Jesus as the propitiation. It is this propitiation that is the one and only specific for the remission of sin. John in the context was underscoring the gravity of sin and the necessity of avoiding the snare of complacency with reference to it. But in that connection it was imperative for him to remind believers that there is no other laver for sin than Jesus' propitiation—there is no other sacrifice for sin. The utmost bounds of human need and the utmost bounds of divine grace know no other propitiation—it is for the whole world.

3. It was necessary for John to remind his readers of the *perpetuity* of Jesus' propitiation. It is this propitiation that endures as such through all ages—its efficacy is never diminished, it never loses any of its virtue. And not only is it everlasting in its efficacy, but it is the perpetual propitiatory for the ever-recurring and ever-continuing sins of believers—they do not plead another propitiation for the sins they continue to commit any more than do they appeal to another advocate with the Father for the liabilities which their continuing sins entail.

Hence the scope, the exclusiveness, and the perpetuity of the propitiation provided sufficient reason for John to say, "not for ours only but also for the whole world."[30]

Murray augments his argument:

It is worthy of note that John in this text speaks of Jesus as the propitiation—"and he is the propitiation for our sins." It is highly probable that this form of statement points to "Jesus Christ the righteous" as not only the one who made propitiation once for all by his sacrifice on the

---

[30]*Ibid.*, p. 83f.

cross, but as the one who is the abiding embodiment of the propitiatory virtue accruing from his once-for-all accomplishment and also as the one who offers to those who trust in him an ever-availing propitiatory.

. . . .

It is because Jesus made propitiation and is the abiding propitiatory that he is the advocate with the Father. If we give to the propitiation an extent far beyond that of his advocacy we inject something which is hardly compatible with this complementation.

. . . .

It is this complex of thought that makes it difficult for us to place even this text in the framework of universal propitiation.[31]

Thus Murray labors long to remove I John 2:2 from "the framework of universal propitiation." The assumptions he makes to accommodate the text to his theology are apparent. Without pausing to comment at length on Murray's treatment of I John 2:2, let us consider a passage which Murray did not treat in his consideration of the question of the extent of the atonement: "But there were false prophets also among the people, even as there shall be false teachers among you, who will secretly bring in damnable heresies, even denying the Lord who bought them, and bring upon themselves swift destruction" (II Pet. 2:1). Calvin comments:

Even denying the Lord that bought them. Though Christ may be denied in various ways, yet Peter, as I think, refers here to what is expressed by Jude, that is, when the grace of God is turned into lasciviousness; for Christ redeemed us, that he might have a people separated from all the pollutions of the world, and devoted to holiness and innocency. They, then, who throw off the bridle and give themselves up to all kinds of licentiousness are not unjustly said to deny Christ *by whom they have been redeemed.*[32]

Murray's position—the Westminster doctrine of an atonement of limited sufficiency—collapses in the face of II Peter 2:1. The

---

[31]*Ibid.*, p. 84f.
[32]Calvin, *op. cit., ad loc.,* latter italics mine.

text is but one of numerous passages militating decisively against his position which Murray did not treat in his chapter "The Extent of the Atonement," passages which demolish his whole construction. Among important passages which Murray did not mention are the following, all of them pertinent to the question of the extent of the atonement:

God was in Christ reconciling the world to himself. (IICor. 5:19)

God desires all men to be saved and to come to the knowledge of the truth. For there is one God, and one mediator between God and men, the man Christ Jesus, who gave himself as a ransom for all. (I Tim. 2:4-6 RSV)

For God so loved the world that he gave his only Son, that whoever believes in him should not perish but have eternal life. For God sent the Son into the world, not to condemn the world, but that the world might be saved through him. (John 3:16f. RSV)

And I, when I am lifted up from the earth, will draw all men to myself. He said this to show by what death he was to die. (John 12:32f. RSV)

The bread of God is he which cometh down from heaven and giveth life to the world. . . . the bread that I will give is my flesh, which I will give for the life of the world. (John 6:33,51)

Behold the Lamb of God, who takes away the sin of the world! (John 1:29 RSV)

For the grace of God has appeared for the salvation of all men. (Titus 2:11 RSV).

The Father sent the Son to be the Saviour of the world. (I Jn. 4:14)

The passages cited above all have specific reference to the redemption wrought by Christ, and all posit universality. They are supported by numerous correlative passages which assert God's will that all men be saved.[33] With the above passages, we

---

[33] Passages in this category will be considered in the following chapter.

would cite in support of the doctrine of unlimited atonement three passages treated by Murray in his chapter:

[Christ] is the propitiation for our sins, and not for ours only, but also for the sins of the whole world. (I Jn. 2:2)

Then as one man's trespass led to condemnation for all men, so one man's acts of righteousness leads to acquittal and life for all men. (Rom. 5:18 RSV)

But we see Jesus, who was made for a little time lower than the angels for the suffering of death ... that he by the grace of God should taste death for every man. (Heb. 2:9)[34]

The import of all the above passages with respect to the extent and sufficiency of the atonement is so obvious that it could be called into question only by those whose theology makes it necessary for them either to ignore the passages or to "interpret" them in some ingenious manner to accommodate them to the necessities of their theology. Among the most fanciful interpretations to be found in theological literature are some imposed on these simple categorical affirmations by advocates of the Westminster doctrine of an atonement of limited sufficiency.

Murray's efforts to find support for his doctrine are completely abortive. His treatment of selected passages is unsatisfactory and totally unconvincing, his omission of most of the really decisive passages raises the question of objectivity, and his whole thesis collapses in the face of II Peter 2:1, a supremely pertinent passage which he does not mention in his chapter or in his book.

In the concluding paragraph of his chapter "The Extent of the Atonement," Murray asserts that

... no conclusive support for the doctrine of universal atonement can be derived from universalistic expressions. The question must be determined on the basis of other evidence. This evidence we have tried to present.[35]

---

[34]We have considered Murray's treatment of I Jn. 2:2 and Rom. 5:18. In a brief paragraph, Murray asserts that "every man" in Heb. 2:9 includes only the elect.

[35]Murray, op. cit., p. 85.

This is to say that, in our attempt to determine whether the atonement is of limited or unlimited sufficiency, the testimony of the many passages of Scripture affirming the universality of the atonement is not to be admitted in evidence. "The question must be determined on the basis of other evidence" than the pertinent categorical affirmations of Scripture. This is indeed a strange plea. "It is easy," continues Murray, "for the proponents of universal atonement to make offhand appeal to a few texts."[36] We deny that appeal to the texts affirming a universal atonement is in any sense "offhand," and we deny that such texts are "few."

Let us state again Georgius's proposition, which Calvin accepted (except from Georgius): "Christ suffered sufficiently for all, but efficiently only for the elect." The Westminster doctrine of the atonement must reduce the proposition to a single clause: Christ suffered sufficiently and efficiently only for the elect. The two-clause proposition, as stated by Georgius, Calvin, and many others, is equally acceptable to advocates of Calvin's doctrine of the atonement and to non-Calvinists.

In their common acceptance of the proposition as stated by Georgius, the only matter that remains to divide the "Calvin" Calvinists and the non-Calvinists is the question of how the identity of the elect, for whom alone the atonement is efficient, is determined. Calvin believed, of course, that the identity of the elect was determined by fiat decree before creation, a decree comprehending every man ever to live and determining the election or reprobation of particular men unconditionally, without regard to anything in any man, either the elect or the reprobate. This assumption is shared both by "Calvin" Calvinists and "Westminster" Calvinists. Others of us believe that the election or reprobation of particular men is determined by means quite other, as we shall consider in the chapters to follow.

Let us state the Biblical proposition with respect to the efficacy of the atonement wrought by Christ: The atonement is

---

[36]*Ibid.*

efficacious for all men potentially, for no man unconditionally, and for the Israel of God efficiently.

The above proposition is demonstrated in the Holy Scriptures in the ordinance of the annual Day of Atonement observed by Israel. Under the old economy, once a year the High Priest entered into the Holy of Holies to sprinkle the blood of a bullock and afterward the blood of a goat on the Mercy Seat and before it "because of the uncleanness of the children of Israel, and because of their transgressions in all their sins" (Lev. 16:16). Laying his hands on the head of the scapegoat, the High Priest "confessed over him all the iniquities of the children of Israel, and all their transgressions in all their sins, putting them upon the head of the goat" (v. 21) that he might bear them away into the wilderness. The design of the ordinance was "to make an atonement for the children of Israel for all their sins once a year" (v. 34). The New Testament, especially the Epistle to the Hebrews, unfolds for us the rich symbolism of the ordinance, typical of Christ and the atonement accomplished "once in the consummation of the ages" through our Lord's offering of Himself once for all for ever. We cannot at this time dwell upon the wonders of holy truth implicit in the ordinance. Only let it be observed that the atonement was made for all the sins of all the people of Israel, without exception. It was an *objective* atonement providing the benefits of grace for all alike, into which the people could enter as individuals only by personal faith. The benefits of the atonement, graciously provided for all, were not conferred on all people or any individuals automatically and indiscriminately. Although the atonement was made for the sins of all the nation, it was of no efficacy for the impenitent in the nation.

Exactly so, on the once-for-all-for-ever Day of Atonement, the Savior of the World offered Himself as the propitiation for the sins of the whole world, making an everlasting atonement that avails for all the penitent faithful, and for them alone. Again we state our thesis: the atonement is efficacious for all men potentially, for no man unconditionally, and for the Israel of God efficiently.

The doctrine of limited atonement (limited by arbitrary decree of God) is a reproach to the Saviour of the World and impugns the majesty of Him who stood one day in old Capernaum and declared, "I am the living bread which came down from heaven: if any man feed on this bread, he shall live for ever: and the bread that I will give is my flesh, which I will give for the life of the world." The fallacious doctrine of limited atonement impugns the majesty of Him who, a few days before His crucifixion, stood in old Jerusalem and quietly said, "And I, if I be lifted up from the earth, will draw all men unto me."

We have seen and do testify that the Father sent the Son to be the Savior of the world.

And he is the propitiation for our sins: and not for ours only, but also for the sins of the whole world.

For there is one God and one mediator between God and men, the man Christ Jesus, who gave himself a ransom for all.

I JOHN 4:14; 2:2, I TIMOTHY 2:5,6

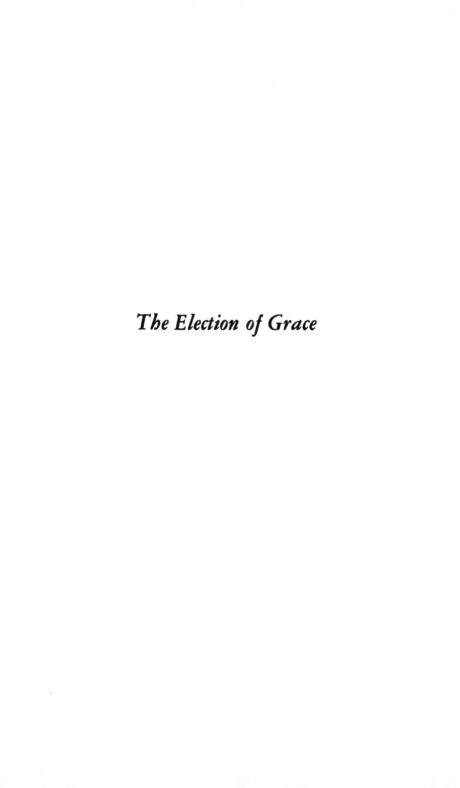

The Election of Grace

For the grace of God has appeared for the salvation of all men.

Titus 2:11 RSV

Therefore as by the offence of one, judgment came upon all men to condemnation, even so by the righteousness of one the free gift came upon all men unto justification of life. For as by one man's disobedience many were made sinners, so by the obedience of one shall many be made righteous.

. . . .

Where sin abounded, grace did much more abound, that as sin has reigned unto death, even so might grace reign through righteousness unto eternal life by Jesus Christ our Lord.

Romans 5:18-21

Even so then at the present time also there is a remnant according to the election of grace.

Romans 11:5

CHAPTER IV

THE ELECTION OF GRACE

FIRST of all," wrote the Prisoner of Jesus Christ at Rome to Timothy at Ephesus, "I urge that supplications, prayers, intercessions, and thanksgivings be made for all men" (I Tim. 2:1 RSV). But of course! What could be simpler?

But have we tried it? Have we ever done it? Have we done more than frame a few pious phrases asking God somehow to bless the whole wide world in general? This is not what the Apostle had in mind. Paul wrote of "supplications, prayers, intercessions" for all men. Have we gone to our knees and buried our faces in our hands and wept before God for all men?—for the mighty and the lowly, the rich and the poor, the well fed and the hungry, the wicked and the "good," the responsible and the lawless, men in the Kremlin and men in Washington, the black, the white, the red, the yellow . . . all men.

When once we truly have prayed for all men, when we have wept for the sins of all men and for what sin has brought to man, when we have remembered that all men alike are of the same clay and that only the grace of "the God of all grace" can save any of us from the just desert of our own doings, we may understand something more of the mercies of "God our Savior, who desires all men to be saved and to come to the knowledge of the truth" (I Tim. 2:4 RSV).

But there are those in the Church, of course, who need not pray for all men, for they are persuaded that it is by no means true that God desires all men to be saved and to come to the

91

knowledge of the truth. The words of the Apostle, as they believe, need not be heeded. Instead, they need only to be interpreted.

Because of the fallacies of his theology, Calvin (as all his disciples) was hard pressed to explain the meaning of I Timothy 2:4. He experienced little difficulty explaining away the import of many affirmations in Scripture of the factor of human agency in salvation through a simple hermeneutical device, as we shall consider. But I Timothy 2:4 and its cognates posed a real problem for him, for here is an assertion—not of anything in man, but of something in God . . . and something which found no place in Calvin's thinking: the will of God for the salvation of all men. Recognition of the will of God for the salvation of all men completely negates Calvin's system of theology. It has been a tragedy for the Church through four centuries and more that Calvin approached I Timothy 2:4 and its cognates, not with candid objectivity, but with untiring ingenuity:

> The difficulty of another place (I Tim. 2.4) is readily solved. Paul tells us that God wills all men to be saved, and also how He wills them to come to the knowledge of His truth. For He joins both together. Now I ask: Did the will of God remain the same from the beginning of the world? For if He willed that His truth be known to all, why did He not proclaim His law also to the Gentiles? Why did he confine the light of life within the narrow limits of Judaea?
>
> . . . .
>
> Did Paul not know that he was prohibited by the Spirit from preaching the word of Christ in Asia and from crossing over into Bithynia where he was proceeding? (Acts 16:6). But as a full treatment of this matter would be too prolix, I content myself with one word more. When He had lit the light of life for the Jews alone, God allowed the Gentiles to wander for many ages in darkness (Acts 14:16). Then this special gift was promised to the Church, that the Lord should rise upon it and His glory be conspicuous in it (Is. 60.2). Now let Pighius asseverate that God wills all to be saved, when not even the external preaching of the doctrine, which is much inferior to the illumination of the Spirit, is made common to all. That passage was long ago brought up by the Pelagians. (E.P. 8:2)

Calvin begins by observing that "Paul tells us that God wills all men to be saved." But after a few lines of comment, it becomes no longer Paul, but only Pighius and the Pelagians who would make such an unfounded assertion. Such are the vagaries of Calvin's polemics.

Calvin's argument ignores the testimony of the Scriptures that the word of God in days of old went into all the earth and to the ends of the world (Rom. 10:16-18, cf. Acts 8:27) and that God left not Himself without witness (Acts 14:17) sufficient for all generations and nations to move them to seek Him and find Him (Acts 17:27, Rom. 2:1-16). He argues, too, from the assumption that the Apostolic witness was virtually confined to Paul, as though there was but one Apostle rather than thirteen. True, Paul did not go to Asia; but Thomas did, and others of the Apostles went elsewhere. The broad range of the Gospel witness in the days of the Apostles is reflected in the words of Paul to the Colossians concerning "the gospel which has come to you, as indeed in the whole world it is bearing fruit and growing" (Col. 1:6). Calvin's argument from *means* against Paul's assertion that God wills all men to be saved crumbles in the face of affirmations of Scripture concerning the scope and authenticity of God's witness to all men in all places in all generations.

Continuing his argument, Calvin contends that the fact that some are not saved proves that God does not desire the salvation of all men. For since God is omnipotent, if He truly desired all men to be saved, then all men would indeed be saved. Here may be detected the fundamental erroneous assumption of Calvin, the fatal flaw in his thinking that determined the construction of his whole system of theology: the assumption that the will of God is monothetic. Proceeding on his false assumption that the will of God has but a single aspect, Calvin continues:

No one unless deprived of sense and judgment can believe that salvation is ordained in the secret counsel of God equally for all. For the rest, the meaning of Paul is quite simple and clear to anyone not bent on contention. He bids solemn prayers be made for kings and princes in authority. Because in that age there were so many dangerous enemies of the Church, to prevent despair from hindering application to prayer, Paul anticipates their difficulties, declaring that God wills all men to be saved. Who does not see that the reference is to orders of men rather than individual men? Nor indeed does the distinction lack substantial ground: what is meant is not individuals of nations, but nations of individuals. At any rate, the context makes it clear that no other will of God is intended than that which appears in the external preaching of the Gospel. Thus Paul means that God wills the salvation of all whom He mercifully invites by preaching to Christ. (*Ibid.*)

Similar are Calvin's comments on I Timothy 2:4 in his *Commentaries.* He begins by asserting that "God has at heart the salvation of all, because he invites all to the acknowledgment of his truth." But after a few sentences, he asserts that

the Apostle simply means that there is no people and no rank in the world that is excluded from salvation; because God wishes that the gospel should be proclaimed to all without exception. Now the preaching of the gospel gives life; and hence he justly concludes that God invites all equally to partake salvation. But the present discourse relates to classes of men, and not to individual persons; for his sole object is to include in this number princes and foreign nations. That God wishes the doctrine of salvation to be enjoyed by them as well as others is evident from the passages already quoted, and from other passages of a similar nature. Not without good reason was it said, "Now, kings, understand," and again, in the same Psalm, "I will give thee the Gentiles for an inheritance, and the ends of the earth for a possession." (Ps. ii. 8,10). In a word, Paul intended to show that it is our duty to consider, not what kind of persons the princes at that time were, but what God wished them to be.[1]

In view of the monothetic will of God which Calvin continually posits, how is it that he writes here of princes' being something other than "what God wished them to be"? How could this be? Calvin was totally unaware that his assertion that the "kind of persons the princes at that time were [was not] what God wished them to be" completely nullifies the point he

---

[1]Calvin, *Commentaries, ad loc.*

was trying to establish concerning the will of God and the salvation of men. If it is possible for princes to be something other than what God wishes them to be, is it not equally possible for men to be lost though God wishes them to be saved? But the point was lost to Calvin in the verbal-smog of his polemics.

Calvin's argument that by "all men" Paul meant only "all classes of men" is without foundation and was only a device by which he sought to evade a simple, categorical affirmation of the Apostle which spells shipwreck for Calvin's whole system of theology.

Calvin's treatment of II Peter 3:9 is equally artificial. He comments

Not willing that any should perish. So wonderful is his love towards mankind that he would have them all to be saved, and is of his own self prepared to bestow salvation on the lost.

. . . .

But it may be asked, If God wishes none to perish, why is it that so many do perish? To this my answer is that no mention is here made of the hidden purpose of God, according to which the reprobate are doomed to their own ruin, but only of his will as made known to us in the gospel. For God there stretches forth his hand without a difference to all, but lays hold only of those, to lead them to himself, whom he has chosen before the foundation of the world.[2]

Thus the will of God that no man perish, as affirmed by Peter, is nullified by "the hidden purpose of God, according to which the reprobate are doomed to their own ruin." Here again is Calvin's fundamental fallacy, the assumption that the will of God is monothetic. His false assumption requires Calvin to assert that in the Gospel "God stretches forth his hand without a difference to all," but with the hidden design of laying hold of only those "whom he has chosen before the foundation of the world." Such deception would be blameworthy in men, and no

---

[2]Calvin, *Commentaries, ad loc.*

less so in God. Thank God, such duplicity is only a figment of Calvinism and not at all a modus operandi of God.

Calvin on John 3:16 offers more of the same:

> *That whosoever believeth on him may not perish.* . . . he has employed the universal term *whosoever,* both to invite all indiscriminately to partake of life, and to cut off every excuse from unbelievers. Such is also the import of the term *World,* which he formerly used; for though nothing will be found in *the world* that is worthy of the favour of God, yet he shows himself to be reconciled to the whole world when he invites all men without exception to the faith of Christ, which is nothing else than an entrance into life.
>
> Let us remember, on the other hand, that while *life* is promised universally to *all who believe* in Christ, still faith is not common to all. For Christ is made known and held out to the view of all, but the elect alone are they whose eyes God opens, that they may seek him by faith.[3]

Here again is an offer to "all," but an offer circumscribed by the "hidden purpose" of the unconditional election and reprobation of particular men. On verse 17 Calvin comments

> *For God sent not his Son into the world to condemn the world.* It is a confirmation of the preceding statement; for it was not in vain that God sent his own Son to us. He came not to destroy; and therefore it follows that it is the peculiar office of the Son of God that *all who believe* may obtain salvation by him. There is now no reason why any man should be in a state of hesitation, or of distressing anxiety, as to the manner in which he may escape death, when we believe that it was the purpose of God that Christ should deliver us from it. The word *world* is again repeated, that no man may think himself wholly excluded, if he only keep the road of faith.
>
> · ·
>
> . . . they who reject the grace offered in him deserve to find him the Judge and Avenger of contempt so unworthy and base. A striking instance of this may be seen in the Gospel; for though it is strictly *the power of God for salvation to every one who believeth,* (Rom. i. 16), the ingratitude of many causes it to become to them death. . . . the Gospel is especially, and in the first instance, appointed for believers, that it may be salvation to them; but afterwards [others] will not escape unpunished who, despising

---

[3]Calvin, *Commentaries, ad loc.*

the grace of Christ, chose to have him as the Author of death rather than of life.[4]

Here Calvin affirms human agency: "they who reject the grace offered in Christ . . . the ingratitude of many causes it to become to them death . . . [they] will not escape unpunished who, despising the grace of Christ, chose to have him as the Author of death rather than of life." But Calvin's affirmations of human agency always are qualified by the a priori assumption (whether expressed, or not) of the divine foreordination of all events and acts of men.[5] Thus, only the *right ones* will believe, and precisely the *right ones* will reject grace, be ungrateful, and choose to have Christ as the Author of death rather than of life.

By resorting to ingenious interpretations of explicit categorical affirmations of Scripture, Calvin manages to save his theology from Paul's declaration that God desires the salvation of all men—a declaration that, for Calvin, somehow becomes only a wild notion of Pighius and the Pelagians.

Calvin's theology to the contrary notwithstanding, the Holy Scriptures affirm that God desires all men to be saved (I Tim. 2:4), not wishing that any should perish (II Pet. 3:9), desiring to have mercy on all (Rom. 11:32), having sent His Son into the world that the world through Him might be saved (John 3:16f.). No "hidden purpose" of arbitrary unconditional reprobation of the mass of mankind exists to impugn the sincerity and infinite compassion with which God addresses Himself to all the sons of men,

There is no God else beside me; a just God and a Saviour; there is none beside me. Look unto me and be ye saved, all the ends of the earth: for I am God, and there is none else. (Isa. 45:21f.)

"The grace of God," wrote Paul to Titus, "has appeared for the salvation of all men" (2:11 RSV). As might be expected,

---

[4]*Ibid.*
[5]Cf. E.P. 10:7-14.

Calvin comments that Paul "does not mean individual men, but rather describes individual classes, or various ranks of life."[6] Fairbairn disagrees:

... the grace of God in its saving design and properties toward men—"that grace of God (as Bishop Beveridge puts it) whereby alone it is possible for mankind to be saved"... presents and offers salvation to all, and in that sense brings it.

. . . .

In a word, the salvation-bringing grace of God is without respect of persons; it is unfolded to men indiscriminately, or to sinners of every name, simply as such.[7]

"Grace... came by Jesus Christ," as John declared (1:17). The whole life of Jesus was a manifestation of the grace of God toward men, especially in the days of His ministry, as reflected in many incidents recorded in the Gospels. But Huther is correct in asserting that "it need hardly be said that [Paul] is speaking here not simply of a revelation of the divine grace by teaching, but also of its appearance *in act*, viz. in the act of redemption."[8]

As we have earlier considered (Chapter II), Christ's act of atonement in His sacrificial death "once in the consummation of the ages" was the authentic act of election, the act whereby He voluntarily concurred in the elective purpose of God and gave to that purpose its eternal realization. We have also considered (Chapter III) that the atonement, which *is* the election, was an objective atonement sufficient "for the sins of the whole world" and potentially efficacious for all men. From these considerations, and as a corollary of the numerous

---

[6]Calvin, *Commentaries, ad loc.*

[7]Patrick Fairbairn, *Commentary on the Pastoral Epistles,* p. 278.

[8]Joh. Ed. Huther, *Critical and Exegetical Handbook to the Epistles to Timothy and Titus,* p. 300.

affirmations of God's desire that all men be saved, it necessarily follows that

I. The Election Comprehends All Men Potentially.

That the election potentially embraces all men becomes evident also when we examine the question of the Fall and the relation of men to the transgression of Adam. The definitive passage on the question is Romans 5:12-21, part of which reads

Wherefore, as by one man sin entered into the world, and death by sin, so death passed upon all men, for all have sinned.

. . . .

Therefore, as by the offence of one judgment came upon all men to condemnation, even so by the righteousness of one the free gift came upon all men unto justification of life. For as by one man's disobedience many were made sinners, so by the obedience of one shall many be made righteous. . . . where sin abounded, grace did much more abound, that as sin has reigned unto death, even so might grace reign through righteousness unto eternal life by Jesus Christ our Lord. (vs. 12,18-21)

The problem of original sin has vexed theologians for generations. That an exact understanding of the matter is not essential to faith may perhaps be inferred from the fact that the Bible affords little light on the question. It is not germane to our present study even to comment on the various theories that have been propounded. Denney's remarks are most practical at this point:

It is not necessary to raise here any of the questions which have been so much discussed as to the primitive state of man. The basis of all theological doctrine is experience, and experience is always of the present. We may have all the experience that is necessary to convince us of the need of reconciliation without having any opinions about the first man, or the state in which he was created, or the connection between his primitive and our present condition.

. . . .

We know immediately and at first hand the only things which are of any consequence: that sin is rooted in our nature so deeply, is so congenital and powerful, that we cannot save ourselves; and on the other hand, that God has made us for Himself and has never left Himself without a witness in our consciences, so that the possibility and hope of reconciliation are not precluded. This is far surer and far more important than anything we can find out about Adam, and it is quite independent of it. What Adam really represents is the unity and solidarity of the human race in sin; and the modern way of expressing this would rather be to say that the unity or solidarity of the human race in sin is involved in the vital organic connection of all men with each other and in the disproportion which actually appears, in all men who have come to moral responsibility, between what they are and what they know they should be.[9]

With respect to the theological problem of original sin, though some questions may remain unanswered in the face of the limited information afforded by the Scriptures, certain facts are made plain. First, it is certain from Romans 5:12-21 that all men were involved in Adam's transgression, and that death and condemnation came upon all men as the consequence. But it is equally certain that all men are comprehended in the redemptive act of Jesus Christ, and that where sin abounded, grace did much more abound. Whatever men's heritage of guilt and condemnation from Adam, it is "much more" offset by the provision of grace through Christ for all men. In I Corinthians 15:21,22, Paul affirms that the resurrection vouchsafed through Christ is coextensive with the death which came upon all men through Adam. In like manner, in Romans 5:12-21 he affirms that the benefit of Christ's act of atonement is coextensive with all that came upon men through Adam's transgression. Thus the benefit of the atonement accrues to all men potentially. This is clear from verse 18: "Then as one man's trespass led to condemnation for all men, so one man's act of righteousness leads to acquital and life for all men" (RSV).

The full import of Romans 5:18 and context is made emphatic when we consider the matter of children and the state of grace which they enjoy. Whatever may be the involvement of mankind in Adam's transgression and the consequences of that

---

[9]James Denney, *The Christian Doctrine of Reconciliation*, pp. 199-201.

involvement, it is clear from the Scriptures that children remain in a state of grace in the years of childhood. Jesus said of children, "of such is the kingdom of heaven" (Matt. 19:14). Again, "Take heed that you despise not one of these little ones, for I say to you that in heaven their angels do always behold the face of my Father who is in heaven" (Matt. 18:10). It is evident from the words of Jesus that children are in a state of grace. This fact in no way negates the fact of original sin. But it does witness that the consequences of mankind's involvement in Adam's transgression are abrogated by Christ's act of atonement for all men. Bengel comments

> Infants are objects of Divine care, not because they have not been under the curse like others, but because they have been rescued from it.... The human race was one mass of perdition, in which infants, even those of better disposition, are also included, on account of original sin; but the whole of it has been redeemed.[10]

Calvin comments on Matthew 19:14

> *Suffer children.* [Christ] declares that he wishes to receive children; and at length, taking them in his arms, he not only embraces, but blesses them by the laying on of hands; from which we infer that his grace is extended even to those who are of that age. And no wonder; for since the whole race of Adam is shut up under the sentence of death, all from the least even to the greatest must perish, except those who are rescued by the only Redeemer.[11]

Calvin's words "except those who are rescued by the only Redeemer" restrict the will of Christ for the salvation of children to the elect (the *particular* unconditionally elect, according to Calvin's definition). But this requires us to assume that Christ had necessarily to be extremely careful about where and when and of *which* children He said such things, for He could not say these things of *all* children who might come into His presence. Such an assumption—artificial, to say the least—is

---

[10]John Albert Bengel, *Gnomon of the New Testament,* Vol. I, p. 346.

[11]Calvin, *Commentaries, ad loc.*

necessary to save Calvin's doctrine of the unconditional election of particular men. Such an assumption leaves him free to write in the *Institutes* that

even infants, bringing their condemnation with them from their mother's womb, suffer not for another's, but for their own defect. For although they have not yet produced the fruits of their own unrighteousness, they have the seed implanted in them. Nay, their whole nature is, as it were, a seed-bed of sin, and therefore cannot but be odious and abominable to God. Hence it follows that it is properly deemed sinful in the sight of God; for there could be no condemnation without guilt. (2:1:8)

Here is condemnation—not for Adam's transgression, as affirmed by Paul in Romans 5:12-21 (where the problem of original sin is raised), but condemnation-in-advance for sins the infants eventually will commit (provided they live to do so). This marks a considerable advance beyond Paul's concept, a thing not uncommon with Calvin.

Certainly God hates sin, as we may judge from the Scriptures. But there is no indication that Jesus regarded sinners whom He encountered as "odious and abominable" (except for the self-righteous Pharisees and Saducees). It was "while we were yet sinners" that God commended His love toward us and Christ died for us—for all the ungodly and all the infants so "odious and abominable to God" (as Calvin believed).

Calvin's position on the question of infant salvation is apparent from the following:

If original guilt is for Pighius not sufficient to condemn men and the hidden judgment of God[12] has no kind of place, what will he make of those infant children who are taken from this life before they could display any such example [of faith and the works of faith] because of

---

[12]Here Calvin contends for the corporate condemnation of men on the ground of Adam's transgression, despite Christ's provision of grace for all men through His voluntary sacrifice as the propitiation "for the sins of the whole world," whereby men are left culpable only for their own personal sins. Calvin's contention constitutes a rejection of Rom. 5:18, easily accomplished through "interpretation" denying the equation between "all men" in the first clause and "all men" in the second clause, interpreting "all men" in the first clause to mean *all* men and in the second clause to mean *some* men—the elect only.

their age? The infants of Sodom and of Jerusalem had the same condition of birth and death, nor was there any disparity in their works. Why then will Christ on the last day separate them to stand some on His right and the others on His left? Who does not here adore the admirable judgment of God by which it is ordained that some are born in Jerusalem and pass thence to a better life, while Sodom, the forecourt of hell, receives the birth of others? But as Christ awards to the elect the recompense of justice, so the reprobate will receive not less fittingly the punishment of their impiety and crimes. Nothing in my teaching goes to show that God by His eternal counsel does not elect to life those whom He pleases and leave others to destruction, or to deny that there are punishments ordained for evil works and a prize laid up for good. (E.P. 8:4)

Such comments as the above have provided warrant for preposterous assertions by zealous Calvinists that millions of infants will forever writhe in everlasting flames in hell—to the eternal praise and glory of God. Many "Calvinists" repudiate such assertions, but they thereby become to that degree not Calvinists, for such assertions are the inevitable corollary of Calvin's doctrine of unconditional particular election. All such unscriptural assertions are seen as outrageous when set over against the gracious words of Jesus, "Let the little children come to me, and forbid them not, for of such is the kingdom of heaven."

Again, on the ground of Calvin's assumption that *particular children only* were invited by Christ to come to Him, it becomes necessary to assume that when Jesus said to the Apostles, who were contending among themselves for the places of greatest honor in the kingdom, "Except you become as little children, you will not even enter the kingdom of heaven" (Matt. 18:3), He had reference—not to children as such, but to particular *elect* children. The inane artificiality of such an assumption is apparent. The sorrows and trials of our Saviour were many and grievous in the days of His flesh when He dwelt among sinners, but at least He was spared the misery of living in the strange, unreal kind of world Calvin's theology would impose on Him. He was free to love all children and to invite all alike to come to Him.

The fact of infant salvation impinges on the question of the nature of election and confirms the election as objective and corporate, efficiently comprehending individuals only in identification and association with the elect body. As we have observed, the atonement was the authentic act of election. The election therefore is coextensive with the atonement, which is efficacious for all men potentially, but only for the Body of Christ efficiently. As participants in the benefit of the atonement, children are efficiently comprehended in the election . . . but only until they ratify sin through personal actual transgression. Paul's description of his own experience is pertinent. In his account of his struggle with sin, recorded in Romans 7, Paul wrote, "I was once alive apart from the law, but when the commandment came, sin revived and I died" (v. 9 RSV). Meyer comments

Paul means *the death-free* (ver. 10) life of childlike innocence[13] where—as this state of life, resembling the condition of our first parents in Paradise, was the bright spot of his own earliest recollection—the law has not yet come to conscious knowledge, the moral self-determination in respect to it has not yet taken place, and therefore the sin-principle is still lying in the slumber of death.

. . . .

This is certainly a *status securitatis,* but one morally indifferent, not immoral, and not extending beyond the childhood unconscious of the *entolē.*[14]

Strong offers a pertinent quotation:

The atonement has come to all men and upon all men. Its coextensiveness with the effects of Adam's sin is seen in that all creatures, such as infants and insane persons, incapable of refusing it, are saved without their consent, just as they were involved in the sin of Adam without their consent. The reason why others are not saved is because when the

---

[13]Here Meyer cites for substantiation Winzer, de Wette and Ewald, Umbreit, Ernesti, Weiss, and Delitzsch.

[14]H. A. W. Meyer, *Critical and Exegetical Handbook to the Epistle to the Romans,* p. 271.

atonement comes to them and upon them, instead of consenting to be included in it, they reject it. If they are born under the curse, so likewise they are born under the atonement which is intended to remove that curse; they remain under its shelter till they are old enough to repudiate it; they shut out its influences as a man closes his window-blind to shut out the beams of the sun; they ward them off by direct opposition, as a man builds dykes around his field to keep out the streams which would otherwise flow in and fertilize the soil.[15]

Coextensive with the atonement, the election comprehends all men potentially. Efficiently, however, it comprehends only those who are actual participants in the benefit of the atonement, either in the *status securitatus* of childhood, or through saving faith in Jesus Christ.

Calvin has these interesting lines concerning the view of Pighius on election:

Pighius expounds his opinion thus: God created all men to salvation by an immutable counsel and without distinction. But as He foresaw the defection of Adam, in order that His election might nevertheless remain firm and stable, He applied a remedy which should be common to all. So the election of the whole human race is made stable in Christ, so that no one may perish except the man who deletes his name from the book of life by his obstinacy. On the other hand, as God foresaw that some would persist to the last in malice and contempt of grace, these He reprobated by His foreknowledge, unless they should repent. This is the source of reprobation, and the wicked deprive themselves of the universal benefit of election outside the counsel and will of God. He declares that all who teach that certain men are positively and absolutely chosen to salvation and others destined to destruction think of God unworthily, attributing to Him a severity alien to His justice and goodness. (E.P. I)

Calvin dismisses Pighius's definition of election as "the trite prattle of a schoolboy." In our own day, all who have read Barth on election will recognize in Calvin's description of Pighius's definition a summary of the central thesis of Barth's doctrine of election. The election, according to Barth, by design

---

[15] Augustus Hopkins Strong, *Systematic Theology*, p. 773. The quotation is from Ashmore, "The New Trial of the Sinner," *Christian Review*, Vol. 26, pp. 245-264.

of God comprehends all men. Every man is elect in Jesus Christ unless he chooses to become

... one who is isolated over against God by his own choice, and who in and with this isolation must be rejected by God.

. . . .

In defiance of God and to his own destruction he may indeed behave and conduct himself as isolated man, and therefore as the man who is rejected by God. (K. D. II:1, p. 316)

There is one principal difference between the definitions of Pighius and Barth. While Pighius (as defined by Calvin) allows for the finality of reprobation by the persistent decision of men (failure to repent), Barth asserts that the choice of the man who deliberately isolates himself against God by his own choice is overruled by God, for "the choice of the godless man is void."[16]

Regardless of the question of the validity of certain aspects of Barth's doctrine of election, there is Biblical warrant for his optimistic dictum that "God is for man." Calvary so declares: "God was in Christ reconciling the world unto himself" (II Cor. 5:19). In Christ and His atoning sacrifice, "the grace of God appeared for the salvation of all men" (Titus 2:11 RSV).

Any suggestion that the grace of God is somehow offered to all men apparently caused Calvin much distress. He sternly protests against anyone "who, by extending the beneficence of God promiscuously to all, does all in his power to diminish it" (E.P. II). Calvin (as his disciples after him) seems somehow obsessed with a great fear that to extend grace to all somehow would "diminish" it so that it no longer would be sufficiently potent to accomplish anything for any man—as if grace were like some sort of soup which, if diluted with too much water to provide for the serving of a larger group of diners, should thereby be weakened so much that it could not satisfy the need

---

[16]*Ibid.*, p. 306. Barth denied universalism, but whether he ever was able to explain the ground of his denial to anyone's satisfaction other than his own may be questioned.

of any man and all should go away hungry. Calvin's tendency often to think of grace, not as an infinite attribute of God, but as some sort of commodity, quantitively limited, is one of the most objectionable and unbiblical aspects of his theological stance. Quite in contrast, when the Apostle Paul wrote that "God has concluded all men in unbelief, that he might have mercy on all" (Rom. 11:32), he gave not the slightest hint of any fear that for God thus to be "promiscuous" with His grace would thereby "diminish" it so that it would become ineffectual.

Reading from Calvin, one detects occasional evidences of his horror at the thought that where sin abounded, grace might much more abound for the salvation of all men. In view of his conviction that there could not be grace enough to meet the needs of all men, Calvin's rejoicing in his own good fortune as one especially favored of God is understandable: "What kind of gratitude is it if, endowed with an incomparable benefit, I only profess myself debtor on equal terms with him who has received hardly a hundredth part of it?" (E.P. II). Calvin is to be commended for his concern for a proper gratitude; but there is a certain smugness about his having been "endowed with an incomparable benefit" so that he is by no means a "debtor on equal terms" with others, having received more than a hundred times as much grace as was bestowed on them.

It is often argued that the doctrine of unconditional particular election is necessary to promote humility. Such a contention is open to serious question. If Calvin's words reflect humility, it is of an arrogant sort, to say the least. Paul does speak of the "exceeding abundant" grace given to him (I Tim. 1:14), but he does not do so as a matter of comparison with grace given to others, and certainly he does not imply that the grace he received is not for others. Shortly after speaking of the exceeding abundant grace given to him, he affirms that God desires all men to be saved and that Christ gave Himself a ransom for all. Elsewhere he speaks of the grace of God given to him as an enduement for service (I Cor. 3:10), but this is in quite another context.

"The grace of God has appeared for the salvation of all men," as Paul affirms. Because grace has appeared for all men, because God desires all men to be saved and to come to the knowledge of the truth, because Christ gave Himself a ransom for all and tasted death for every man, the election comprehends all men potentially. But it is also true that

II. The Election Comprehends No Man Unconditionally.

"God was in Christ reconciling the world to himself," wrote Paul to the Corinthians (II:5:19). Having declared God's act of universal reconciliation, accomplished for all men once for all for ever in the historical act of atonement wrought by Christ, Paul immediately posits the personal response whereby each man must ratify the reconciliation for himself as an individual: "be ye reconciled to God" (v. 20). In Christ and His redemptive act, God has done all that needs to be done for the reconciliation of all men to Himself—except what men themselves must do. Thus the gracious provision for the reconciliation of all men is limited in its application by one factor alone: the personal response of individual men. Meyer comments on II Corinthians 5:19

It applies to *the whole human race.* . . . The reconciliation *of all men* took place objectively through Christ's death, although the subjective appropriation of it is conditioned by the faith of the individual.[17]

In Romans 5:18, Paul affirms a universal atonement and reconciliation comprehending all men: "so one man's act of righteousness leads to acquital and life for all men" (RSV). But actuation of the universal atonement for *individual men* is contingent on personal appropriation: "much more will those who receive the abundance of grace and the free gift of righteousness reign in life through the one man Jesus Christ" (v. 17 RSV). What is provided "for all men" benefits only "those who receive."

---

[17]H. A. W. Meyer, *Critical and Exegetical Handbook to the Epistles to the Corinthians,* p. 537, italics his.

"God so loved the world that he gave his only begotten Son," declared John (3:16). Here is universal provision; but it must be complemented by individual appropriation: "that whoever believes in him should not perish, but have everlasting life."

"God sent not his Son into the world to condemn the world, but that the world through him might be saved." Again, here is universal provision; but it must be complemented by individual appropriation: "He that believeth on him is not condemned, but he that believeth not is condemned already, because he has not believed in the name of the only begotten Son of God." (Jn. 3:17f.).

"The bread of God is that which comes down from heaven and gives life to the world . . . I am the bread of life." Here is universal provision; but it must be complemented by individual appropriation: "he who comes to me shall not hunger, and he who believes in me shall never thirst" (Jn. 6:33, 35 RSV).

"The bread which I shall give for the life of the world is my flesh." The universal provision must be complemented by individual appropriation: "if anyone eat of this bread, he will live for ever" (Jn. 6:51 RSV).

"He came to his own, and his own received him not." The universal offer had to be complemented by individual appropriation: "to as many as received him, to them gave he power to become the sons of God, even to them that believe on his name" (Jn. 1:11f.).

"Go into all the world and preach the gospel to the whole creation." The universal offer must be complemented by individual appropriation: "he who believes and is baptized will be saved, but he who does not believe will be condemned" (Mk. 16:15f. RSV).

Through the universal provision of grace, God is "the Savior of all men" (I Tim. 4:10), but "specifically of those who believe," because of the necessity of personal appropriation by faith.

The complementary relation of God's provision and man's appropriation appears throughout the Scriptures, confirming the fact that "without faith it is impossible to please God" (Heb. 11:6). Thus the Scriptures posit faith as the condition of election, the condition whereby the election potential for all men becomes realized in individual men: "Therefore, being justified by faith, we have peace with God through our Lord Jesus Christ, by whom also we have access by faith into this grace wherein we stand" (Rom. 5:1f.).

The complementary relation between God's provision and man's appropriation is apparent in Ephesians 2:8: "For by grace are you saved through faith, and that not of yourselves; it is the gift of God." Calvin's comments are excellent:

> For by grace are ye saved. This is an inference from the former statements. Having treated of election and of effectual calling, he arrives at this general conclusion, that they had obtained salvation by faith alone. First, he asserts that the salvation of the Ephesians was entirely the work, the gracious work of God. But then they had obtained this grace by faith. On one side, we must look at God; and, on the other, at man. God declares that he owes us nothing, so that salvation is not a reward or recompense, but unmixed grace. The next question is, in what way do men receive that salvation which is offered to them by the hand of God? The answer is, by faith; and hence he concludes that nothing connected with it is our own. If, on the part of God, it is grace alone, and if we bring nothing but faith, which strips us of all commendation, it follows that salvation does not come from us.
>
> Ought we not then to be silent about free-will, and good intentions, and fancied preparations, and merits, and satisfactions?[18]
>
> •   •   •   •   •   •   •   •   •   •   •   •   •   •   •   •   •   •
>
> When, on the part of man, the act of receiving salvation is made to consist in faith alone, all other means on which men are accustomed to rely are discarded. Faith, then, brings a man empty to God, that he may be filled with the blessings of Christ. And so he adds, not of yourselves; that, claiming nothing for themselves, they may acknowledge God alone as the author of their salvation.[19]

---

[18]Though we may well be silent about "merits and satisfactions," we must not be altogether silent about intentions and preparations, for Scripture has some important things to say about these matters. And certainly we must by no means be silent about "free-will," or to use Scripture's grand term, "whosoever will."

[19]Calvin, Commentaries, ad loc.

It cannot be questioned that the Scriptures categorically affirm that salvation proceeds from the grace of God and comes to man by faith. But the question arises, Whence comes faith? There is in the Scriptures an apparent paradox: faith is exhibited as a gift of God which He graciously bestows on men; at the same time, faith is exhibited as something in man which is *of* man, of which God takes full account in His dealings with men.

Among passages cited as affirming that faith is a gift of God are Romans 12:3, I Corinthians 12:9, and Galatians 5:22. With respect to these passages, however, context implies that the faith in view is not faith for salvation, but faith for Christian living and service. Ephesians 2:8 is sometimes cited, but the "gift of God" in view is not faith itself, but the whole complex of salvation-by-grace-through-faith. *Touto* has reference, not to faith, and certainly not to grace, but to the whole clause "by grace are you saved through faith."[20] The fact that *touto* is neuter and *pisteōs* feminine forbids *faith* to be the antecedent of *that.* Many exegetes are agreed on this point, including Calvin.

The assumption that the above passages posit saving faith as a gift of God has been strengthened by appeal to certain passages which assert that to some it is not given to know and believe holy truth (e.g., Matt. 13:10-16, John 12:37-40), by assertions that men can come to Christ only as the Father draws them (John 6:37,44,65), and by Acts 13:48, Acts 16:14, II Timothy 2:25, and I Peter 2:8. These passages (which will be considered in the following chapter under the questions of reprobation and the call to faith) lend no support to the passages cited in the above paragraph, for the passages cited in the above paragraph do not posit *saving* faith as a gift of God. However, they do lend support to the passages cited below.

The definitive passage positing saving faith as a gracious gift is II Peter 1:1, and Acts 18:27 and Philippians 1:29 may well be understood as doing so (though not necessarily so). In addition, I Corinthians 3:6 and context may be regarded as doing so by

---

[20]Cf. Meyer, Bloomfield, Lange *ad loc.*

inference. These passages, supported by the passages cited in the above paragraph, establish that saving faith is a gracious gift of God, a fact which lends emphasis to the joyful affirmation "by grace are you saved."

Passages that affirm or imply that faith is something in man which is *of* man, of which God takes full account in His dealings with men, are to be found throughout the Scriptures. Representative of such passages in the New Testament are the passages cited in the footnote below (the list is not complete).[21]

The Scriptures affirm that faith is the gracious gift of God to man, and they also affirm that faith is something in man which is *of* man, of which God takes account. But the paradox is only apparent, rather than real, and is resolved when all the facts are recognized, as we shall observe later.

It is evident from his writings that Calvin's thinking and his treatment of the Scriptures were thoroughly conditioned by the dominance of the concept of faith as a gift of God to man. While he recognized the presence of the other concept exhibited in the Scriptures—faith as a factor in man of which God takes account and which is the condition governing salvation—he completely accommodated it to the concept of faith as the gift of God. This accommodation is evident in his treatment of passages of Scripture which affirm or imply faith as the condition governing salvation. In his treatment of such passages, he customarily begins by acknowledging the obvious meaning of the text—which negates his theology, then proceeds to extricate himself, either by burying the point in a mass of theological

---

[21]Matt. 8:10f.; Jn. 1:7,11f. (the question of agency in the faith posited in Jn. 1:12 is determined by v. 7 rather than v. 13, which properly has reference to Christ; cf. my work *Life in the Son,* footnote p. 91); Jn. 2:50; Jn. 3:14-18; Jn. 5:32-47; Jn. 6:32-35,51; Jn. 7:17; Jn. 8:24 and context; Jn. 10:37f.; Jn. 12:32,44-50; Jn. 16:8f.; Acts 10:34-43; Acts 13:38-41; Acts 14:22; Acts 17:24-34; Acts 28:23-38; Rom. 1:16-20; Rom. 3:21–5:2; Rom. 16:26; Gal. 2:16–3:29; I Thess. 2:13; I Thess. 3:1-8; I Tim. 2:4; I Tim. 4:16; I Tim. 6:9-14; II Tim. 2:12; II Tim. 2:18; II Tim. 4:1-4; Heb. 2:1-4; Heb. 3:1–4:16; Heb. 5:9; Heb. 6:4-15; Heb. 10:19-39; Heb. 11:1–12:29; Heb. 13:7-17; Jas. 1:18-21; Jas. 2:14-26; II Pet. 1:10f.; II Pet. 2; II Pet. 3:16-18; I Jn. 1:5–2:6; I Jn. 2:23-25,28; Jude 20f.; Rev. 2:10f.; Rev. 2:17; Rev. 2:25-29; Rev. 3:4-6; Rev. 3:11-13; Rev. 3:19-22; Rev. 22:14-19.

verbalsmog, blowing up peripheral and tangential considerations as though they were the heart and essence of the matter under consideration in the text, or by candidly asserting the existence of a "hidden purpose of God" supposedly assumed by the Biblical writer—which serves to make the passage merely rhetorical rather than categorical (and often casts the Biblical writer in the role of an exceedingly subtle writer who presumed much on the intuition of his readers).[22] Such accommodation is found again and again in Calvin's treatment of Scripture passages which negate his theology. His ingenious treatment of contrary passages proceeded, we believe, not from insincerity, but from his zeal to find uniformity in the Scriptures and complete substantiation for what he believed to be the teaching of the major definitive passages bearing on the question of election.

It is apparent from his frequent and extensive appeals to Romans 9:6-29 that Calvin considered it the cardinal definitive passage on election. Unfortunately, as in the case of some before him, his misconstruction of the passage, together with his confusion of predestination with election, furnished him with three false premises on which he erected his doctrine of election and to which he accommodated all contrary passages of Scripture: (1) that the will of God is monothetic, having but one aspect; (2) that the unconditional election and reprobation of particular men is an inevitable corollary of the sovereignty of God; and (3) that in the impartation of salvation to individual men, God takes account of nothing in men (monergism). Calvin's erroneous assumptions so completely conditioned his approach to the Scriptures that he found no place for the candid acceptance of the many affirmations of Scripture positing faith as a factor in man of which God takes account in salvation, and instead labored to accommodate the Scriptures in toto to the affirmations of faith as a gift of God to men. This is reflected in many passages in his works. The following are representative:

---

[22]Cf. *Commentaries*, II Pet. 3:9.

Certainly they are far from honoring the grace of God as it merits who declare that, while it is common to all, it effectually resides in them because they have embraced it by faith. For all the time they would keep the cause of faith out of sight, namely that, elected to be sons by grace, they have afterwards bestowed upon them the spirit of adoption. (E.P. II)

... the faith by which the children of God enter into possession of their salvation is ... derived from election as its origin. (E.P. 9:2)

How do we prove that some men are gratuitously elect, unless because God illumines whom He will by His Spirit, so that by faith they are engrafted into the body of Christ? But divine election is the origin and cause of our faith. ... election is prior to faith, but is learnt by faith. (E.P. 8:6)

There is no place in any of the above quotations for faith as something in man of which God takes account. Calvin has resolved the paradox by repudiating the affirmations of faith as a factor in man of which God takes account in salvation and election—affirmations which receive far more emphasis in the Scriptures than the equally valid affirmations of faith as a gift of God. Thus faith becomes symbolic rather than probative and loses the determinative aspect that Scripture everywhere posits for it—rendering unintelligible such affirmations as "without faith it is impossible to please God . . . he is a rewarder of them that diligently seek him" (Heb. 11:6), and rendering merely rhetorical such major definitive passages as Romans 3:21—5:2 and Galatians 2:16—3:29 and all other affirmations of faith as the condition of salvation, which affirmations are many and emphatic.

The paradox is to be resolved, not by repudiating one or the other of the affirmations, but by recognizing that the election is corporate rather than particular, that it comprehends all men potentially, that God wills to have all men to be saved and none to perish or to fail to come to repentance, and that His gracious gift of saving faith is available to all men who will accept it. Let us observe at this point that, though saving faith is a gift of God, it does not follow that God must be arbitrary in the bestowal of the gift. The fact that He is not arbitrary becomes clear from an objective analysis of Romans 9-11.

Many have pored over Romans 9:6-29 and proceeded to draw final conclusions on the question of election on the assumption that the passage says all that needs to be said on the question. That Calvin so assumed is evident, not only from the frequent and extensive appeals he makes to the passage, but also from his reference to the passage as "that memorable passage from Paul which alone ought easily to compose all controversy [concerning the doctrine of election] among sober and compliant children of God" (E.P. 5:3). There is full warrant for Calvin's doctrine of unconditional particular election and reprobation in Romans 9:6-29 if it is considered "alone" and is accepted as essentially all that the Bible has to say on the subject of election. But no passage of Scripture stands in isolation from its context, and the context of Romans 9:6-29 forbids the conclusions that Calvin drew from the passage, as we shall see.

First, let us observe that the Epistle to the Romans, regarded by many as Paul's greatest epistle, speaks to one cardinal thesis: the just (righteous) shall live by faith (1:17). Following his salutation and an expression of his interest in the church at Rome, the Apostle states the principal proposition of the epistle:

... the gospel of Christ ... is the power of God unto salvation to every one who believes, to the Jew first, and also to the Greek. For therein is the righteousness of God revealed from faith to faith: as it is written, The Just shall live by faith. (1:16f.)

In the dogmatic portion of the epistle (1:16—11:36), Paul considers the principle of justification by faith in its relation to mankind in general, and as Gentile and Jew (1:18—3:20); in its relation to Christ, through whom redemption has come to man and who is now the object to which faith must be directed (3:21-31); in its relation to Abraham, the father and archetype of all the faithful (4:1-25); in its relation to Christ, who has recovered for all men all that was lost through Adam's transgression, and through whom "where sin abounded, grace much more abounds" (5:1-21); and in its relation to all true believers in Jesus Christ (6:1—8:39). Finally, Paul considers the principle of justification by faith in its relation to Israel collectively (9:1—11:36), a consideration of urgent concern to many in the churches of that day.[23]

*   *   *

In the days of the Apostles, the Gospel of Christ was truly "to the Jew first." Wherever the Apostles went, it was customary for them to enter the synagogues and preach the Gospel first to the Jews of the community. Many Jews became believers, and assemblies which were predominantly Gentile usually had strong nuclei of Jewish converts. This was the situation at Rome. Writing to believers at Rome, Paul addresses them sometimes as Gentiles (1:13-15; 11:13ff.) and sometimes as Jews (2:17ff.; 4:1ff.; 7:1ff.).

Having reached a glorious climax in his consideration of the cardinal questions of sin, and of salvation, justification, and righteousness by grace through faith in Jesus Christ, Paul turns to a consideration of the present circumstance of Israel—a question of utmost concern for Jewish believers. They had accepted Jesus as the promised Messiah and now anticipated the fulfillment of the Messianic promises concerning Israel—perhaps soon (Acts 1:6,7; 3:19-26). But grounds for their hope seemed to be fading. Why the delay? Had Israel been cast away? Were the glorious promises of God to the fathers to be ignored? More and more, it seemed either that the promises must fail, or that Jesus was not really the promised Messiah. The question was of more than academic concern. Doubts arising from incomplete understanding and nourished by disappointment threatened to destroy the faith of many. It was a vexing question among Jewish believers everywhere, and one which required a firm and positive answer. Paul doubtless had often met the question

---

[23]Some of the material which follows is taken from my work *Life in the Son: A Study of the Doctrine of Perseverance*, pp. 340-344.

elsewhere, and he now writes at length to answer it for Jewish converts at Rome. Let us consider a brief analysis of his answer:
1. [9:6-13] God's word has not been proved ineffective. There is an "Israel" *within* Israel—even as, historically, only the descendants of Isaac and Jacob were reckoned as the children of the covenant-promise, to the exclusion of all other descendants of Abraham.
2. [9:14-31] God is sovereign and therefore has the right to do as He pleases with individuals and nations. He is free to bestow favors on some, and to deny them to others, without becoming answerable to any creature. This absolute sovereignty extends to Isaac and Ishmael (vs. 7-9), to Jacob and Esau (vs. 10-13), to Moses (vs. 15,16), to Pharaoh (v. 17), to all other individual men (vs. 18-24), and, collectively, to Israel and the Gentiles (vs. 25-31). God, as sovereign, has an absolute right to make of the common lump of humanity some vessels to honor, and others to dishonor; some for wrath and destruction, and others for mercy and glory. He has an absolute right to say of Israel, "not my people." It is not for men to call God into question. (To do so is not only presumptious; it is positively dangerous, since such an attitude is incompatible with faith. Hence the sharpness and vigor of Paul's reply to presumed objectors.)
3. [9:30-10:21] Israel's failure to "arrive," however, is not at all due to some absolute unconditional decree arising arbitrarily from the fact of the sovereignty of God, without respect to anything in men. The cause of Israel's present frustration is their own unbelief and disobedience. They have only themselves to blame. God continues to stretch forth His hands toward them, but in vain.
4. [11:1-6] Actually, despite the allegations of some, God has not cast away His people. Even though Israel, nationally, is "not my people," God still has His remnant in Israel-after-the-flesh. Paul, himself, is one among them (11:1). As in past generations, God has His "Israel" *within* Israel. Jewish believers in Christ constitute His present remnant in Israel and are of the election, not of works, but of grace.

5. [11:7-10] The present hardening of Israel, nationally—far from being the consequence of an arbitrary act of God in casting them off (11:1,2)—is the consequence of their own failure to obtain the righteousness which they sought. Their failure (as Paul has affirmed, 9:31-10:21) stemmed from the fact that they sought righteousness by their own works, rather than by faith, thus stumbling over Christ, whom they found an offence. Their stumbling and consequent hardening were foretold by Isaiah and David (as well as others).

6. [11:11,12,15] God is able to turn Israel's present lapse to good account, both for the immediate proclamation of salvation among the Gentiles, and for the ultimate recovery of Israel herself. Having accomplished good through their lapse, God will multiply blessing for all nations through the recovery and restoration of Israel.

7. [11:13-24] During the present lapse of Israel, nationally, the salvation of individuals, both Jews and Gentiles (10:12,13), remains a separate and distinct consideration, entirely independent of the question of the circumstance of Israel, nationally. It is evident from vs. 14,23,24 that the "hardening" of "the rest" (as distinguished from "the election," v. 7) is not the consequence of an arbitrary decree of unconditional reprobation; it is not absolute, but only relative.

8. [11:25-27] The recovery and restoration of Israel, nationally, is certain in the purpose of God. They will again become "my people" (9:25,26).

9. [11:28,29] Even in the present era of national unbelief, while "enemies concerning the gospel," Israel-after-the-flesh is still beloved for the fathers' sake, and God's promises to the fathers will yet be honored and fulfilled.

10. [11:30-32] God's constant sincere purpose is to have mercy on all, both Jews and Gentiles, and includes any and all individual men, as they believe (10:12, 13; 11:20-24).

Many have failed to recognize that Paul's consideration in Rom. 9:6-29 is the question of the circumstance of Israel, rather than the personal salvation of individual men, and that his argument serves only to affirm that God, as a sovereign

Creator, is free to order all things as He pleases and to bestow or deny favors as He chooses without becoming answerable to men—a truth which Paul earnestly desired to establish in the minds of Jewish Christians who were profoundly disturbed over the question of the circumstance of Israel and in danger of denying the wisdom and righteousness of God. Paul asserts only the inherent freedom of God, as a sovereign Creator, to act without becoming accountable to His creatures. But this must not be construed to mean that God is not governed by moral principles inherent in His own holy character and that He is at liberty to be arbitrary or capricious. God is governed in His actions, not by the judgment of His creatures, but by the moral integrity of His own Person. Those who have assumed that Rom. 9:6-29 affirms that God is merely arbitrary in His dealings with men, including the unconditional choice of some to salvation and the arbitrary consignment of others to perdition, have misconstrued the passage. They have also ignored much that follows in Rom. 9-11 and the consistent testimony of the Holy Scriptures, including categorical assertions that God wills to have all men to be saved and does not will that any should perish, but that all should come to repentance.

Liddon comments

"Throughout this section (ix. 6-29) no attempt is made by the Apostle to harmonize the absolute Freedom and Omnipotence of God with man's self-determination and responsibility. For the moment, the former truth is stated with such imperious force that the latter appears to be quite lost sight of: and the necessity for this 'one-sidedness' of statement lay in the presumption entertained by the Jews, that in virtue of their theocratic position God *must* be gracious to them. Without attempting to determine the relation of interdependence which exists between Divine and human freedom, (secured by the truth that the former is ruled by God's essential Sanctity and is consequently conditioned by moral facts on the side of man), S. Paul passes on to consider the other side of the phenomenon before him, viz. the responsibility of the Jews themselves for their failure to attain the [righteousness of God].[24]

* * *

---

[24]H. P. Liddon, *Explanatory Analysis of St. Paul's Epistle to the Romans*, p. 174.

Arbitrary election and reprobation is consistent with the fact of the sovereignty of God, as Paul affirms in Romans 9:6-29. But it is not consistent with the moral and ethical nature of God, and therefore it is not the modus operandi of God's dealings with men, as the rest of Romans 9-11 clearly establishes. Consider another brief analysis of the remainder of Paul's extended passage dealing with the relation of Israel to the principle of justification by faith:

1. [9:30-33] The real reason for Israel's fall is unbelief.
2. [10:1-17] Israel's fall is not final, not even necessarily so for Paul's own generation.
3. [10:18-21] Israel's unhappy state is the consequence of her own rejection of the gracious appeals and overtures of God.
4. [11:1-6] Despite Israel's fall, God has not cast away His people: there is yet an *Israel* within Israel, elect by grace.
5. [11:7-24] The rest of Israel-after-the-flesh, though blinded and not now included (efficiently) in the election of grace—not part of *Israel,* are not beyond recovery if they will turn from unbelief.
6. [11:25-36] The ultimate recovery of Israel collectively, still beloved for the fathers' sakes, and the blessing of Israel together with the Gentiles is certain in the purpose of God.

One point made by Paul in the passage requires emphasis, for it is decisive on the question of the nature of election. Paul affirms that the majority of Israel stumbled over Christ and rejected Him (9:30—10:21) and thus "Israel failed to obtain what it sought" (11:7 RSV)—righteousness before God (10:3). But "the elect obtained it, but the rest were hardened" (v. 7). Here Paul divides Israel into two groups—the elect, "a remnant according to the election of grace" (v. 5), and "the rest [who] were hardened." But what was the basis for the election of some and the hardening of the rest? Was the choice of some and the repudiation of the rest predicated on something in men, or was it predicated simply on the arbitrary will and pleasure of God? Calvin affirms the latter. Of numerous passages in his works which might be cited, the following is representative:

... the Jews, deprived of the light of understanding, fell into horrible darkness and thus suffered the just punishments of their wicked contempt of divine grace. Nor does [Paul] conceal the fact that this blindness was inflicted on all the reprobate. For he teaches that the remnant were saved according to gratuitous election, and all the rest were blinded (Rom. 11:5). If all the rest, whose salvation is not governed by the election of God, are blinded, it is clear that the same people who provoked the wrath of God by their rebellion and procured fresh blindness for themselves were already from the beginning devoted to blindness. (E.P. 9:3)

Thus, according to Calvin, "the remnant were saved according to gratuitous election" because they were unconditionally elect from eternity, and "all the rest were blinded" because they "were already from the beginning devoted to blindness," and therefore, by decree of God, "this blindness was inflicted on all the reprobate." Calvin's thesis is in full accord with the erroneous assumptions he deduced from Romans 9:6-29, but it is in radical conflict with the affirmations Paul makes about "the rest [who] were blinded." Far from writing them off as unconditionally reprobate by eternal decree of God, Paul dedicates himself to efforts directed toward their recovery, in the hope and expectation that he "might save some of them" (v. 14). Though "some of the branches" were broken off from the olive tree (the elect *Israel*), "they were broken off because of their unbelief," and Paul declares that they, "if they do not persist in their unbelief, will be grafted in, for God has the power to graft them in again," and in the saving purpose of God in the election of grace, "these natural branches [will] be grafted back into their own olive tree . . . *if* they do not persist in their unbelief" (vs. 17-24 RSV). God desires to have mercy on all (v. 32), and their recovery and return to *Israel* and the election of grace only awaits their turning from their present unbelief to faith in Jesus Christ.

The affirmations Paul makes concerning "the rest [who] were blinded" prove (1) that they were still *potentially* comprehended in the election of grace, and their reprobation was neither unconditional nor necessarily final; (2) that *efficiently* the election of grace is corporate rather than particular and comprehends individual men only in identification and association with the body, "the Israel of God" (Gal. 6:16); and (3) that *efficiently* the election of grace comprehends no man unconditionally.

Calvin's doctrine of unconditional particular election and reprobation collapses at Romans 11:7,14,17-24,32. The election is here proved to be potentially universal, corporate rather than particular, and conditional rather than unconditional.

The total lack of objectivity with which Calvin approached the Scriptures, completely conditioned as he was by the false assumptions which he deduced from Romans 9:6-29, is reflected in his comments on Romans 11 in his *Commentaries.* His comments on verse 14 reflect no recognition that the "some of them" whom Paul hoped to save were some of "the rest [who] were blinded" (v. 7). In his treatment of verses 17-24, he evades the issue by shifting the frame of reference from individual Jews and Gentiles to Israel and the Gentiles corporately—despite Paul's explicit reference, not to Israel corporately, but to "some of the branches." Commenting on verse 21 he asserts that

... the discourse is addressed generally to the body of the Gentiles, for the excision of which he speaks could not apply to individuals, whose election is unchangeable, based on the eternal purpose of God. Paul therefore declares to the Gentiles that if they exulted over the Jews, a reward for their pride would be prepared for them; for God will again reconcile to himself the first people whom he has divorced.[25]

Thus Calvin salvages his "unchangeable election of individuals" by shifting the frame of reference, casually repudiating Paul's reference to "some of the branches" and other evidences that Paul's frame of reference is personal and individual rather than national and corporate. Calvin's apologists in our own day still resort to the same sort of devious devices in their abortive efforts to achieve the impossible—to find uniform Biblical substantiation for Calvin's unbiblical theology.

---

[25]Calvin, *Commentaries, ad loc.*

(Reflecting on Calvin's belief that the mass of Israel were not of the elect and were instead unconditionally and eternally reprobate by the will and good pleasure of God, one is left to wonder what Calvin conceived to be the real import of Paul's expressions of profound sorrow and compassion for Israel-after-the-flesh and his intense yearning for their salvation (9:1-3 and 10:1). Why should Paul have "great heaviness and sorrow" for those for whom God had no such sorrow? Why should he even wish himself accursed from Christ for those who were reprobate by the design and will of God? Why should Paul care so much for those for whom God cared nothing—whom even He hated (as Calvin presumed Paul to understand and teach). Why should Paul pray to God for Israel, that they might be saved, when (as Calvin presumed Paul to understand and teach) he knew that "the rest were blinded" and consigned to everlasting perdition—for which, alone, they had been created by the immutable will of God and for His eternal praise and glory! Why should the Apostle endure such anguish of heart and spend himself in such profound yearning of spirit in prayer to God for the salvation of men whom God had created only to be the objects of His everlasting hatred and wrath? Why did not the Apostle pause to consider what God must have thought about such foolish agonizings and pleadings for men whom he knew to be forever excluded from His saving purpose? Why did not Paul get in step with God and stop insulting him with ridiculous prayers for something he knew to be contrary to His will?)

Rejecting Paul's affirmation of God's purpose to "have mercy upon all" (v. 32), Calvin asserts that "Paul simply means that both Jews and Gentiles do not otherwise obtain salvation than through the mercy of God."[26] Having asserted that "God in the dispensation of his grace is under no restraint that he should not grant it to whom he pleases," Calvin continues, "It is indeed true that this mercy is without any difference offered to all, but every one must seek it by faith."[27] Thus, "mercy is without

[26]*Ibid.*
[27]*Ibid.*

any difference offered to all," and men must "seek it by faith"... but God is "under no restraint that he should not grant it to whom he pleases," and according to Calvin, He by no means pleases to "have mercy upon all." Certainly the Bible teaches that, though all have not sinned alike, all men alike have sinned and come short of the praise of God. The election is "the election of grace," and it is only by the grace of God that any man is saved. In the eternal purpose of God to elect, that grace was "given to us in Christ Jesus before the world began" (II Tim. 1:9). In the unfolding of God's eternal saving purpose, historically that grace "came by Jesus Christ" (Jn. 1:17), and it came for all men alike: "for the grace of God has appeared for the salvation of all men" (Titus 2:11 RSV) and God "desires all men to be saved and to come to the knowledge of the truth" (I Tim. 2:4 RSV). That some men are lost reflects the fact that salvation, offered to all by the grace of God, is not unconditional.

Calvin, of course, taught that election is unconditional. Finding support in Romans 11:5f., he comments

So then at this time, &c. He applies the example [of the remnant of 7,000 faithful men in Elijah's day—vs. 2-4] to his own age, and to make all things alike, he calls God's people a remnant, that is, in comparison with the vast number in whom impiety prevailed ... he expressly calls them a remnant that survived through the grace of God: and thus he bore witness that God's election is unchangeable....

. . . .

... those are saved by God's power whom he has chosen with no regard to any merit. The *election of grace* is a Hebrew idiom for gratuitous election.

6. *If through grace, it is no more by works, &c.* This amplification is derived from a comparison between things of an opposite character; for such is the case between God's grace and the merit of works, that he who establishes the one overturns the other.

. . . .

Now, though he speaks here of election, yet as it is a general reasoning which Paul adopts, it ought to be applied to the whole of our salvation; so that we may understand that whenever it is declared that there are no merits of works, our salvation is ascribed to the grace of God; or rather, that we may believe that the righteousness of works is annihilated, whenever grace is mentioned.[28]

Certainly all agree that Romans 11:5f. posits that the election is not of works, but of grace. But this does not establish that election is unconditional. Rather, it establishes only that election is not conditioned on works. That election is conditioned on faith is clearly affirmed in the Scriptures. Consider the following propositions:

Romans 11:6 says in effect, Not of *works,* but of *grace.*

Romans 4:1-5 says, Not of *works,* but of *faith.*

The Bible nowhere says, Not of *faith,* but of *grace.*

Romans 4:16 says, By *faith,* so that by *grace.*

Ephesians 2:8 says, By *grace,* through *faith.*

Consider Romans 4:16: "Therefore [justification] is of faith, that it might be by grace." So decisive is this verse that we may well observe it in another translation: "[That is why it] depends on faith, in order that the promise may rest on grace" (RSV). The contention that faith as a *condition* nullifies grace, often urged by Calvinists, collapses at this point. Paul affirms precisely the opposite: faith, as a condition, establishes grace and is its sine qua non as a modus operandi. "By grace . . . through faith."

It may be argued that God, acting in grace, need not have posited any condition whatever for election. At least this may be argued dialectically (though not ethically, in view of (1) the witness of the Scriptures to the moral nature of God, His economy, and His kingdom and (2) the fact that faith *has* been posited as a condition). But the issue is not what God *could* do, but rather what God has done and does do, as disclosed in the Scriptures. We have earlier observed that the Bible contains many categorical affirmations positing faith as a factor in man of which God takes account in salvation. The many emphatic affirmations are confirmed by Romans 4:16 and also by Romans 11:7,14,17-24, which passage establishes that the

---

[28]Calvin, *Commentaries, ad loc.*

election of individual men is not unconditional and is predicated on faith, as we have observed.

The above considerations unmistakably posit the validity of the thesis of synergism as against monergism. The considerations involved in the question of synergism are well defined by Berkouwer in his brief résumé of the development of Melanchthon's understanding of the place of man's will in his personal salvation:

> In Lutheran theology the problem appears especially in the development of Melanchthon's thinking. As did Luther, he at first declined all synthesis or cooperation between the acts of God and of man and based conversion exclusively on the deciding grace of God. Later, however, Melanchthon began to emphasize the factor of man's free will and with that he began to reflect on the relation between the human will and offered grace. Accordingly, in his *Loci Communes* (1535), he speaks of three causes of salvation–Scripture, the Holy Spirit, and the will of man who does not reject Scripture but accepts it. In this reflection on the human will a direct interrelationship among the questions regarding predestination becomes visible.[29] For the issue with Melanchthon is the how and where of the decision of man's salvation. The issue is Melanchthon's rejection of any interpretation of human decision in which the superiority of God's predestination and sole activity would leave no room for any activity on man's part. This development in Melanchthon is clear in that he at first rejected the anthropological aspects (*liberum arbitrium*) in justification and predestination (the two terms by which the sovereignty of grace is necessarily indicated), but later resisted any viewpoint which made man "passive" and ruled out his responsibility. The Word of God, the Holy Spirit, and man's will–this was Melanchthon's combination, a combination which has well been called "suspect."

To be sure, Melanchthon did not intend to give up the sovereignty of grace, or the *sola gratia* of justification, but he came nevertheless to this co-ordination whereby a synergistic equalization could no longer be avoided. The predestination that Luther accepted was not completely

---

[29]Many "questions regarding predestination" no longer exist when we abandon the fallacy of confusing predestination with election, and when we recognize that the election is corporate rather than particular, and conditional rather than unconditional. The question of predestination will be considered later in the chapter.

disregarded; rather, it lost its prominence through this co-ordination. Such a loss, according to Melanchthon, cannot be avoided, for when one person believes while the other does not, the reason for this difference must be "within us." Melanchthon's defense against determinism is understandable, but we must agree with Kawerau when he writes, "As commendable as the practical direction was which Melanchthon by this doctrine gave, it was nevertheless in error since by the combination of the three causes he combined the divine and human activity in such a way that salvation comes to pass by the addition of a human acitivity to God's. This resulted in synergism. . . .[30]

It is understandable that, for anyone committed to Calvin's hypothesis of unconditional particular election, Melanchthon's thesis is "suspect" and *synergism* is a word with dire connotations. Despite the fact that Melanchthon's synthesis of the Word of God, the Holy Spirit, and man's will as co-ordinate elements in the realization of conversion is "commendable [for] the practical direction" it affords, synergism can have no place in Calvin's system of theology. Along with the Bible's affirmations that Christ died " for the sins of the whole world" and that God desires all men to be saved and none to perish, the Bible's affirmation of faith as a condition of salvation must be rejected. Faith, in Calvin's system, must finally be only symbolic rather than authentic. Man, according to Berkouwer, can only be "completely passive in the process of conversion," and there can be no "cause within men for their different reactions to the gospel."[31]

For Calvinists, there need be no real correspondence between doctrine and proclamation. Indeed, there cannot be. For Calvinists, in the everyday real-world vocation of the Gospel ministry, what is true will not do. "A pastoral emphasis on man's responsibility," writes Berkouwer, "does not imply criticism of the monergism of grace, but Melanchthon's 'three causes' certainly do imply this."[32] Which of Melanchthon's "three causes" is so objectionable to Berkouwer? such a threat

---

[30]G. C. Berkouwer, *Divine Election*, p. 32f.

[31]*Ibid.*, p. 34.

[32]*Ibid.*

to grace? Is it "man's will"? If so, then what is this "man's responsibility" of which Berkouwer speaks that properly requires "pastoral emphasis"? If, as Berkouwer assures us, man is "completely passive in the process of conversion," what is the nature and scope of his "responsibility"? Responsibility for what?

What is this "man's responsibility" which Berkouwer commends for "pastoral emphasis" and which "does not imply criticism of the monergism of grace"? Is it real? If not, how can it be the object of "pastoral emphasis"? If it is real, then in his reference to "man's responsibility," Berkouwer posits synergism, for this is all that synergism proposes: recognition of man's responsibility, a responsibility that is real and authentic rather than imaginary, hypothetical, and symbolic.

Berkouwer poses a question: "Does our redemption depend on God's decision, or does it depend on ours?"[33] But the question which confronts us in the debate over monergism as against synergism is not the question put by Berkouwer, but rather, Does our redemption depend on God's decision alone, or does it depend on God's decision and ours? Synergism posits no false dilemma of God's decision vs. man's decision. But irrespective of which way the question is put, Berkouwer opts for the former proposition rather than the latter, though he advocates that "pastoral emphasis" be given to the latter rather than the former. Berkouwer's difficulty arises from the fact that he knows nothing of an objective atonement. In his chapter "Election and the Preaching of the Gospel" (which essentially is a 35-page projection of the difficulty posed in his sentence commending "a pastoral emphasis on man's responsibility" and deploring Melanchthon's "three causes"), Berkouwer writes

Universalism should not simply be identified with the doctrine of general reconciliation. There is also a universalism which takes into account the rejection of the gospel on the part of man, so that the

---

[33]*Ibid.*, p. 28.

universal offer does not become realized and effective in every individual. This universalism leads to the conclusion that the decision lies with man.

· ·

God becomes a waiting God who in His powerlessness has actually been humanized. Thus the question naturally arises whether this universalism is true to the Scriptural testimony regarding God's free election.[34]

Obviously not consonant with Calvin's doctrine of unconditional particular election, advocated by Berkouwer, the universalism he describes is indeed true to the Scriptural testimony regarding God's "free election"—an election that comprehends all men potentially, no man unconditionally, and the Israel of God efficiently. Though by no means powerless, God in a true sense is "a waiting God,"[35] and His long patience speaks of infinite grace. There is a majesty about the patience of God that commends His grace as few things could. And it was a "humanized" God, the Word made Flesh, who wept for Jerusalem and cried with broken heart, "Oh, Jerusalem, Jerusalem! how often would I . . . but you would not . . ." Here is infinite compassion. Here, too, is obvious synergism.

"Under the influence of Melanchthon," writes Berkouwer (quoting Althaus), "the old Lutheran orthodoxy abandons unconditional predestination,"[36] and faith, foreseen, became recognized as the condition of election. "In such a notion," according to Berkouwer, "God's decision is made dependent on man's decision."[37] This would be true if the election were particular. But the election is corporate, and Berkouwer's contention therefore is unfounded.

The fact remains that both God and man have a decision in election. We have observed (Chapter III) that Matthew 26:53

---

[34]*Ibid.*, p. 229.

[35]"A Waiting God"—what a wonderful title for a sermon! The theme points to rich lodes of gracious truth in the Holy Scriptures—Rom. 10:21; Isa. 1:18; 55:6; I Pet. 3:20; II Pet. 3:7-9,15; Jas. 5:7—the list of pertinent texts is long, for this is a great Bible theme.

[36]Berkouwer, *op. cit.*, p. 42.

[37]*Ibid.*

discloses that Jesus accepted the death of the cross, not only by the Father's decision, but also by His own decision, a decision in which He was completely free and in which the Father would have concurred immediately, either way. In like manner, God made His decision of election before the foundation of the world (II Tim. 1:9, Eph. 1:4, I Pet. 1:20), a decision positing an objective election comprehending all men potentially and reflected in His desire to have all men to be saved and none to perish (I Tim. 2:4, II Pet. 3:9). By the free decision of Jesus, in which He voluntarily concurred with the Father's decision, the purpose of election was given substance and realization on the Cross where "God was in Christ reconciling the world to himself" (II Cor. 5:19). All that remains is man's decision: "be ye reconciled to God" (v. 20). As Meyer affirms (as we have earlier observed), "The reconciliation *of all men* took place objectively through Christ's death, although the subjective appropriation of it is conditioned by the faith of the individual."[38]

Commenting further on Lutheran theology's recognition of faith as the condition of election, Berkouwer protests

The initiative and the majesty of God's grace is overshadowed.

. . . .

For is it possible that this self-consciousness, unavoidable in connection with man's cooperation, still leaves room for a full recognition of God's sovereign grace? Is not grace, as God's decree and gift, limited and obscured by such cooperation and self-consciousness?[39]

Quite to the contrary, Paul did not assume that faith as a condition "limits and obscures" grace or takes anything away from the initiative of God's grace: "[justification] depends on faith, in order that the promise may rest on grace" (Rom. 4:16 RSV). Faith as *condition* is the *way* of grace and in no sense an antithesis.

Again, Berkouwer writes

---

[38]Meyer, *op. cit.*, p. 537, italics his.
[39]Berkouwer, *op. cit.*, p. 42f.

... the Roman Catholic Church confesses the free will of man, defends it emphatically against the Reformation[40] and places it over against the *sola gratia.* Grace is necessary and active, but man must cooperate with it and affirm it. Grace comes first (praeveniens), but it is not irresistible. "Scripture never teaches that grace works all things by itself in the sense that man's free will can contribute nothing to the salvation of man. Both factors work in such interrelation that neither of the two will encroach upon the other." The Roman Catholic Church wants to emphasize that in relation to salvation man cannot be completely passive, and it supports its position by quoting Scripture passages that call man to activity. From this position arises the problem of whether grace is, or is not, decisive in character.[41]

Berkouwer here implies that if salvation is by grace, there can be no condition—a contention which we already have shown to be without foundation. He also implies that grace is irresistible.

The doctrine of the irresistibility of grace is an essential corollary of the doctrine of unconditional particular election. Representative of many passages in the writings of Calvin and his apologists is the following from the *Institutes:*

When [God] is pleased to save, there is no free will in man to resist. Wherefore, it cannot be doubted that the will of God ... cannot be resisted by the human will or prevented from doing what he pleases, since with the very wills of men he does so. (3:23:14)

The saving purpose of God in election has been fixed from eternity and cannot be altered. But the election is corporate rather than particular, and how individual men relate themselves to God's purpose in election is quite another matter. "God was in Christ reconciling the world to himself ... be ye reconciled to God."

Calvin's concepts of both God and grace are in some respects strange. Following Augustine, he asserts that God "does not convert the obstinate because he does not exert that more

---

[40]"... against the Reformation"? Are Melanchthon and Oecolampadius no longer part of the Reformation?

[41]Berkouwer, *op. cit.,* p. 31. The quotation is from F. Diekamp, *Kathlolische Dogmatik nach den Grundsätzen des heiligen Thomas,* II, 452.

powerful grace, a grace which he has at command, if he were disposed to use it" (3:23:1). Here is a mechanical sort of concept of both God and grace in which grace becomes, not an attribute of God, but some sort of device or apparatus wholly *other* to God Himself, which He "uses" on whatever persons and to whatever extent He pleases. Similar is his concept of grace as quantitive: "before they were born [God] had the grace which he designed to bestow upon [the elect] set apart for their use" (3:22:2). We have earlier alluded to Calvin's distress over those who "by extending the beneficence of God promiscuously to all" would thus "diminish it," and to his gratitude for having been "endowed with an incomparable benefit" so that he was by no means "on equal terms with him who has received hardly a hundredth part" as much saving grace as Calvin had received (E.P. II). Such concepts of grace as quantitive entity and mechanical apparatus are in radical conflict with the Biblical concept of grace as an attribute of God intrinsic in His being. It is true that the term *grace* is not used uniformly in the Scriptures and is often spoken of as an entity when it has reference, for example, to such things as a spiritual gift for enduement for service (Rom. 15:15), a Christian virtue (II Cor. 8:7), the status of right relation with God (Rom. 5:2), or by metonymy for salvation (I Pet. 1:10,13). But with respect to God and His saving purpose, grace is not at all something extrinsic to His being which He arbitrarily manipulates or which He distributes quantitively from some sort of inventory. Contrary to many of Calvin's explicit affirmations and the obvious implications of many others, the grace of God is infinite because *God* is infinite, and "the grace of God has appeared for the salvation of all men" (Titus 2:11 RSV).

But grace is not irresistible. To the Galations (2:21), Paul wrote, "I do not frustrate the grace of God" (by seeking righteousness through the works of the law rather than through faith in Christ). To the Corinthians he wrote (II:6:1), "We then, as workers together with God, beseech you also that you receive not the grace of God in vain" (by failing to go on with God in the unfolding of His redemptive purpose for them, cf. chap. 6,7).[42]

With respect to Calvin's hypothesis of irresistible grace, it is noteworthy that Hebrews 10:29 warns against "doing despite to the Spirit of grace." That the designation "Spirit of grace" appears in the context of Hebrews 10:19–12:29, the longest of the five hortatory sections of the Epistle to the Hebrews which treat the peril of apostasy with such profound urgency, strongly forbids any assumption of the irresistibility of grace.

"My spirit shall not always strive with man," declared God in the days of Noah (Gen. 6:3). If the men of Noah's generation were foreordained to damnation, as Calvin believed, in what sense did the Spirit strive with them, since they were but fulfilling their foreordained role in refusing the testimony of Noah? If no man, either elect or reprobate, can resist the will of God, against whom or what is the Spirit striving when He "strives with man"? If there is in man no faculty of decision which God takes into account, any striving of the Spirit that fails to bring man to submission proves God incapable of performance. Any "striving" not intended to eventuate in the submission of man would be a farce and prove God hopelessly insincere. If decision rests with God alone, any striving at all is totally superfluous.

"You always resist the Holy Spirit!" was Stephen's charge against his persecutors (Acts 7:51). If Calvin's hypothesis of irresistible grace were true, how could this be? If they were reprobates by eternal decree of God, in what sense could they be resisting the Holy Spirit by fulfilling their foreordained role in opposing the Gospel? Only as potential objects of election could it be possible for them to resist the Holy Spirit; and the record stands that they did indeed resist the Spirit of Grace. The doctrine of the irresistibility of grace is a theological fiction.

---

[42]For a consideration of the significance of II Cor. 7:8-11 in this connection, cf. *Life in the Son*, pp. 192-195.

"Paradoxical as it may sound," writes Berkouwer, "one can truly speak of cooperation only when synergism has been completely denounced."[43] This is paradoxical indeed since, as Berkouwer defines it, synergism is the "idea of cooperation."[44] It is as though Berkouwer were saying that "one can speak of cooperation only when cooperation has been completely denounced." However we may view his statement, it is difficult to find in it any real meaning, especially coming, as it does, from a staunch advocate of monergism, which categorically denies cooperation. But completely understandable—and totally objectionable—is his assertion that "only then will sanctification not lead to the self-conceit which can be correlated with the merit of good works."[45] This is an unfair misrepresentation. Synergism posits, not "the merit of good works," but faith, which renounces all confidence in merit and good works. There is no place in Melanchthon's formula for confidence in "the merit of good works," as Berkouwer must know.

Berkouwer rejects any "correlation which makes the election of God dependent on our act of faith" and "every interpretation of the election in Christ in which faith would become the condition of election."[46] Yet in his chapter "Election and Rejection," struggling to relieve God of responsibility for sin, he writes

Theology does not afford a separate dogmatic *gnosis* with which it can proceed further than the average believer in understanding salvation, or in comprehending better the acts of God with man. The dogmatician may not live secretly with a theory of parallelism or symmetry, as if he were allowed to work with other and deeper causes than those given to us in prayer, faith, and confession of sins.[47]

Berkouwer rejects symmetry (parallelism)—unconditional reprobation as the concomitant of unconditional election. But

---

[43]Berkouwer, *op. cit.*, p. 50.
[44]*Ibid.*, p. 47.
[45]*Ibid.;* p. 50.
[46]*Ibid.*, pp. 26,144.
[47]*Ibid.*, p. 216.

his rejection of unconditional reprobation imposes on him the problem of finding some basis for "God's rejection" which relieves God of responsibility for that rejection, and the only "causes" seem to be "prayer, faith, and confession of sins" . . . which are not causes of rejection, and therefore can only be causes of election.

Acknowledgment of "causes–prayer, faith, and confession of sins" is an uncomfortable position for one who elsewhere rejects any "correlation which makes the election of God dependent on our act of faith" and "every interpretation of the election in Christ in which faith would become the condition of election." (Not faith? Then how about "prayer, faith, and confession of sins"?) Berkouwer becomes so uncertain in the face of his problem that he writes

> Every hesitation about or hidden resistance against the sovereign freedom of God, every form of indeterminism which defends man's cooperation against the divine act, will suffer shipwreck on Romans 9.[48] But also every attempt to press the divine act into a deterministic framework and thus to make it the powerful competitor of man's acts will ever be doomed. For every form of competition is made impossible. There are relations here which have no human analogies.
>
> The struggle between determinism and indeterminism in the doctrine of election is a futile one, and he who has discerned the dangers of indeterminism may not go over to determinism as though the explanation of God's freedom were to be found in the concept of causality.[49]

Thus, according to Berkouwer, the election involves neither determinism nor indeterminism. Herein is a wonderful thing: though determinism and indeterminism are mutually exclusive, and though one or the other must be true (no neutral ground is possible), Berkouwer asks us to reject both. We have here what seems to be some sort of theological shell game.[50]

---

[48]Yes, unless Rom. 9 is seen in the light of Rom. 10 and 11. To turn off our thinking at Rom. 9:29 is to miss the point of 9:6-29 and to come away with fatal misconstructuions that are in radical conflict with all the rest of Rom. 9-11 and the cardinal thesis of the whole epistle: "The just shall live by faith."

[49]Berkouwer, op. cit., p. 216.

[50]We cast no disparagement on Professor Berkouwer, a brother in Christ and a gentleman and a scholar. Rather, we make these observations only because it is

After rejecting both determinism and indeterminism (left with what?), after both rejecting "the concept of causality" and positing "causes—prayer, faith, and confession of sins," Berkouwer retreats to more certain ground, asserting that

. . . one will not limit God's freedom and counsel in electing and rejecting. Only with humbleness and veneration we may say after Augustine: what was *contra voluntatem Dei* was not *praeter voluntatem Dei.*[51]

Berkouwer's endorsement of Augustine's well known assertion that what was *against* the will of God was not *beyond* the will of God is noteworthy, for elsewhere he rejects the fact of duality in the will of God. Struggling with I Timothy 2:4, II Peter 3:9, I John 2:2 and other texts positing universalism, fettered as he is by his commitment to Calvin's doctrine of unconditional particular election, he writes

The attempt has repeatedly been made to escape the difficulty—God's will and its efficacy—by presupposing a certain duality in the will of God. But

---

[51]*Ibid.,* p. 217.

germane to our study that we survey briefly the difficulties and contradictions which engulf those whose commitment to Calvin's hypothesis of unconditional particular election requires them to reject synergism and defend monergism, a commitment which involves them in insoluble problems of doctrinal synthesis as well as frequent instances of hermeneutically unsound exegesis.

In his struggle to avoid accepting synergism, Berkouwer becomes involved in numerous self-contradictions. For instance, on page 201 he commends Calvin for "his fervent defense against Pighius, as if Calvin had taught the fall to be one of the acts of God." On page 257 he commends Calvin because he "taught that the fall was comprised in the counsel of God [as against] Bullinger, who did not dare to go that far, but wanted to speak only of *praescientia.* " Thus, while asking us on page 216 to reject both determinism and indeterminism, Berkouwer on page 201 commends Calvin for positing indeterminism and on page 257 for positing determinism. We are to reject both, but Calvin does well to accept both.

Berkouwer sometimes contradicts himself within the limits of a single paragraph. Thus, on page 201, after defending Calvin against the charge of determinism—"as if Calvin had taught the fall to be one of the acts of God"—Berkouwer closes his paragraph (four sentences later) with a rhetorical question calling for the *acceptance* of determinism: "who is able to maintain concepts like *praescientia* and *permissio* at the cross of Christ?"

Again, on page 190 he endorses Calvin's rejection of *permission:* "Calvin confesses that . . . it is impossible ever to give a solution here by means of the concept of the

this unsatisfactory solution is soon put aside, the more so since it affects the urgent power of all these passages. Then again the conclusion has been drawn that behind this "will" is hidden a real will which actually desires something else, or that it is a provisional will (universal and *antecedens*) which ultimately is delimited again by man's free decision.

. . . .

If those whom God wants to bring to salvation with His *voluntas consequens* are the predestinated, the question arises about the seriousness of the *voluntas antecedens* which comes to the fore in such urgent references in Scripture.[52]

In other words, God really cannot be serious about His desire that all men be saved and none perish, despite His affirmations to that effect. For, after all, "those whom God wants to bring to salvation [are only] the predestinated." Thus, on the assumption of Calvin's hypothesis of unconditional particular election, duality in the will of God—accepted on page 217—is rejected on pages 238 and 239. Such are the vagaries of the polemics of Calvinism.

---

[52]*Ibid.*, pp. 238f.

---

praescientia or permission." But on page 191, citing Article 13 of the Belgic Confession, he concurs that "there is nothing contradictory in speaking of God's ordinance and at the same time of His 'allowing' sin." Thus Berkouwer commends Calvin for rejecting *permission* and, a few lines later, commends the Belgic Confession for accepting *allowance.*

Again, on page 34 Berkouwer defends the validity of the thesis of monergism and deplores Melanchthon's concern with the will of man as a factor in personal salvation: "A pastoral emphasis on man's responsibility does not imply criticism of the monergism of grace, but Melanchthon's 'three causes' certainly do imply this." But on page 50 he takes a different view of the matter: "In the light of the gospel it is foolish to let man's acts and decision shrink to nothingness in a system of monergism." Melanchthon asks nothing more than that we not "let man's acts and decision shrink to nothingness," to use Berkouwer's words. But coming from Melanchthon, the words would be rank heresy, while coming from Berkouwer, they are sound doctrine and truly Biblical.

Berkouwer's troubles derive from his commitment to Calvin's fallacy of unconditional particular election, a commitment that imposes on him the necessity of defending a thesis for which there is no warrant in the Scriptures: monotheism-determinism-monergism, a thesis which denies the authenticity of the moral agency of man.

Despite the fact that monothetism is an essential corollary of unconditional particular election, Calvinists (including Calvin himself) are inexorably driven to accept dualism when they face the problem of responsibility for sin. For example, Berkouwer writes that

Bavinck accepts that fall, sin, and punishment are "incorporated" in the counsel of God and "in a sense, are willed by God. But then only in a certain sense, and certainly not in the same manner as grace and salvation."[53]

Here is duality, a positive will for the salvation of the elect and a permissive will for the damnation of the reprobate. This duality is found throughout the literature of Calvinism (with the exception of the literature of hyper-Calvinism which, in contrast with main-stream Calvinism and Calvin himself, remains consistent with the foundation of Calvin's system of theology: the misapprehension of Romans 9:6-29, which forbids indeterminism).

Calvin was plagued with this problem of responsibility for sin and rejection, a problem with which Augustine wrestled. No consistency is to be found in Calvin on the matter. Reading him on the question, one is reminded of the celebrated report of the Irish railroad engineer to his trainmaster: "Off again, on again, gone again, Flannigan." So it is with Calvin on the question of determinism. Writing on the question, he is off again, on again, gone again, where again? The following passages are representative:

[Calvin posits indeterminism] . . . that cannot be done without His will which is yet done contrary to His will. For it would not be done if He did not permit it, and permission is given, not without, but by His will. (E.P. 4)

[Calvin posits determinism] . . . how foolish and frail is the support of divine justice afforded by the suggestion that evils come to be, not by His will, but merely by His permission. . . . It is a quite frivolous refuge to say

---

[53]*Ibid.*, p. 177.

that God otiosely permits them, when Scripture shows Him not only willing, but the author of them. (E.P. 10:11)

[Calvin posits indeterminism] Therefore the great works of the Lord are contrived according to His desire, so that in a wonderful and ineffable way what is done against His will is yet not done beyond His will; for it would not be done did He not allow, and allow it not unwillingly, but willingly. (E.P. 10:14).

[Calvin posits determinism] But of all the things which happen, the first cause is to be understood to be His will, because He so governs the natures created by Him as to determine all the counsels and the actions of men to the end decreed by Him. (E.P. 10:12)

[Calvin posits indeterminism] In a wonderful and ineffable way, what was done contrary to His will was yet not done without His will, because it would not have been done at all unless He had allowed it. So He permitted it not unwillingly but willingly. For the principle that here operates cannot be denied: men and angels as to themselves did what God did not will . . . in sinning, they did what God did not will in order that God through their evil will might do what He willed. (E.P. 8:5)

[Calvin *abhors* indeterminism] The distinction commonly made in the schools of a twofold will we by no means admit. The sophists of the Sorbonne talk of a regulative and an absolute will of God. This blasphemy is rightly abhorrent to pious ears but is plausible to Pighius and those like him. (E.P. 8:4)

[Calvin posits determinism] Here they recur to the distinction between will and permission, the object being to prove that the wicked perish only by the permission, but not by the will of God. But why do we say that he permits, but just because he wills? Nor, indeed, is there any probability in the thing itself—viz. that man brought death upon himself, merely by the permission, and not by the ordination of God; as if God had not determined what he wished the condition of the chief of his creatures to be. (3:23:8)

[Calvin posits indeterminism] I always affirm that the nature of man is at first created upright, lest the depravity which he contracted should be ascribed to God; and similarly that the death to which, though formerly the heir of life, he rendered himself subject, proceeded from his own fault so that God cannot be considered its author. (E.P. 8:5)

[Calvin posits determinism] Who does not tremble at these judgments with which God works in the hearts of even the wicked whatever He will, rewarding them none the less according to desert? Again it is quite clear from the evidence of Scripture that God works in the hearts of men to incline their wills just as He will, whether to good for His mercy's sake or to evil according to their merits. (E.P. 10:11)

[Calvin posits indeterminism] Adam voluntarily deprived himself of the rectitude he had received from God, voluntarily gave himself to the service of sin and Satan, and voluntarily precipitated himself into destruction.... For the proper and genuine cause of sin is not God's hidden counsel but the evident will of man. (E.P. 8:5)

Other passages could be cited, but these suffice to show Calvin's confusion on the question of determinism, which in reality is the question of the nature of the will of God. The doctrine of unconditional particular election and its supporting corollaries of limited atonement, total depravity, irresistible grace, and inevitable perseverance require the assumption of determinism and a monothetic will of God. But the point of difficulty for Calvinism is the question of responsibility for sin. In the face of this consideration, determinism is not an acceptable position, for it places the onus for sin on God rather than man.

The problem for Calvinism is how to relieve God of responsibility for sin and rejection and still retain the thesis of monothetism. This is the problem with which Berkouwer struggles in his chapter "Election and Rejection": "On the one hand, we want to maintain the freedom of God in election, and on the other hand, we want to avoid any conclusion which would make God the cause of sin and unbelief."[54]

It is easy to opt for monothetism and determinism when one takes Romans 9:6-29 as a starting point, interprets it in

---

[54]*Ibid.*, p. 181.

isolation from the rest of Romans 9-11 and the cardinal thesis of the Epistle, and carries away from the passage a fatal misapprehension to use as a hammer to beat into submission every contrary passage in the Holy Scriptures. Thus mentally conditioned, Calvin could opt for monothetism and determinism, with unconditional reprobation as the inevitable corollary of unconditional particular election. Thus he asserts that

The predestination by which God adopts some to the hope of life, and adjudges others to eternal death, no man who would be thought pious ventures simply to deny. (2:21:5)

... there could be no election without its opposite reprobation.

. . . .

Those therefore whom God passes by he reprobates, and that for no other cause but because he is pleased to exclude them from the inheritance which he predestines to his children. (3:23:1)

The above passages are representative of many which posit the central thesis of Calvin's system of theology: unconditional particular election and reprobation.[55] It is a thesis for which support can be found in the Scriptures only by resorting to irresponsible proof-texting and ingenious interpretations and applications, and a thesis that involved Calvin in much confusion and self-contradiction. As we may judge from his on-again, off-again comments on the question of determinism, he never solved the problem . . . or perhaps we should say that he never accepted the solution which continually confronted

---

[55] Tillich (A History of Christian Thought, pp. 263ff.) denies that "the doctrine of predestination is the main point" in Calvin's system of theology, asserting that "for Calvin, the central doctrine of Christianity is the doctrine of the majesty of God." But Tillich goes on to show that Calvin saw in providence—God working in all things to display His glory—the implementation of the majesty of God. He then asserts that predestination is the essential and "final fulfillment of providence." But as the essential expression of providence, which is the implementation of God's majesty, predestination (more precisely, election and reprobation) thereby becomes the central thesis of the whole system, with which all segments must be correlated, though the doctrine of the majesty of God may be the starting point (as Tillich believed).

him in his struggle with the problem: to abandon the unbiblical thesis of monothetism, sincerely accept duality, and stop fleeing back and forth from one to the other. But the price of the real solution was too high: to abandon monothetism and determinism is to abandon monergism and accept synergism . . . and to abandon the doctrine of unconditional particular election.

Calvin's theological heirs have fared no better in their struggle with the problem of responsibility for sin, as we may judge from Berkouwer's chapter. Numerous quotations and references to individuals and doctrinal confessions reflect the fact that the problem of determinism vs. indeterminism—really the issue of monothetism vs. duality and monergism vs. synergism—has tormented thoughtful Calvinists for generations. Berkouwer, certainly among the ablest Calvinist theologians of our day, finds no solution for the problem and ends his 45-page chapter on a note of complete indecision and confusion, advocating the impossible: to reject both determinism and indeterminism, and to reject causality while positing causes. As did Calvin before him, he takes refuge in the question-begging escape device to which Calvinists always resort when their dialectal vehicle collapses: appeal to the inscrutability of the ways of God. He concludes

As the Canons put it, this way [to walk in the presence of the electing God] cannot be trod by those who speak lightly of election (CD, I, 13), but those who do walk upon it will understand why Paul concludes by giving praise. That praise is not that of the *visio Dei*. The ordinances of God are inscrutable and His way cannot be comprehended (Rom. 11:33). In a mirror we still see darkly (I Cor. 13:12), but those riddles are spoken of in a song of love. There is no other and higher point of view. It is precisely faith and love that know of God's freedom, His election and mercy.[56]

We cannot agree that, by concluding with a paean of praise his long and detailed consideration of the relation of Israel to the principle of justification by faith, Paul gives us to

---

[56]Berkouwer, *op. cit.*, p. 217.

understand that the election of grace must remain obscure and that all that he had written on the subject is designedly unintelligible. Rather, we believe that Paul intends only to praise God for His wonderful works of grace, great beyond all that man could conceive.

Although, under the pressure of the problem of responsibility for sin, Berkouwer on page 216 actually espouses synergism and conditional election by positing "causes—prayer, faith, and cònfession of sins," elsewhere, concerned for the defense of the sovereignty of God, he protests that

... synergism must have its effects on the confession of the doctrine of election. It will always make it ... a conditional election, whereby the "high tension" of God's sovereign election is reduced to the level of human decision.

. . . .

Only when we reject synergism ... shall we be able to obtain the correct religious insight into the sovereignty of God's merciful election.[57]

Calvin, of course, posits unconditional particular election and reprobation as a necessary corollary of the sovereignty of God:

God has always been at liberty to bestow his grace on whom he would, [variously distributing] favours as seems to him meet, [retaining] the free right of electing and reprobating. (3:22:1)

Calvinists find the sovereignty of God in Romans 9, and well they should, for certainly it is there; this is precisely Paul's point in 9:6-29. But the sovereignty of God is equally present in 11:32, Titus 2:11, I Timothy 2:4, II Peter 3:9, and other texts positing universalism. One of the great fallacies of Calvinism is the assumption that unconditional particular election is an essential corollary—virtually the sine qua non—of the sovereignty of God. This is by no means so, and the assumption should be examined and seen for what it is: an *assumption,* and one without warrant.

---

[57]*Ibid.,* pp. 44,50.

The sovereignty of God does not need to be established. As an essential aspect of His being and person, it is in no way contingent. The sovereignty of God does not depend, for either its existence or its manifestation, on either the fact or the mode of election. God is sovereign, regardless of whether He elects, or does not elect . . . whether he elects some, or all . . . whether election is conditional, or unconditional. Neither the *fact* of election nor the *mode* of election nor the *extent* of election affects the fact of the sovereignty of God, and the assumption that unconditional particular election is necessary for the preservation of the sovereignty of God is a theological humbug which for generations has been used by Calvinists to beg the question.

Another humbug to which Berkouwer resorts is the assumption that synergism fosters pride:

. . . the real problem of synergism [is that] it results in a certain amount of human self-conceit.

  . . . .

With synergism . . . one cannot—even if one wants to—escape the contradiction between true prayer and self-esteem.

  . . . .

Nor is it clear why man's decision may and should not be honored—even in his self-esteem—once synergism has been accepted.[58]

Conceit and self-esteem for what, Professor Berkouwer? For totally renouncing all claim to self-righteousness? For completely repudiating all dependence on good works? For renouncing all claim to personal merit? For abjectly humbling oneself before God as a broken sinner, deserving of death, helpless, unable to save himself? For casting oneself on the mercies of God and hoping only in the merits and grace of Jesus Christ? These are the elements that are of the essence of saving faith, and where true faith exists, there can be no pride or self-esteem. Pride and faith are mutually exclusive.

---

[58]*Ibid.,* pp. 42ff.

In the case of the assumption of unconditional election, it is quite otherwise. It was precisely the fact of election and the assumption of its irrevocability that fostered such smugness, self-conceit, and reprehensible pride in Israel and encouraged presumptious indifference toward God. And where could one find a more flagrant example of obvious pride than Calvin himself, with his assumption that he was "endowed with an incomparable benefit" so that he was not at all "on equal terms with him who has received hardly a hundredth part" as much grace? No countenance can be given to any equation of synergism with pride, which is simply another theological humbug with which Calvinists for generations have shamelessly begged the question.

We have observed that the doctrine of unconditional particular election finds support in a misconstruction of Romans 9:6-29 which ignores the significance of the rest of Romans 9-11, a misconstruction that collapses in the face of Romans 11:7,14,17-24,32. The thesis of monothetism-determinism-monergism is refuted by many explicit passages of Scripture which posit human responsibility and agency, and faith as the condition of salvation. However, as we have observed, Calvin evades the obvious import of such passages—by ingenious "interpretation" whenever possible, or by burying the point of the passage beneath an avalanche of theological verbalsmog dealing with peripheral and tangential considerations far removed from the essential issue of the passage, or by candidly asserting the existence of a "hidden purpose of God" supposedly assumed by the Biblical writer, making the passage merely rhetorical rather than categorical. Reading from his theological heirs, one must conclude that they learned well the hermeneutical methods of their mentor. But there are certain passages which forbid such wonderfully ingenious treatment, as we shall observe.

Calvin taught that repentance is a gift from God:

Moreover, that repentance is a special gift of God, I trust is too well understood ... to require any lengthened discourse. Hence the Church extols the goodness of God and looks on in wonder, saying, "Then hath

God also to the Gentiles granted repentance unto life" (Acts xi. 18); and Paul, enjoining Timothy to deal meekly and patiently with unbelievers, says, "If God peradventure will give them repentance to the acknowledging of the truth, and that they may recover themselves out of the snare of the devil" (2 Tim. ii. 25, 26). (3:3:21)

And if repentance were placed at the will of man, Paul would not say, "If God peradventure will give them repentance" (2 Tim. ii, 25). (3:24:16)

First, let us observe that, in view of Isaiah 45:22 and numerous cognates in the Old Testament, it was by no means a new thing that the Gentiles should be called to repentance. Instead, it was an old thing newly discovered by the Jewish Christians (and a thing difficult for many of them to learn, including Peter). Acts 17:30,31 posits not a new commandment to repent, but an emphatic reiteration of the commandment already given (Rom. 1:18ff., Jonah 3, etc.) in view of the fuller knowledge of God now made available to the nations and a warning that God's patience, already so well demonstrated in history, is not without limit and judgment must come.

Many have joined Calvin in the appeal to II Timothy 2:25f. to contend that God does not wish all men to repent and withholds repentance from some. There is a solemn consideration that impinges on the question of whether, under certain circumstances, it remains possible for particular men to repent, as we may judge from the word of the Lord against the house of Eli (I Sam. 3:11-14).[59] But II Timothy 2:25f. must be understood in the light of Revelation 2:21, Romans 2:4f., and II Peter 3:9, which passages forbid the assumption that II Timothy 2:25f. posits a general proposition of unconditional particular reprobation.[60] Consider the words of Christ to the church at Thyatria concerning the prominent woman referred to as "Jezebel" and His servants, who were practicing immoral-

---

[59]See the chapter "Is Apostasy Without Remedy?" in my work *Life in the Son: A Study of the Doctrine of Perseverance.*

[60]The questions of reprobation and depravity will be considered in the following chapter.

ity and pagan customs, doubtless in a religious context after the manner of the pagan cults:

I have a few things against you, because you allow that woman Jezebel, who calls herself a prophetess, to teach and to seduce my servants to commit fornication and to eat things sacrificed to idols. And I gave her space to repent of her fornication, and she repented not. Behold, I will cast her into a bed, and them that commit adultery with her into great tribulation, except they repent of their deeds. (Rev. 2:20-22)

Consider especially the words of our Lord, "I gave her space [time, opportunity] to repent . . . and she repented not." If Calvinism's thesis of monergism is correct, if repentance hinges on the decision of God alone, if man repents only as a consequence of a special immediate act of God, we are left to wonder why Christ gave Jezebel *opportunity* to repent without giving her *repentance*. If her failure to repent was the consequence of His own decision, in what sense did He give her opportunity to repent? If He did not choose for her to repent, why did He do something directed toward repentance? If He did something directed toward repentance, why did He not do everything needed? If the repentance of Jezebel and His servants hinged on His own decision rather than theirs, where is any sincerity in His warning of dire consequences to come "except they repent"? No logic, no reason, no sensible meaning can be found in the text if it be denied that there is latitude in the will of God and that man's agency and responsibility to repent are authentic rather than artificial, imaginary and symbolic, as monergism insists. Monergism collapses in the face of Revelation 2:21. Bloomfield is correct in his observation that " the reading supplies, as Wordsworth observes, a strong text for the freedom of the human will, against necessitarian doctrines."[61] The text is decisive, admitting no qualifications or assumptions.

Of the many universalist texts forbidding Calvinism's hypothesis of unconditional particular election and reprobation, II Peter 3:9 is especially relevant: God is "not willing that any

[61]S. T. Bloomfield, *The Greek Testament with English Notes, ad loc.*

should perish, but that all should come to repentance." In his Epistle to the Romans, Paul affirms that the goodness of God is leading to repentance (the verb is conative, expressing endeavor) even those who, with hard and impenitent hearts, are refusing to repent and instead are storing up wrath for the day of judgment to come (2:4). It is evident from these passages that the will of man is free and his responsibility in the matter of repentance is real rather than hypothetical and symbolic.

Another decisive text against monergism is Luke 7:30: "But the Pharisees and the lawyers rejected the purpose of God for themselves, not having been baptized by [John]" (RSV). That the Pharisees and lawyers were able to reject the will of God for them establishes both the fact of duality in the will of God and the validity of synergism. As the text demolishes the thesis of monothetism (the central assumption underlying his system of theology), Calvin attempts to evade the import of the verse through translation and interpretation:

Despised the counsel of God within themselves.

. . . .

Literally, Luke says that they *despised* AGAINST THEMSELVES; and indeed I do not disapprove of the meaning which is preferred by some, that the scribes were rebellious to their own destruction. But as Luke's narrative is simple, and as the proposition *eis* is often used in the sense of *en*, I have chosen rather to translate it, *within themselves,* as meaning that although they did not openly and expressly contradict, yet as they inwardly swelled with hidden pride, they despised within themselves.[62]

There is no warrant for Calvin's rendering of *ēthetēsan* as *despised.* Although he concedes the acceptability of "the meaning which is preferred by some, that the scribes were rebellious to their own destruction,"[63] he rejects it in favor of

---

[62]Calvin, *Commentaries, ad loc.*

[63]Such a proposition is easily explained in terms of Calvin's thesis of proximate and remote causes (E.P. 10:14): "Hence, since the criminal misdeeds perpetrated by men proceed from God with a cause that is just, though perhaps unknown to us, though the first cause of all things is His will, I nevertheless deny that He is the

his own translation-interpretation, "despised the counsel of God within themselves," which allows the assumption that the Pharisees and lawyers did not thwart the will of God for *themselves,* but instead simply held in disdain the will of God for *others*—all those who were baptized by John. Thus, according to Calvin, it was actually the will of God for the Pharisees and lawyers *not* to believe the testimony of John and be baptized. But his assumption is in radical conflict with the explicit declaration that John was sent from God to bear witness of the Light "that all men through him might believe" (John 1:7). In the face of John 1:7, no legitimate choice remains other than to accept the obvious import of Luke 7:30—that in refusing to be baptized by John, the Pharisees and the lawyers rejected God's will for them.

We may inquire of Calvin, Did the "great company of the priests" who later "were obedient to the faith" (Acts 6:7) and the "certain of the sect of the Pharisees who believed" (Acts 15:5) include no one who earlier had refused John's testimony and baptism? If the "great company of the priests" who later believed and obeyed the Gospel were all priests who were baptized earlier by John, where were they during the public ministry of Jesus, especially in the closing days at Jerusalem? If the "great company of the priests" and the "certain of the sect of the Pharisees" were not baptized by John because (as Calvin assumed) they were reprobate by the eternal, immutable will of God, how did it later become the eternal, immutable will of

---

author of sin. What I have maintained about the diversity of causes must not be forgotten: the proximate cause is one thing, the remote cause is another."

Calvin's thesis of proximate cause and remote cause offers nothing valid against synergism. Unless the proximate cause is left free of necessity and confronts valid options with authentic agency, it ceases to be *cause* and becomes only the *consequence* of the remote cause. If the proximate cause is *cause* rather than consequence, the assumption of monothetism-determinism-monergism collapses.

There is no help for Calvin in his problem of responsibility for sin short of honestly repudiating monothetism and accepting the fact of the duality of the will of God—which he sometimes "abhors" as the invention of "the sophists of the Sorbonne," but which he himself often posits temporarily in his frustrations over the problem of responsibility for sin, as we have observed.

God for them to be elect? To attempt to flee the obvious import of Luke 7:30 by resorting to ingenious translation and hermeneutical manipulation leads only to a theological impasse.

To His auditors in the temple at Jerusalem, some of whom were receptive and others antagonistic, Jesus said, "If any man's will is to do [God's] will, he shall know whether the teaching is from God or whether I am speaking on my own authority" (Jn. 7:17 RSV). Two cardinal truths, closely related, are implicit in our Savior's words.

First, a moral element enters into the reception and knowledge of holy truth. "If any man wills to do his will, he shall know ... " Only those who will to do God's will may know His saving truth, and indeed His truth to any appreciable degree in any of its context. "Had you believed Moses," said Jesus on another occassion, "you would have believed me, for he wrote of me. But if you believe not his writings, how will you believe my words?" (Jn. 5:46f.) A moral element enters into faith and the reception of holy truth.

Second, whatever is moral necessarily involves the will: men, as moral agents, are free and therefore responsible to choose to do the will of God. The will of God, who wills that all men be saved and come to the knowledge of the truth and that none perish or fail to come to repentance, in its central saving essence is the same for every man, an objective entity to which men relate themselves or from which they isolate themselves by their own moral decisions in response to "the Light that lights every man" (Jn. 1:9), to the Gospel, and to the Holy Spirit, who convicts the world of sin, righteousness, and judgment (Jn. 16:8). If we face the implications of our Lord's solemn declaration, we can only conclude that men are free to choose to comply, or not to comply, with the will of God, on which decision the fulfillment of His saving purpose in Jesus Christ hinges for every man.

Calvin, following Augustine, asserts that

in the very head of the Church we have a bright mirror of free election, lest it should give any trouble to us the members—viz. that he did not become the Son of God by living righteously, but was freely presented with this great honor, that he might afterwards make others partakers of his gifts. (3:22:1)

True . . . as far as it goes. But Calvin stops short of the full measure of truth. Jesus Christ was indeed born Son of God. But that fact did not of itself make Him the Savior of men. If we may believe the testimony of the Holy Scriptures, the incarnation did not of itself make Him the Elect and the Elector: "Although he was a Son, he learned obedience through what he suffered; and being made perfect, he became the source of eternal salvation to all who obey him" (Heb. 5:8 RSV).

Little can we know of all it cost Jesus to become the Savior of men—the Elect and the Elector. There are passages which afford some insight, among them:

We have not a high priest who is unable to sympathize with our weaknesses, but one who in every respect has been tempted as we are, yet without sinning. (Heb. 4:15 RSV)

Consider him who endured from sinners such hostility against himself . . . resisted to the point of shedding blood. (Heb. 12:3f. RSV)

In the days of his flesh, Jesus offered up prayers and supplications, with loud cries and tears, to him who was able to save him from death, and he was heard for his godly fear. (Heb. 5:7 RSV)

. . . my flesh, which I will give for the life of the world . . . this is my body . . . this is my blood of the new covenant, which is shed for many for the forgiveness of sins. (Jn. 6:51, Matt. 26:26,28)

. . . the cup which my Father has given me, shall I not drink it? (Jn. 18:11)

My God, my God, why hast thou forsaken me? . . . He poured out his soul unto death . . . his soul [was made] an offering for sin. (Matt. 27:46, Isa. 53:12,10)

I thirst! . . . It is finished! . . . Father, into thy hands . . . (Jn. 19:28,30, Lk. 23:46)

This was the "free election." Decreed by the Father, it was an election which Jesus ratified in history by His deliberate, free decision (Matt. 26:53f.), as we have observed (Chapter III). Jesus became the Savior of the World—the Elect and the Elector—at infinite cost to Himself beyond all our power to appreciate. The saving act of Christ in history was authentic, not symbolic pageantry. The response of men to His saving act of election must be equally authentic. No one who understands the implications of Matthew 26:53f. will reject the thesis of synergism.

Other passages which completely negate the thesis of monergism will be considered in the following chapter. In the face of passages already considered, passages positing human agency which forbid ingenious interpretation or any assumption of a "hidden purpose of God" that makes them merely rhetorical rather than categorical, it is evident that there is no warrant in the Holy Scriptures for Calvinism's assumption of monothetism-determinism-monergism. The many passages positing authentic decision as the free moral response of man to "the grace of God that appeared for the salvation of all men" and faith as the condition of salvation must be accepted at face value.

Comprehending all men potentially, comprehending no man unconditionally,

III. The Election of Grace Comprehends the Israel of God Efficiently.

At the close of his letter to the churches of Galatia, the Apostle Paul writes "peace be . . . upon the Israel of God" (6:16). The Israel of God—such is his designation of the body of the faithful, all who "walk according to this rule"—the principle of life as new creatures, not through circumcision or ceremonial ordinances and observances, but through faith in Jesus Christ, in whose cross was Paul's boast and rejoicing (vs. 14-16). It is in the Israel of God—the corporate body of the just who live by faith[64]—that the election of grace, potential for all men, is realized.

That the Israel of God is composed of individuals is obvious. But the election is of the body and comprehends individual men only in association and identification with the body, as we have observed. While the election of particular men is contingent on the condition of faith, the election of the body is unconditional in the sense that election is an eternal purpose of God—the kingdom purpose of God which antedates creation.

Some have objected that, apart from the unconditional election of particular men, God could not have been certain that there would be an elect body. Such an assumption, which proceeds on the fallacy of monothetism-determinism-monergism, implies that the foreknowledge of God could comprehend nothing of which He is not the immediate and sole cause. Such an assumption thus consigns to God all blame and responsibility for sin and denies the moral agency of man and of Jesus Christ. Such an assumption denies the veracity of Christ's affirmation that the Father would have concurred immediately in His decision either for or against the cross, as readily for one option as for the other (Matt. 26:53). Such an assumption must have as its corollary the assumption that Christ's propitiatory offering of Himself once for all for ever for the sins of the whole world was merely symbolic rather than authentic, necessary rather than voluntary. Such an assumption proceeds on a make-it-happen concept of prophecy, a concept negated by Matthew 26:53 and the whole experience of Jesus in the days of His flesh.[65]

The passages positing foreknowledge (I Pet. 1:2, Rom. 8:28-30; 11:2) and predestination (Eph. 1:3-14, Rom. 8:28-30) obviously comprehend individuals, but only within the context of the corporate election of the Israel of God. To assume that

---

[64]Hab. 2:4, Rom. 1:17, Gal. 3:11, Heb. 10:38.

[65]For a consideration of the relation of prophecy and free agency, as illustrated in the experience of Jesus, see my work *Life in the Son: A Study of the Doctrine of Perseverance*, pp. 246-250.

the individuals comprehended in the passages are unconditionally elect is to ignore context and the whole concensus of the Holy Scriptures.

In the same passage in which Paul writes of foreknowledge, predestination, calling, justification, and glorification in conformity to the image of God's Son (Rom. 8:28-30), he writes also of fateful contingencies confronting his readers and all believers: glorification with Christ only on condition of suffering with Him (v. 17), spiritual life only on condition of living after the Spirit rather than after the flesh (vs. 12f.), and sonship only on condition of walking after the Spirit (v. 14).

After praising God for the gracious election in Christ and the predestination to sonship in the kingdom through Christ (Eph. 1:3-14), Paul warns the Ephesians against the peril of being deceived by those who with vain words would seek to persuade them that they were unconditionally secure in the kingdom of Christ and of God (5:1-7). It is noteworthy that, as Bible scholars generally believe, Paul wrote his Epistle to the Colossians at the same time he wrote the Epistle to the Ephesians, perhaps dictating Colossians 1:21-23 the same day he dictated Ephesians 1:3-14. In any event, the Ephesian doxology is not to be interpreted in isolation from the solemn warning in the Colossian passage.

Peter, who addresses his First Epistle to "the strangers scattered . . . elect according to the foreknowledge of God" (1:1f.), in his Second Epistle exhorts his readers, who "have obtained like precious faith with us" (1:1), to "give diligence to make your calling and election sure" (1:10).

As we have observed, Romans 11:7,14,17-24,32 forbids any definition of the election of grace as unconditional and particular, as do also the many passages warning against apostasy and the many passages positing faith as the condition of election. Thus it is evident that the passages positing foreknowledge and predestination must be understood as having as a frame of reference *primarily* the corporate body of the Israel of God and *secondarily* individuals, not unconditionally, but only in association and identification with the elect body, the Body of Christ (the Israel of God)—an identification that is contingent on identification with Christ Himself through abiding faith (John 15:1-6).

Melanchthon's doctrine of election posits the thesis of *praescientia* and *praevisa fides,* making the election of particular men foreknown to God on the ground of their foreseen faith. Certainly if God foreknew particular men as elect, if He foreknew *anything* about them, He foreknew their faith and their personal response to His law of righteousness-by-faith. But, while the Scriptures disclose God's specific foreknowledge of certain particular men whose activities were especially germane to the implementation of His purposes in human history, whether God has actively foreknown each individual— both the elect and the reprobate—may remain a moot question. The Biblical doctrine of election does not require such efficient particular foreknowledge, for the election is primarily corporate and objective and only secondarily particular. The passages positing foreknowledge and predestination of the elect may be understood quite as well one way as the other.

We have earlier suggested that much misunderstanding has arisen from the fallacy of confusing predestination with election. Calvin continually confused the two. Representative of many passages exhibiting his confusion of predestination with election are the following:

The predestination by which God adopts some to the hope of life and adjudges others to eternal death no man who would be thought pious ventures simply to deny. . . . By predestination we mean the eternal decree of God, by which he determined with himself whatever he wished to happen with regard to every man. All are not created on equal terms, but some are preordained to eternal life, others to eternal damnation; and accordingly as each has been created for one or other of these ends, we say that he has been predestinated to life or to death. (3:21:5)

[God engrafts] those who are elect in Christ into His body . . . calling and justifying in His own time those who were predestined before the foundation of the world. (E.P. 8:4)

Of the Eternal Election, by Which God Has Predestinated Some to Salvation and Others to Destruction. (The title of 3:21)

Calvin's theological heirs have followed in his footsteps in confusing predestination with election. The two, while closely related and mutually involved, are not the same. Both election and predestination are acts of determination, but the election is God's choice of men *per se,* whereas the predestination looks beyond the fact of the election itself to the *purposes and objectives* comprehended in election.

It is noteworthy that the verb *eklegō*[66] appears in the New Testament only in the middle voice[67] (*eklegomai,* to choose out for one's self). The use of the middle voice, representing God as acting with reference to Himself in the election of men, is in marked contrast with the New Testament usage of the verb *pro-oridzō*[68] (to predetermine, decide beforehand), which never appears in the middle voice. The contrast is significant.

Thus, election is the act whereby God chose men for Himself, whereas predestination is His act determining the *destination* of the elect whom He has chosen. Predestination is God's predetermination of the eternal *circumstance* of election: sonship and inheritance as joint-heirs with Christ (Eph. 1:5,11) and glorification together with Christ in full conformity to His image (Rom. 8:28-30). In Ephesians 1:3-14, the *election* is in view in verse 4 ("he has chosen us in him before the foundation of the world") and the *predestination* is not to election and salvation, but to the *circumstance* of election: adoption as children of God (v. 5) and participation in an eternal inheritance (v.11). In Romans 8:28-30, the *election* is concomitant with God's foreknowledge, and the *predestination* is not to election and salvation, but to conformity to the image of His

---

[66]Eph. 1:4, Mk. 13:20, and numerous other references, including references to Christ's choosing the Apostles.

[67]Possible exception: Lk. 9:35, where the text is in doubt. In any event, the reference is to Christ rather than to men.

[68]Rom. 8:29, Eph. 1:5,11, Acts 4:28, I Cor. 2:7.

Son (v. 29), a predestination to be realized through calling, justification, and ultimate glorification (v. 30).

Calvin went so far afield in his confusion of election and predestination that he sometimes made election the consequence of predestination:

[God] does not adopt promiscuously to the hope of salvation, but gives to some what he denies to others [and thus] elects those whom he has predestined. (3:21:1)[69]

Here Calvin has matters exactly backward. God does not elect those whom He has predestined; rather, He has predestined (to sonship, inheritance, glorification) those whom He elects.

Unfortunately, in Calvin's thinking election became *predestination*—the predestination of some men to salvation and of all other men to everlasting damnation. The error has persisted among his theological heirs. Uncritical usage of the term *predestination* for *election,* a fault found everywhere in the writings of Calvinists, has contributed to gross confusion and lent credence to Calvin's hypothesis of unconditional particular election and reprobation, an assumption for which there is no warrant in the Holy Scriptures.

Election and predestination, coextensive, are corporate and comprehend individuals only in association and identification with the elect body. Election and predestination comprehend all men potentially, no man unconditionally, and the Israel of God efficiently.

Romans 11:7,14,17-24,32, a passage to which we have made several references, affords conclusive evidence that the election of grace is corporate rather than particular. Paul affirms that, because of unbelief, "some of the branches" were broken off—not from Israel-after-the-flesh, but from the *Israel* within Israel, the true Israel where the election of grace resides. Although many individuals were broken off through unbelief, the election of grace remained intact and precisely what it was

---

[69]Cf. Berkouwer, *op. cit.,* p. 239: "... those whom God wants to bring to salvation ... are the predestinated."

and always is: the corporate election of the Israel of God—all the faithful. As Paul affirms, the branches broken off through unbelief may be grafted in again—if they do not continue in unbelief. Thus, the way is open for them again to become participants in the election of grace, through faith, and Paul dedicates himself to the recovery of as many as possible (v. 14). In the Israel of God, which comprehends all by-faith sons of Abraham and all sons and daughters of the Jerusalem which is above, comprehending the Israel within Israel and all the Gentiles who are called by His name; in the household of God and of faith, in which there is neither Jew nor Gentile, but one body and one Spirit, confessing one hope, one Lord, one faith, one baptism, one God and Father of us all; in the Church which is His body, the fulness of Him who fills all in all, reconciled to God in one body through the cross, built together into a holy temple in the Lord for a dwelling place of God in the Spirit; in the Kingdom gathering together many from the east, the west, the north, and the south—a great host which no man could number, from all nations and tribes and peoples and tongues; in the people of God, among whom He will dwell for ever—the Israel of God, forever blessed—is realized the election of grace.

> Remember me, O Lord, with the favor that thou bearest unto thy people. Visit me with thy salvation, that I may see the good of thy chosen, that I may rejoice in the gladness of thy nation, that I may glory with thine inheritance.
>
> PSALM 106:4,5

The Called According to His Purpose

And we know that all things work together for good to them that love God, to them who are the called according to his purpose. For whom he did foreknow, he also did predestinate to be conformed to the image of his Son, that he might be the firstborn among many brethren. Moreover, whom he did predestinate, them he also called; and whom he called, them he also justified; and whom he justified, them he also glorified.

ROMANS 8:28-30

CHAPTER V

THE CALLED ACCORDING TO HIS PURPOSE

SHE WAS a widow. Less than a week had passed since we had made our sorrowful way out to the cemetery to bury the body of her teen-aged daughter, her only child, victim of an illness of only a few days. In the evening prayer service in the village church, she rose to testify. "And we know," she quietly said, tears coursing down her cheeks, "that all things work together for good to them that love God, to them who are the called according to his purpose."

Do we really know this? Someone has said that Romans 8:28 is the hardest verse in the Bible to believe. But what a joyful affirmation when, in simple faith that does not demand to understand and sometimes dwells in a broken heart, we can say, "We know that in everything God works for good with those who love him, who are the called according to his purpose."

Who are these favored ones, thrice blessed and marked for everlasting glory—these who are "the called according to his purpose"? Paul identifies them as "those who love God."[1] But the question arises, especially in view of Romans 8:29,30, why do some love God, while others do not? Have men a choice whether to love God? Or, has God predestined some men to love Him and others to despise Him or, at best, to be indifferent toward Him?

---

[1] What great blessings are promised to those who love God!—present providential care (Rom. 8:28), eternal life (Jas. 1:12), glorification together with Christ (Rom. 8:29f.), and blessings beyond imagination in eternity to come, vouchsafed now to believers by the Holy Spirit (I Cor. 2:9f.).

These questions raise again the question of the validity of Calvinism's assumption of monothetism-determinism-monergism, an assumption which we considered in Chapter IV and found to be a fallacy without warrant in the Holy Scriptures, a fallacy which has involved Calvinists in endless contradictions and confusion in their synthesis of the doctrine of election.

We also considered in Chapter IV the matter predestination, affirmed in Romans 8:28-30 and Ephesians 1:3-14, and found it to be not a decree of unconditional election and reprobation marking certain men for salvation and all others for damnation, as Calvin and his disciples have assumed, but rather God's predetermination of the purposes and objectives and eternal *circumstance* of election: sonship, inheritance, and glorification with Christ.

We have observed that the election is corporate rather than particular and comprehends all men potentially, no man unconditionally, and the Israel of God (all the faithful) efficiently.

The above considerations imply the authentic universality of the Gospel call as against Calvinism's thesis of a "general" call addressed to all men and a hidden "special" call arbitrarily granted to some men and withheld from others. However, we shall now address ourselves more especially to this question and to the passages of Scripture that have been cited in support of Calvin's thesis of unconditional particular reprobation and its corollary, the thesis of a merely representative general call to all men, designedly ineffectual apart from a hidden effectual call arbitrarily reserved for the unconditionally elect. Our present concern with respect to the call of God in the Gospel is to determine from the Scriptures

I. Whom He Called.

The Holy Scriptures bear abundant testimony that the call to salvation is a universal call to all mankind. God's gracious word to all men everywhere is

There is no God else beside me; a just God and a Saviour; there is none beside me. Look unto me and be ye saved, all the ends of the earth: for I am God, and there is none else. (Isa. 45:21f.)

In His final words to John in the Apocalypse, the Risen Christ declares

And the Spirit and the Bride say, Come. And let him who hears say, Come. And let him who is athirst come. And whosoever will, let him take the water of life freely. (Rev. 22:17)

The words are the age-long echo of the gracious invitation of Jesus spoken one autumn day in old Jerusalem on the final day of the Feast of Tabernacles, only a few months before His crucifixion:

If any man thirst, let him come to me and drink. He that believeth on me, as the scripture has said, "Out of his heart shall flow rivers of living water." (Jn. 7:37f.)

The gracious invitations of Jesus are universal in scope: "whosoever will . . . any man." God so loved the world (*kosmos,* the whole human race) that He gave His only begotten Son, that *whoever* believes in Him should not perish but have eternal life. For God sent His Son that the *world* through Him might be saved (Jn. 3:16f). The Gospel commission given by our Lord to His disciples is to "all nations . . . all the world . . . every creature" (Matt. 28:19, Mk. 16:15). The Gospel call is as broad as the command to repent—to "all men everywhere" (Acts 17:30).

But is the general call to salvation authentic? According to Calvin (most of the time) it is not. As we have observed, Calvin posits indeterminism whenever he is confronted by the problem of responsibility for sin, in which case the general call to salvation becomes authentic. But when not struggling with the problem of responsibility, Calvin posits determinism— unconditional particular reprobation as well as election: "God chose out of the condemned race of Adam those whom He pleased and reprobated whom He willed" (E.P. 8:5). Thus the general call to salvation becomes only a representation, totally devoid of authenticity. Representative of Calvin's conception of the purpose of the general call to salvation are the following passages:

... there are two species of calling—for there is a universal call by which God, through the external preaching of the word, invites all men alike, even those for whom he designs the call to be a savour of death and the ground of a severer condemnation. (3:24:7)

[God] invites all to [life] by His word. Now this is not contradictory of His secret counsel, by which He determined to convert none but His elect. He cannot rightly on this account be thought variable, because as lawgiver He illuminates all with the external doctrine of life, in this first sense calling all men to life. But in the other sense, He brings to life whom He will, as Father regenerating by the Spirit only His sons. (E.P. 8:2)

... however universal the promises of salvation may be, there is no discrepancy between them and the predestination of the reprobate, provided we attend to their effect. We know that the promises are effectual only when we receive them in faith, but, on the contrary, when faith is made void, the promise is of no effect. If this is the nature of the promises, let us now see whether there be any inconsistency between the two things—viz. that God, by an eternal decree, fixed the number of those whom he is pleased to embrace in love and those on whom he is pleased to display his wrath, and that he offers salvation indiscriminately to all. I hold that they are perfectly consistent, for all that is meant by the promise is just that his mercy is offered to all who desire and implore it, and this none do save those whom he has enlightened. Moreover, he enlightens those whom he has predestinated to salvation. Thus the truth of the promises remains firm and unshaken, so that it cannot be said there is any disagreement between the eternal election of God and the testimony of his grace which he offers to believers. But why does he mention all men? Namely, that the consciences of the righteous may rest the more secure when they understand that there is no difference between sinners, provided they have faith, and that the ungodly may not be able to allege that they have not an asylum to which they may betake themselves from the bondage of sin, while they ungratefully reject the offer which is made to them. (3:24:17)

Thus the call, addressed by God to all, by design of God is *not* to all, but only to some. The ungodly have "an asylum to which they may betake themselves from the bondage of sin," and they are utterly without excuse for not doing so–despite the fact that God by immutable decree has rendered them totally unable to do anything other than to "ungratefully reject the offer which is made to them." When God asks, "Why will you die?" the real answer is that God has so ordained. "God so loved the world" that He determined that few shall believe and be saved. "Look unto me and be ye saved, all the ends of the earth," cries God to a lost world . . . while making certain that most men do not comply. "Whosoever will, let him come," pleads the Risen Christ . . . while the Father makes certain that most men will not come. "God sent not his Son into the world to condemn the world, but that the world through him might be saved" . . . but He has effected a "hidden" arrangement ensuring that most of the world *shall not* be saved. Thus, according to Calvin,

> . . . when God, after making a covenant of eternal life, invites any people to himself, a special mode of election is in part understood, so that he does not with promiscuous grace elect all of them.

. . . .

We say, then, that Scripture clearly proves this much, that God by his eternal and immutable counsel determined once for all those whom it was his pleasure one day to admit to salvation, and those whom, on the other hand, it was his pleasure to doom to destruction. (3:21:7)[2]

---

[2] Calvin, who insists that it is God's good pleasure to doom to destruction the great mass of mankind, quotes Augustine with hearty approval: "Because we know not who belongs to the number of the predestinated, or does not belong, our desire ought to be that all may be saved; and hence every person we meet, we will desire to be with us a partaker of peace" (3:23:14). But why? If this be not God's desire, why should it be Calvin's? Why does Calvin wish to be more gracious than God? Since Calvin asserts that God is not "promiscuous" with grace and is pleased to save the few and damn the many, why does he assert that "our desire ought to be that all may be saved"? What inconsistency! It is tragic, especially in view of the baneful effects on the Church and the cause of the Gospel through four centuries and more, that Calvin's theology prevented him from acknowledging that God desires what Calvin himself desired: the salvation of all men. Instead, his theology required him to repudiate every affirmation of Scripture that God desires all men to be saved and none to perish.

Several passages of Scripture are cited in support of the thesis that the general call is merely a representation and that the *effectual* call is a "hidden" call granted only to particular individuals arbitrarily chosen of God for salvation. Certain passages, on casual examination, may be so construed. But in every case, there are alternative constructions, constructions which are required—sometimes by the demands of context, and always by the necessity of avoiding radical contradiction of passages positing God's will for the salvation of all men: such "universal" passages as I Timothy 2:4-6, I Timothy 4:10, II Peter 3:9, Romans 5:18, Romans 11:32, II Corinthians 5:19, Titus 2:11, Colossians 1:20, John 3:14-17, John 6:33,51, John 7:37, Revelation 22:17, Acts 17:30, I John 2:2, and Isaiah 45:22, among others.

Among passages cited in support of the thesis of a "hidden" call granted only to chosen individuals and a general call designed only to augment the condemnation of the mass of mankind are Isaiah 6:9,10 and its New Testament cognates: Matthew 13:13-15, Mark 4:12, Luke 8:10, John 12:37-40, and Acts 28:25-27. The passage in Isaiah reads

Go and tell this people, Hear ye indeed, but understand not; and see ye indeed, but perceive not. Make the heart of this people fat, and make their ears heavy, and shut their eyes, lest they see with their eyes, and hear with their ears, and understand with their heart, and turn and be healed.

The Scriptures bear abundant witness that Judah, which profited nothing from the example of Israel's spiritual declension and consequent judgment from God at the hands of the Assyrians, well deserved the divine censure announced in Isaiah 6:9,10 and the judgment declared in verses 11 and 12. The censure sounds so final and irremediable. But it must be observed that Isaiah, commissioned to declare such solemn censure and to announce judgment to come, was also called of God to declare some of the most compassionate appeals to repent and most gracious promises of forgiveness and restoration found in all the Holy Scriptures, among them such entreaties as 1:16-19; 43:25,26; 44:22; 45:22; and 55:6,7. The import of the solemn national censure recorded in Isaiah 6:9,10 must be understood in the light of the many appeals and gracious promises of God also declared through His servant Isaiah.

Isaiah 6:9,10 must be understood also in the light of the message of Jeremiah to Judah a century and more after Isaiah. Through His servant Jeremiah, God again charges Judah with having eyes which see not and ears which hear not:

Hear now this, O foolish people, and without understanding, which have eyes and see not, which have ears and hear not. . . . To whom shall I speak and give warning, that they may hear? Behold, their ear is uncircumcised, and they cannot hearken: behold, the word of the Lord is unto them a reproach; they have no delight in it. (5:21; 6:10)

But Judah's blindness, deafness, and hardness of heart is attributed, not to any arbitrary divine interdiction, but to human volition, and God's gracious appeal to Judah is predicated on the fact of man's moral agency:

Fear ye not me? saith the Lord: will ye not tremble at my presence? . . . But this people hath a revolting and a rebellious heart; they are revolted and gone. Neither say they in their heart, Let us now fear the Lord our God. . . . Your iniquities have turned away these things, and your sins have withheld good things from you. . . . Be thou instructed, O Jerusalem, lest my soul depart from thee; lest I make thee desolate, a land not inhabited. . . . Thus saith the Lord, Stand ye in the ways and see, and ask for the old paths, where is the good way, and walk therein, and ye shall find rest for your souls. But they said, We will not walk therein. Also I set watchmen over you, saying, Hearken to the sound of the trumpet. But they said, We will not hearken. Therefore, hear, ye nations, and know, O congregation, what is among them. Hear, O earth: behold, I will bring evil upon this people, even the fruit of their thoughts, because they have not hearkened to my words, nor to my law, but rejected it. . . . Thus saith the Lord of hosts, the God of Israel, Amend your ways and your doings, and I will cause you to dwell in this place. . . . For if ye thoroughly amend your ways and your doings . . . then will I cause you to dwell in this place, in the land that I gave to your fathers, for ever and ever. (5:22-25; 6:8,16-19; 7:3,5,7)

In wrath God remembers mercy, and gracious pardon is promised for all who turn from their wicked way to seek His face.

The New Testament cognates of Isaiah 6:9,10, which on a casual reading seem to lend support to the thesis of a general call designed only to augment condemnation for all but a favored few arbitrarily and unconditionally chosen of God for salvation, on careful examination are found to afford no such support. Let us consider Matthew 13:11-15, which follows Matthew's account of our Lord's Parable of the Sower. In reply to the disciples' question why He spoke to the multitude in parables,

Jesus answered and said to them, Because it is given to you to know the mysteries of the kingdom of heaven, but to them it is not given. For whoever has, to him shall be given, and he shall have more abundance; but whoever has not, from him shall be taken away even what he has. Therefore I speak to them in parables, because seeing they see not, and hearing they hear not, neither do they understand. And in them is fulfilled the prophecy of Isaiah which says, Hearing, you shall hear and shall not understand, and seeing, you shall see and shall not perceive. For this people's heart has grown dull, and their ears are hard of hearing, and their eyes they have closed, lest at any time they should see with their eyes and hear with their ears and understand with their heart and turn, that I should heal them.

First, let us observe that the Parable of the Sower was in no sense intended by Jesus to be a proclamation of the Gospel. There had been ample preaching of the Gospel in the area. Several months had elapsed since He had taken up residence in Capernaum as headquarters for an extended ministry in Galilee, the burden of which is indicated in Mark's introductory summary, "Jesus came into Galilee preaching the kingdom of God and saying, The time is fulfilled and the kingdom of God is at hand: repent ye, and believe the gospel" (1:14f.). Jesus Himself summarized His labors in the cities of Galilee in His words to the two disciples of John, "Go and show John the things you hear and see: the blind receive their sight, the lame walk, the lepers are cleansed, the deaf hear, the dead are raised, and the poor have the gospel preached to them." (Matt. 11:4f.).

But the preaching of Jesus had met with so little acceptance (Matt. 11:16-19) that He was moved to pronounce severe condemnation on the three principal cities of the area "in which most of his mighty works were done"—Chorazin, Bethsaida, and Capernaum (Matt. 11:20-24). When all the facts are taken into consideration, it becomes evident that the inability of the multitude at Capernaum to understand the parable derived from their own past rejection of the preaching of Jesus, especially as we consider the import of the solemn principle declared by our Lord: "For whoever has, to him shall be given, and he shall have more abundance; but whoever has not, from him shall be taken away even what he has" (13:12). The principle is vividly expressed in Mark 4:24,25:

Take heed what you hear: with what measure you give, it shall be measured to you, and to you that hear shall more be given. For he who has, to him shall be given, and he who has not, from him shall be taken even that which he has.

Reception of holy truth as it is offered is the indispensable prerequisite for understanding additional truth. The multitude at Capernaum had rejected the preaching of Jesus, and thus had rendered themselves incapable of understanding His parables of the kingdom. All such "mysteries of the kingdom of heaven" would remain enigmatic and unintelligible to them as long as they continued to reject the Gospel proclaimed by Christ.

Despite His severe rebuke and condemnation of Chorazin, Bethsaida, and Capernaum, Jesus yet proclaimed mercy and saving grace. It was to the same multitudes whom He rebuked so severely, who in the past months had adamantly rejected His preaching and teaching, that Jesus yet addressed His gracious invitation

Come unto me, all ye that labor and are heavy laden, and I will give you rest. Take my yoke upon you, and learn of me: for I am meek and lowly in heart, and you shall find rest for your souls. (Matt. 11:28f.)

Thus it is evident that the spiritual dullness of the multitude and their inability to understand our Lord's parables derived, not from some divine interdiction arbitrarily imposed on them because they were by eternal decree unconditionally excluded from grace and salvation (which would be radically contrary to I Timothy 2:4-6, II Peter 3:9, Titus 2:11, John 3:14-17, Romans 5:18, etc.), but rather from their own rejection of the preaching and teaching of Jesus during His ministry among them in the previous months, a rejection which was not necessarily final, as we may judge from our Lord's gracious invitation in Matthew 11:28-30. In the light of all the attendant facts, Matthew 13:11-15 no more lends support to the thesis of a general call designed only to augment the condemnation of all but a favored few than does Isaiah 6:9,10 when viewed in the context of the many calls to repentance and promises of forgiveness which accompanied God's severe censure of Judah in Isaiah's day.

Another passage cited by advocates of the thesis that the general call is only a representation really intended only to augment the guilt of the mass of mankind is John 12:37-40:

But though he had done so many miracles before them, yet they believed not on him, that the saying of Isaiah the prophet might be fulfilled which he spoke, Lord, who has believed our report? and to whom has the arm of the Lord been revealed? Therefore they could not believe, because Isaiah said again, He has blinded their eyes and hardened their heart, that they should not see with their eyes nor understand with their heart and be converted, and I should heal them.

Westcott comments on verses 39 and 40:

The fact which has been already noted (*they did not believe*) is now traced back to its ultimate origin, which lay in the divine action. They did not believe, and they could not believe, for *that Isaiah said again: He* (that is God) *hath*. . . The want of belief was involved in the necessary truth of the prophetic word. This fulfillment again involved in the incredulous an inability to believe consequent upon the actual working of God according to His fixed laws. Comp. Rom. x. 16. And yet, further, this working of God, as we look at it in the order of succession, was consequent upon man's prior unbelief. The Jews were already in an unnatural and diseased state when the prophet was sent to them. Then came the punishment whereby those who would not give glory to God by willing faith were made to subserve to His glory. The revelation of Christ, like the preaching of Isaiah, was the very power by which the existing form of unbelief was carried to its full development.

. . . .

With regard to the general scope of the passage it may be observed that: 1. As a fact, disregard of impulses and motives to right-doing makes it more and more hard to obey them. 2. We may regard this law as acting mechanically; or we may see in it, in relation to man, the action of a divine power. The latter supposition introduces no new difficulty, but on the other hand places this stern law in connexion with a wider scheme of action, which makes hope possible. This divine "cannot" expresses a moral and not an external or arbitrary impossibility.[3]

As Westcott observes, the proscription in view in John 12:37-40 is predicated on a moral rather than an arbitrary impossibility, and therefore is not without remedy—which is precisely the circumstance we have already observed in our consideration of Isaiah 6:9,10 and Matthew 13:11-15.

The "proscription" passages which are the subject of our present consideration are relevant to the whole question of the hardening of men's hearts, as disclosed in the Scriptures, especially the question of the agency or agencies which effect the hardening of men's hearts against holy truth. It is evident from the Scriptures that both God and men themselves effect the hardening of men's hearts. In his chapter "Election and the Preaching of the Gospel," Berkouwer says many good things in his discussion (pp. 244-253) of "what Scripture calls the 'hardening of the heart.' " He writes

He who reflects on what Scripture teaches about hardening of the heart will certainly not be able to find the solution by speaking only of the self-hardening of man's heart in sin and unbelief. To do that, the testimony in Scripture would have to be drastically reduced, for it speaks often of God Himself who does the hardening. It is typical of the

[3] B. F. Westcott, *The Gospel According to St. John*, p. 185.

testimony in Scripture that it speaks of both man's self-hardening and God's hardening of the heart.[4]

As Berkouwer declares, the Scriptures affirm both man's self-hardening and God's hardening of the heart. Let us observe at this point, however, that God's hardening of the heart never occurs apart from man's self-hardening, and God does nothing in this solemn matter that is not consonant with His earnest appeal "Harden not your heart" (Ps. 95:8, Heb. 3:8). Dealing with Isaiah 6:9,10 and many cognate passages, Berkouwer asserts

It is almost incomprehensible that Isaiah 6:9,10 has been quoted as "proof" for the hardening of the reprobate from eternity.

. . . .

In Scripture the issue in hardening is never an arbitrary, causal matter. The divine hardening is closely related to the message of salvation, to the preaching of the gospel which evokes a decision.

. . . .

The gospel does not leave unchanged the person who does not listen and remains disobedient; it compels him to go the way of estrangement and judgment. In that way we see the ripening process, and when it is said that "they could not believe," that inability is not the result of a decree by a *potentia absoluta* but the holiness of the judgment of God, which is increasingly realized in such unbelief.

. . . .

. . . hardening is not the result of a fateful decree, but an act of God which manifests its judgment upon man's sinful self-determination. And for that reason hardening is forever distinguished from fate. Behind fate stands the impersonal power of determinism, but behind hardening of the heart stands a God who repeats: "Do not harden your hearts!"[5]

Thus Berkouwer departs from Calvin in his rejection of reprobation as a positive decree comprehending particular men unconditionally from eternity. What Calvin regarded as decreed

---

[4]G. C. Berkouwer, *Divine Election*, p. 245.

[5]*Ibid.,* pp. 248-251.

from *eternity* Berkouwer regards as accomplished in *time* by the self-determination of men.

But Berkouwer arrives at the same destination as Calvin by indulging in a popular fallacy of contemporary Calvinists: the assumption that there can be an unconditional election of particular men without a corresponding unconditional reprobation of all other men. Let it be observed that the election of particular men constitutes no rejection of other men *only* if the election is not unconditional. Any unconditional choice of particular men constitutes per se a rejection of all men not chosen.

Although Berkouwer insists on the reality and determinative character of human agency and volition in the hardening of men's hearts, and though he insists that "human inability [to believe the Gospel] comes about only through sinful response to the preaching of the gospel" and that the hardening of man's heart results, not from "a fateful decree," but rather from "man's sinful self-determination,"[6] Berkouwer nullifies his contention by insisting on "a free and sovereign election," by which he means Calvin's unconditional election of particular men . . . according to which thesis, except as God visits particular men here and there with a "hidden" effectual call, the only course open to men is to harden their hearts against Him by their own "sinful self-determination." Thus, according to Berkouwer, men have power to respond negatively to the Gospel, for which they incur increased guilt, but they have no power to respond affirmatively.

But we must insist that "self-determination" (which Berkouwer posits) is impossible if only one course is open to man. A choice without alternatives is not a *choice*. Agency without viable options is not *agency*.

What kind of God, we may well inquire, does Berkouwer worship? If God alone has power to act to reverse men's wayward course, if men can exercise no authentic personal decision for God and salvation, if men have no power of

---

[6]*Ibid.*, p. 251.

responding affirmatively to God apart from an immediate particular act of enabling which God in His sovereignty grants unconditionally to some and withholds from others, then in the case of every man who does not turn to Him, God's appeals to men to "turn ye from your evil ways . . . turn you at my reproof . . . turn thou unto me . . . let the wicked forsake his way . . . let him return unto the Lord . . . seek ye the Lord . . . why will ye die?" and all such appeals and admonitions constitute the most abhorrent, the most reprehensible, the most malicious and despicable deceptions that ever can be conceived, and God Himself constitutes the most abominable curse that ever can be visited on His own creation.

"But Oh, thank God for God!"[7] Praise be to God for Himself . . . and for the *kind* of God He is! All His admonitions and invitations are offered in good faith, and there is not the slightest semblance of duplicity in any act or word of our God . . . for men are free to act, and there are valid alternatives before them, as the Gospel and all God's gracious appeals and invitations imply. The general call to salvation is authentic, for men are free to respond affirmatively, if they will.

It is understandable that Romans 9:15-24 has been cited as proof that God Himself hardens the hearts of particular men arbitrarily, without regard to any consideration other than His own good pleasure—His own whimsy, we might say. Certainly Paul affirms in this passage that God has a perfect right to act in mercy or in wrath, in grace or in judgment, in favor or in repudiation, toward every man without becoming answerable to any of His creatures. But as we have already observed (Chapter IV), Romans 9 must be understood in the light of Romans 9:30—11:36, in which Paul affirms that, instead of acting arbitrarily toward men (as He has a right to do as sovereign Creator), God is governed in His actions by His purpose of grace toward all men (Romans 11:32, Titus 2:11, etc.). On the significance of Romans 9-11, Berkouwer asserts

---

[7]Joyce Kilmer, in "Thanksgiving."

It is being accepted more and more that this passage is not concerned primarily with establishing a *locus de praedestinatione* as an analysis of individual election or rejection, but rather with certain problems which arise in the history of salvation.

. . . .

The meaning of Romans 9-11 is . . . misjudged when one explains these chapters deterministically, reading into them a system of cosmology in which everything is deduced from God as prime cause, making human activity of no significance. Such a concept of God is certainly not what Paul tries to give us.

. . . .

It must be said, however, that many no longer agree with Calvin's exegesis of Romans 9:14-24, not because they wish to minimize the sovereignty of God, but because they recognize that Paul's words cannot legitimately bear this interpretation.

. . . .

Again, this is not an independent analysis of the destiny of individual man; it shows, rather, the acts of the electing God through the course of history.[8]

Berkouwer's comments on Romans 9-11 merit careful reading.

As we have observed (Chapter IV), Romans 11:7-24 forbids any interpretation of Romans 9:6-24 as establishing Calvin's thesis of unconditional particular election and reprobation. It also forbids any interpretation of Isaiah 6:9,10, Matthew 13:11-15, John 12:37-40, and cognate passages as supporting the thesis of the arbitrary unconditional interdiction of particular men and the thesis that the general call to salvation is merely representative rather than authentic, the design of which is to augment the guilt and condemnation of men not arbitrarily chosen to be the recipients of a "hidden" effectual call.

Another passage which has been cited in support of the thesis that the general call is merely a representation and that the "hidden" effectual call is reserved for particular men arbitrarily and unconditionally chosen of God is found in John 6:

_____

[8] Berkouwer, *op. cit.*, pp. 210-214.

All that the Father gives me shall come to me. . . . No man can come to me except the Father which hath sent me draw him. . . . No man can come to me except it were given to him of my Father. (vs. 37,44,65)

Rejecting "the synergistic idea of cooperation" as irreconcilable with "the sovereignty of election and grace," Berkouwer writes

How can the solution of synergism—also in its interest in the anthropological freedom of will—maintain itself over against the unequivocal words of Christ spoken in a moment of crisis for His people: "No man can come to me, except the Father that sent me draw him" (John 6:44)?

The word *draw* which Christ uses here has always attracted much attention. Kittel says that when it refers to man it has the meaning of *to compel,* of *irresistible superiority,* as in James 2:6 where the rich *drag* the poor before the judge, and as Paul and Silas are *dragged* into the market place in Acts 16:19.

Criticism of synergism has often—and not incorrectly—proceeded from the radical, the unequivocal nature of this word *draw.* And indeed, the word touches the core of the doctrine of election.[9]

Berkouwer's whole case here rests on an assumed significance of the word *draw* . . . and collapses in the face of the fact that the same word (*elkuō*) is used in John 12:32, where Jesus declares, "And I, if I be lifted up from the earth, will draw all men unto me."

While rejecting synergism, Berkouwer asserts that "This 'drawing' of the Father is not at all an act that rules out all human activity; rather, says Kittel, it rules out all that is coercive and magical."[10] Thus, according to Kittel (and Berkouwer), the "drawing" is a matter of *compelling,* but it is not at all *coercive.* No explanation is given of how God can *compel* without being *coercive.* Obviously, both propositions cannot be true, for they are mutually exclusive. Truth rests with the latter proposition: the Father's "drawing" is not coercive. And if God does not coerce, it follows that in man's response to the Gospel, something is left to man's volition. That this is so is implied in John's passage. Having asserted that "no man can

[9]*Ibid.,* pp. 47f.
[10]*Ibid.,* p. 48.

come to me except the Father which hath sent me draw him" (v. 44), Jesus immediately declared,

It is written in the prophets, And they shall all be taught by God. Every one who has heard and learned from the Father comes to me. (v. 45 RSV)

As Christ affirmed, all are *taught.* But only those who choose to *hear* and *learn of the Father* come to Him. Robertson comments on verse 45

And hath learned (kai mathōn).... It is not enough to hear God's voice. He must heed it and learn it and do it. This is a voluntary response. This one inevitably comes to Christ.[11]

Jesus' words "no man can come to me except the Father who sent me draw him" are especially significant in the context in which they appear. He had spoken repeatedly of God as His Father, claiming that the Father had sent Him into the world—a claim which most of His hearers rejected (vs. 41f). Affirming that "no man can come to me except the Father who sent me draw him" and that "every man who has heard and has learned from the Father comes to me," Jesus implied that the coming of every man who comes to Him constitutes a certification of His divine Sonship, a Sonship of which men must be persuaded before they can come to Him in the true sense of the term.

The passage affords no support for the thesis of a merely representative Gospel call not intended to constitute an authentic call to salvation for all men. Nor is such support afforded by two other verses often cited by advocates of such a thesis:

No one knows the Father except the Son and anyone to whom the Son chooses to reveal him. (Matt. 11:27 RSV) As the Father raises the dead and gives them life, so also the Son gives life to whom he will. (John 5:21 RSV)

On casual reading, our Lord's words may seem to imply that He does not wish all men to be saved and that His auditors were

---

[11]A. T. Robertson, *Word Pictures in the New Testament, ad loc.*

under some sort of divine proscription rendering them incapable of believing His Gospel. However, that this is not so is clear from the context of John 5:21. To His hearers, who were condemning Him for "violating" the Sabbath and were scoffing at His claim to be the Son of God (v. 18), Jesus declared

You search the scriptures, because you think that in them you have eternal life; and it is they that bear witness to me, yet you refuse to come to me that you may have life. (vs. 39f. RSV)

Thus Jesus implied that they were at liberty to come to Him, if they would. What really prevented them from believing in Him and coming to Him was not some divinely imposed proscription, but rather their own doings—their ultimate rejection of the testimony of John (vs. 32-35), their rejection of the testimony of Jesus' mighty works (v. 36), their rejection of the witness and word of the Father and the Scriptures (vs. 37-40), their repudiation of the love of God (v. 42), and their rejection of the testimony of Moses (vs. 46f.). Again we see the principle we have already observed: reception of holy truth as it is offered is the indispensable prerequisite for understanding and receiving additional truth. That His critics were not prevented from coming to Him by some eternal decree unconditionally marking them for destruction rather than salvation is clear from Jesus' words to them, "these things I say, that you might be saved" (v. 34). It is evident that Jesus entertained hope that even yet His critics might turn from their unbelief and become receptive to the truth and saving grace.

Elsewhere, Jesus made plain who they are to whom He is pleased to reveal the Father: "If a man love me, he will keep my words: and my Father will love him, and we will come to him and make our abode with him" (John 14:23).

There is no support in John 5:21 and Matthew 11:27 for the thesis that the true call to salvation is "hidden" and reserved for only a favored few, arbitrarily and unconditionally chosen for salvation, to the exclusion of all other men. Nor is there support for such thesis in the following passages from John's Gospel, all of which have been cited as evidence of an arbitrary and unconditional interdiction of particular men:

1. "You believe not, because you are not of my sheep" (10:26). That their unbelief did not derive from some eternal, irrevocable decree of God is evident from the fact that to the same men Jesus appealed, "believe [my] works, that you may know and believe that the Father is in me, and I in him" (v. 38).

2. "The wind blows where it wills, and you hear the sound of it, but you do not know whence it comes or whither it goes; so it is with every one who is born of the Spirit" (3:8 RSV). Some have assumed that our Lord's words here imply that the Holy Spirit visits some men with saving grace, but not others, because God wishes to save only some men rather than all. It is assumed that the words rule out all possibility of the existence of any pertinent condition or factor in men of which the Holy Spirit takes cognizance in effecting the new birth. Certainly the new birth is a divine operation—the action of Spirit on spirit—and not in any sense something man does for himself. But our Lord's words in John 3:8 must be understood as *descriptive* rather than *proscriptive*.[12] Human condition and agency, far from negated in Christ's discourse to Nicodemus, are categorically affirmed: "you do not receive our testimony. If I have told you earthly things and you do not believe, how can you believe if I tell you heavenly things?" (v. 11f. RSV) Nothing is more emphatic in verses 14-21 than the condition "whoever believes" and the affirmation of authentic human agency in the face of valid practicable options.

3. "He that is of God hears God's words: you therefore hear them not, because you are not of God" (8:47). But Jesus regarded their perdition as yet contingent: "if you believe not that I am he, you shall die in your sins" (v. 24).

4. "For judgment came I into this world, that they which see not might see, and that they which see might be made blind" (9:39). Context (vs. 40f.) indicates that those who were made blind by the coming of Christ into the world and the stream of

---

[12]For comment on the significance of Jn. 3:8, see *Life in the Son*, p. 87.

human events were those who were so very sure that they "saw" and were well instructed in the Scriptures. Romans 11:7 and context discloses that the blindness visited on men through their rejection of Christ was occasioned only by their own unbelief, and in the grace of God was not without remedy. The blindness and hardness of men's hearts does not derive from the will and good pleasure of God, else Jesus would not have been "grieved for the hardness of their hearts" (Mark 3:5), for the Father's will was His delight.

5. "You did not choose me, but I chose you and appointed you that you should go and bear fruit and that your fruit should abide" (15:16 RSV). The choice of which Christ speaks is to the Apostolate rather than to salvation (cf. Mk. 3:13ff., Lk. 6:13ff., Acts 1:2, etc.), a choice which Christ made among His larger body of disciples (Lk. 6:13).

6. "You are not of the world, but I chose you out of the world, therefore the world hates you" (15:19). Christian discipleship (the circumstance of salvation) by its very nature invites the enmity of the world (I Pet. 4:1-5, Eph. 5:1-16), especially in the case of the Apostles (I Cor. 4:9-13). The choice to the Apostolate, as well as the call to salvation, imposed the circumstance of ethical separation from the world, and this is the import of Christ's words rather than fiat reprobation of most of the world for whom He was about to die.

7. "I pray not for the world, but for those whom thou hast given me, for they are thine" (17:9). Although the burden of our Lord's prayer for the moment was for His Apostles, His concern went beyond them to include all who would believe through their word (v. 20) and extended to all the world (that the world may believe and know, vs. 21,23), a world for whose life He soon would give His flesh in sacrifice (6:51), being nailed to His cross and lifted up to die, that He might draw all men to Himself (12:32).

Among passages in the Acts of the Apostles that have been cited in support of the thesis of a merely representative general call, ineffectual apart from a hidden call arbitrarily reserved for the chosen few, is 2:39, "For the promise is unto you, and to your children, and to all that are afar off, even as many as the Lord our God shall call." Although the Gospel promises find fulfillment only in those who obey the Gospel, to assume that the words "even as many as the Lord our God shall call" did not potentially comprehend all of Peter's auditors at Pentecost and all who come under the sound of the Gospel call is to reject the testimony of I Timothy 2:4 that God desires that all men believe and obey the Gospel and the testimony of many cognate "universal" passages. That men who refuse to obey God's call thereby reject His will and counsel for them is clear from Luke 7:30, "The Pharisees and the lawyers rejected the purpose of God for themselves, not being baptized of [John]."

Another passage often cited in support of the thesis of a hidden call without which the general call of the Gospel remains ineffectual is Acts 16:14, "And a certain woman named Lydia, a seller of purple, of the city of Thyatira, who worshipped God, heard us: whose heart the Lord opened, that she attended to the things which were spoken by Paul." A cognate passage if Luke 24:45, "Then opened he their understanding, that they might understand the scriptures"—the gracious ministry of the risen Lord to His Apostles and other disciples. Another pertinent passage is found in Ephesians 1:17, 18, in which is recorded Paul's prayer for the Ephesians that "the eyes of your understanding [may be] enlightened" through the gracious operation of God.

It is evident from these and other Scriptures that all spiritual enlightenment comes to men through divine enablement, by the grace of God, as implied in Acts 18:27, "those who through grace had believed" (RSV). It is only by the grace of God that any man can believe and respond affirmatively to His call. But to assume that God wills that only a few shall believe and heed His call is to reject the testimony of I Timothy 2:4 that God wills that all men shall come to the knowledge of the truth and be saved, and the testimony of Titus 2:11 that "the grace of God has appeared for the salvation of all men" (RSV), and the testimony of many other categorical assertions in the Holy Scriptures. To assume from Acts 16:14 that Lydia and her household were all that God was pleased to save of the group who heard Paul by the riverside near Philippi on that day long ago is to ignore or reject many plain affirmations of Scripture.

Luke depicts Lydia as one who sincerely "worshiped God," and it may well be inferred that she was one who exemplified the principle declared by Jesus, "If any man's will is to do [God's] will, he shall know whether the teaching is from God" (John 7:17 RSV). It must be remembered also that Jesus laid the responsibility for unbelief on men themselves (as we have already observed) and, in the case of men who rejected His words, indicated both the possibility and His desire and concern for their salvation: "these things I say, that you might be saved" (John 5:34).

There is nothing in Acts 16:14 and 18:27 which nullifies the many passages affirming the universal will of God for the salvation of all men and the purpose of Christ to draw all men to Himself (John 12:32). That there is an "inner" call given to men which makes the spoken call of the Gospel effectual is clearly implied in the Scriptures, but that it is arbitrarily bestowed on some and denied to others unconditionally cannot be assumed without doing violence to many categorical assertions in the Holy Scriptures.

The appeal to Acts 16:14 and 18:27 in the interest of the thesis of a hidden call arbitrarily reserved for particular men has been supplemented by appeal to Romans 12:3, "God has dealt to every man the measure of faith," and Ephesians 2:8, "For by grace are you saved through faith; and that not of yourselves: it is the gift of God." With reference to the former passage, it need only be observed that context discloses that faith, as considered here, is concerned with Christian living and service rather than with salvation. With respect to the latter passage, Robertson states an essential grammatical consideration observed by many commentators:

And that (kai touto). Neuter, not feminine *taute*, and so refers not to *pistis* (feminine) or to *charis* (feminine also), but to the act of being saved by grace conditioned on faith on our part.[13]

Paul depicts not faith, but the whole economy of salvation-by-grace-through-faith as being God's gracious gift to men. Thus salvation itself becomes a gracious gift of God, a gift which men could not earn by good works or merit (v. 9) and which comes to them by faith.

Another passage to which men have appealed in support of the thesis of a "hidden" call arbitrarily reserved for particular men unconditionally elect is Acts 13:48, "And when the Gentiles heard this, they were glad and glorified the word of the Lord; and as many as were ordained to eternal life believed." The appeal to this passage is understandable, for the passage appears to lend strong support to the thesis in question. However, the support is only apparent rather than real, and on careful examination the passage is found to be not in conflict with I Timothy 2:4 and its many cognates which affirm the desire of God for the salvation of all men.

Commentators are divided on the question of the precise significance of *tetagmenoi*, which the Authorized Version (following the Vulgate) renders "ordained," as do most English versions, including the Revised Standard Version. As in the case of many words, *tasso* possesses latitude, and the determination of its meaning in any instance becomes a matter of interpretation. It is imperative that full consideration be given to context in determining the precise meaning of *tetagmenoi* in Acts 13:48. This men have failed to do who have presumed to find in the verse support for the thesis in question. Alford comments:

The meaning of [*tetagmenoi*] must be determined by the context. The Jews had *judged themselves unworthy of eternal life*: the Gentiles, as many as were disposed to eternal life, believed. *By whom* so disposed is not here declared: nor need the word be in this place further particularized. We know that it is God who worketh in us the will to believe, and

---

[13]A. T. Robertson, *Word Pictures in the New Testament, ad loc.*

that the preparation of the heart is of Him:[14] but to find in this text
pre-ordination to life asserted is to force both the word and the context to
a meaning which they do not contain. The key to the word here is the
comparison of [I Cor. 16:15 and Rom. 13:1] in both of which places the
agents are expressed, whereas here the word is absolute. See also ch. xx.
13.... Wordsworth well observes that it would be interesting to enquire
what influence such renderings as this of *praeordinati* in the Vulgate
version had on the minds of men like St. Augustine and his followers in
the Western Church in treating the great questions of free will, election,
reprobation, and final perseverance: and on some writers in the Reformed
churches who, though rejecting the authority of that version, were yet
swayed by it away from the sense of the original here and in ch. ii. 47. The
tendency of the Eastern Fathers, who read the original Greek, was, he
remarks, in a different direction from that of the Western School."[15]

Wordsworth's observations merit serious reflection. The fact
that the Greek fathers, thoroughly conversant with the Greek
text as their native tongue and the language of daily use, found
in the passage nothing to suggest the doctrinal concept implied
by the Latin rendering *praeordinati* indicates that the transla-
tors of the Vulgate erred in their rendering of *tetagmenoi* in
adding the prefix *prae* to *ordinati,* not only in view of the fact
that *tetagmenoi* is without the prefix *pro* (the word is *tassō*, not
protassō), but also by reason of the fact that, as Alford has
observed, the word is absolute, with no assertion of the
particular agency involved. The fact that human agency is
explicit asserted in verse 46—"since you thrust [the word of
God] from you and judge yourselves unworthy of eternal
life"—strongly militates against any assumption of divine agency
in verse 48 and of an eternal decree of unconditional particular
election, an assumption invited by the unfortunate and unwarranted addition of the prefix *prae*. Pertinent to these considerations is the comment of Meyer on Acts 13:48:

---

[14]But in so doing, God does not act arbitrarily, which would be in radical
contradiction of I Tim. 2:4, II Pet. 3:9, and the many cognate passages affirming the
will of God for the salvation of all men.

[15]Henry Alford, *The Greek Testament,* pp. 153f.

It was dogmatic arbitrariness which converted our passage into a proof of the *decretum absolutum.* For Luke leaves entirely out of account the relation of 'being ordained' to free self-determination. . . . Indeed, the evident relation in which this notice stands to the apostle's own words, *epeide . . . zoes,* ver. 46, rather testifies *against* the conception of the absolute decree, and *for* the idea, according to which the destination of God does not exclude, comp, ii. 41, individual freedom. . . . [16]

Both Alford and Meyer (above) have alluded to the significance of verse 46, "since you thrust [the word of God] from you and judge yourselves unworthy of eternal life." The judging (*krinō*) is determinative. Contrary to the ingenious interpretations of some, there is no warrant for the assumption that the word *krinō* can mean *to show, exhibit, display, or manifest*—an assumption that rests on appeal, not to lexicographers, but rather to the necessities and conveniences of theology.

The question arises, In what sense did they judge themselves unworthy of eternal life? Certainly Paul did not assert that they judged themselves unworthy of eternal life in their own estimation of themselves. Much to the contrary, they doubtless considered themselves not only worthy, as good Jews faithful to Moses and zealous for the Law, but also as quite *certain* of eternal life, especially if they faithfully opposed such heretics as Paul.

Again, they did not prove themselves unworthy of eternal life in the judgment of Paul, for he himself had resisted the Gospel of Christ far more strenuously and for a much longer time than these Jews of Antioch, and yet grace had availed for him. Paul, who with profound deliberation had rejected the preaching of the Gospel of Christ and so persecuted His followers that he later felt himself to be "the chief of sinners" and lamented that he had "persecuted the church of God," could not so lightly and abruptly dismiss these erring Jews as forever unworthy of the grace which he himself had experienced.

---

[16]Meyer, *Critical and Exegetical Hand-Book to the Acts of the Apostles, ad loc.*

There is but one other possibility: by thrusting the word of God from them and rejecting the Gospel preached by Paul, they "judged themselves unworthy of eternal life" in God's sight. The judgment was not necessarily final as yet, but rather was only in progress, as implied by the linear quality of the present indicative verb. As in the case of Paul, the judgment could be altered if they would "not persist in their unbelief" (Rom. 11:23 RSV). But their present course could end only in disaster, and Paul left them with a solemn warning to ponder.

The fact and significance of human agency and self-determination is quite apparent in verse 46, and verse 48 must be understood in the light of its context. The unfortunate rendering of *tetagmenoi* as *praeordinati* in the Vulgate encouraged Augustine and others in the Western church (very much in the minority) in an erroneous construction of doctrine for which no support exists in the Greek text as understood by the Greek fathers, men most fully conversant with the language of the original text.

Rotherham translates Acts 13:48, "And they of the nations, hearing this, began to rejoice and to be glorifying God, and they believed—as many as had become disposed for life age-abiding."[17] Rotherham's rendering "had become disposed" is fully warranted. Citing examples, Bloomfield asserts (as do others) that the passive voice of *tasso* often conveys the middle sense and that the use of the passive

does not necessarily suppose any over-ruling impulse from without. The expression *tassesthai eis* may here have the sense it sometimes bears, 'to be *thoroughly disposed for,* or purposed for, bent on,' like the similar one *euthetos einai eis,* 'to be *fitly disposed for.'* Of this signification several examples are adduced by Krebs and Loesner . . . in all of which passages the middle sense is very apparent. Chrysostom goes so far as to say that the expression *tetagmenoi* is employed to intimate that the thing is not a matter of *necessity*, or what is *compulsory.* And thus, far from favouring the system of an absolute decree, the words would lead to the *opposite*

[17]Joseph Bryant Rotherham, *The Emphasized New Testament.*

conclusion, that the Creator, while 'binding nature fast in fate, left free the human will.'[18]

Bartlet comments on Acts 13:48

ordained to eternal life. A bad rendering, as suggesting that human choice had no real part in such belief. The idea is simply that of preparedness of heart, without any thought as to how this came about. This is clear from the account of the Jews' unreadiness: they 'judged themselves unworthy' (in the sense of Matt. xxii. 8, 'The wedding is ready, but they that were bidden were not worthy'–i.e. as making light of it, verse 5). Thus all is conceived to turn ultimately on man's own choice. Like the Pharisees in Luke vii. 30, the Jews 'rejected for themselves the *counsel* of God.' No divine 'decree' ordained the result either way. The best rendering then would be, 'were (found) disposed to eternal life,' which preserves the exact shade of the verb ('to set in order, arrange, dispose')[19] and has just that degree of ambiguity which belongs to the original.[20]

All who assume that *tetagmenoi* in Acts 13:48 implies that those who believed the Gospel at that particular time and place did so as the consequence of an eternal decree of unconditional particular election unwittingly embrace a second assumption, completely absurd: all present in the synagogue who ever were to believe the Gospel did so at once; there could be no further opportunity to consider the Gospel, and no man who failed to believe that moment could ever subsequently believe. A preposterous assumption! Such a pattern fits neither the case of Paul himself nor the universal experience of the Church through all generations.

The above considerations strongly militate against the thesis of Augustine, Calvin, Beza, and men of their school. Finally decisive against their thesis is the fact that it is in radical contradiction of the categorical affirmations of I Timothy 2:4, II Peter 3:9, Titus 2:11, and the many cognate passages affirming the desire and provision of God for the salvation of all men through Christ.

[18] S. T. Bloomfield, *The Greek Testament with English Notes, ad loc.*
[19] Cf. Thayer.
[20] J. Vernon Bartlet, *The New Century Bible: The Acts* (Walter F. Adeney, edit.), *ad loc.*

The thesis of a hidden call arbitrarily reserved for particular men unconditionally elect is a corollary of the doctrine of positive reprobation, advocated by Calvin, as we have observed. Foremost among passages adduced in support of the doctrine of unconditional reprobation is Romans 9:6-29. As we have observed in Chapter IV, while the passage affirms God's right as a sovereign Creator to deal with any and all of His creatures in whatever manner He pleases, either for good or for ill, without becoming answerable to any man, context (9:30–11:36) discloses that, quite to the contrary, in His dealings with both Israel and the Gentiles, God is governed by His desire to have mercy on all and takes full account of men's response to His overtures of grace and calls to repentance. In the light of its immediate context, in the light of the cardinal thesis of the Epistle to the Romans ("the just shall live by faith," 1:17), and in the light of the general concensus of the Holy Scriptures, Romans 9:6-29 lends no support to the doctrine of positive reprobation.

Another passage adduced in support of the doctrine of positive reprobation is I Peter 2:7,8, "to those who are disobedient, the stone which the builders rejected [is made] a stone of stumbling and a rock of offence to those who stumble at the word, being disobedient, to which also they were appointed."

Because of the textual ambiguity of I Peter 2:8, grammatically the passage may be construed either as supporting, or as not supporting, the doctrine of positive reprobation. The matter hinges on the reference assumed for the phrase "to which also they were appointed." Was the appointing to *disobedience,* or to both *stumbling and disobedience,* or to *stumbling* as the consequence of disobedience? All three assumptions have their advocates, and all are admissible grammatically. As Canon Cook observes,

Commentators are divided, rather in accordance with their doctrinal views than as a result of grammatical and critical inquiry, some referring the words [*whereunto also they were appointed*] to the unbelief of the Jews, others to the punishment which followed justly upon their unbelief.[21]

From the standpoint of grammar alone, as Huther observes, *eis ho*

may be referred either to *apeithein* (Calvin, Beza, Piscator, and others) or to *proskoptein* and *apeithein* (Estius, Pott, De Wette, Usteri, Hofmann, Wiesinger, etc.), or, more correctly, to *proskoptein* (Grotius, Hammond, Benson, Hensler, Steiger, Weiss), since on the latter (not on *apeithein*) the chief emphasis of the thought lies, and *eis ho, k.t.l.,* applies to that which is predicated of the subject, that is, of the *apeithountes,* but not to the characteristic according to which the subject is designated. The *proskoptein* it is to which they, the *apeithountes,* were already appointed, and withal on account of their unbelief, as appears from the *tōi logōi apeith.* This interpretation alone is in harmony with the connection of thought, for it is simply the *pisteuontes* and *apeithountes,* together with the blessing and curse which they respectively obtain, that are here contrasted, without any reference being made to the precise ground of faith and unbelief.[22]

Huther's contention that immediate context militates against any assumption of support from I Peter 2:8 for the doctrine of unconditional reprobation is augmented by an evidence that must be regarded as finally decisive: such a doctrine radically contradicts the many explicit, categorical affirmations of Scripture of God's desire and provision for the salvation of all men. The great body of "universal" passages dictates the rejection of all interpretations (and translations) of I Peter 2:8 which, though grammatically allowable, are inadmissible in the light of the context of the whole body of the Holy Scriptures. Any assumption that the appointing was to *disobedience* or to both *disobedience and stumbling* is in radical contradiction of I Timothy 2:4 and its many cognates. In view of the necessities imposed by context, Robertson's comments are well founded:

---

[21] F. C. Cook, *The Holy Bible, with an Explanatory and Critical Commentary, ad loc.*

[22] Joh. Ed. Huther, *Critical and Exegetical Handbook to the General Epistles of James, Peter, John, and Jude* (Meyer's *Commentary*), *ad loc.*

Tōi Logōi can be construed with *apeithountes* (stumble, being disobedient to the word). *Whereunto also they were appointed* (*eis ho kai etethēsan*). First aorist passive indicative of *tithēmi*. . . . "Their disobedience is not ordained, the penalty of their disobedience is" (Bigg). They rebelled against God and paid the penalty.[23]

J. B. Phillips's translation effectively conveys the gist of the passage: "Yes, they stumble at the word of God, for in their hearts they are unwilling to obey it—which makes stumbling a foregone conclusion."

When all the facts are observed, it is evident that the "appointing" of I Peter 2:8 was not of particular men as under the necessity of disobeying the word and stumbling (which would be in radical contradiction of I Tim. 2:4, II Pet. 3:9, Titus 2:11, Rom. 5:18, and many other passages), but rather of the circumstance and principles of the moral economy in which men live, especially the moral test inherent in the proclamation of the Gospel and in the existence and reality of Christ and His redemptive ministry, Who, by the nature of His person and mission, was "set for the fall and rising of many in Israel" and is "a stone of stumbling and a rock of offense" to some and "the chief cornerstone, chosen and precious" to others. God wills that all men be saved and come to the knowledge of the truth; but in the nature of the moral economy as God Himself has ordained it, men are free and responsible agents, and many are offended by Christ and disobedient to the saving Word, thus "rejecting the purpose of God for themselves" (Luke 7:30 RSV).

Advocates of the doctrine of positive reprobation have also cited Jude 4, "certain men . . . who were of old ordained to this condemnation. . . . " Whether the passage is considered to lend support to such doctrine hinges on the significance assumed for *progegrammenoi*, rendered "ordained" in the Authorized Version and "designated" in the Revised Standard Version.

The word *prographein* means only "to write, designate, or declare beforehand." There is no warrant for any assumption

---

[23]A. T. Robertson, *Word Pictures in the New Testament, ad loc.*

(implied especially in AV's "ordained") that the word somehow requires the predetermination of the historical personal identities of the "ungodly persons" referred to by Jude. Bloomfield comments

The expression [*progegrammenoi eis touto to krima*] does not imply any predestination of the persons, but merely imports that they were long since foretold, and thereby designated, as persons who should suffer.[24]

The appearing of false leaders is predicted in Matthew 24:11, Acts 20:29f., II Peter 2:1, and I Timothy 4:1, in none of which passages is there any suggestion of the predetermination of personal identities. Nor is there any such suggestion in the Greek text of Jude 4. The words *hoi palai progegrammenoi* simply reflect the fact that the wicked careers and just condemnation of such men were foretold by Enoch (vs. 14f.) and others of old. To assume that the personal identity of such men was predetermined and that they were therefore predestined to such a course is to set Jude in radical contradiction to the many passages affirming the desire of God for the salvation of all men.

We must conclude that the passages cited in support of the doctrine of a merely representative Gospel call which most men by divine decree are prohibited from answering affirmatively have been misconstrued by the advocates of Calvinism's determinism, which assumption involves the fallacy of unconditional reprobation. As we have earlier observed, when confronted with the question of responsibility for sin, Calvin abandoned determinism and resorted to indeterminism. But when not consciously confronting the question of responsibility for sin, Calvin advocated determinism. Representative of numerous declarations of the doctrine of unconditional reprobation are the following:

God chose out of the condemned race of Adam those whom He pleased and reprobated whom He willed (E.P. 8:5).

---

[24]S. T. Bloomfield, *The Greek Testament with English Notes, ad loc.*

... they ... remain sunk in this corruption because, reprobate by the secret counsel of God before they were born, they were not delivered from it (E.P. 5:5).

God ... determined with himself whatever he wished to happen with regard to every man. All are not created on equal terms, but some are preordained to life, others to eternal damnation; and accordingly as each has been created for one or the other of these ends, we say that he has been predestinated to life or to death (3:21:5).[25]

Calvinists often attempt to repudiate the doctrine of unconditional reprobation while retaining the doctrine of unconditional particular election. For example, Berkouer writes, "God may be called, in our human language, the author and cause of our salvation (cf. *Inst.* III, xxi, 5), but every attempt will fail to construct here a parallel with rejection."[26]

Calvin, however (despite the fact that he abandoned determinism whenever he confronted the question of responsibility for sin), is correct in his observation that "there could be no election without its opposite reprobation" (3:23:1). This is true if one accepts Calvin's thesis of unconditional particular election, and "Calvinists" who accept unconditional election and at the same time propose to reject unconditional reprobation are radically inconsistent. God's act of election, if it be unconditional and particular (as Calvinists assert), constitutes per se the repudiation of all men not chosen. Whether such repudiation is just is irrelevant to the fact, and the plea that reprobation is not unconditional because men deserve it is futile. The question is not, What do men deserve? but rather, How wide is the mercy of God? It is not, How great are the sins of men? but rather, How great is the grace of God?

The attempt has been made to temper the doctrine of unconditional reprobation by asserting that, while election is a

---

[25] Here again, as so often, Calvin confounds predestination with election—an error that, as we have observed (Chapter IV), renders impossible a correct construction of the Bible doctrine of election.

[26] Berkouwer, *op. cit.*, p. 190.

deliberate act of God, reprobation is not: God simply leaves the lost to their just desert. Thus Calvin writes

God of his mere good pleasure [elects some and] passes by others (3:22:1).

Those therefore whom God passes by he reprobates, and that for no other cause but because he is pleased to exclude them from the inheritance which he predestines to his children (3:23:1).

But we must protest that a god who, while rescuing some, simply "passes by" others in the same lost circumstance is so little like the Good Samaritan in our Lord's parable and so much like the priest and the Levite that he cannot be the God who desires to have all men saved and none to perish. Such a god constitutes a total contradiction of the spirit of the words of James, "To him who knows to do good and does it not, to him it is sin" (4:17). If God simply "passes by" the mass of humanity in unconcern, His creation of man was the most dastardly act of infamy ever perpetrated, for He thus damned into irremediable perpetual misery and despair the great mass of mankind created in His own image, and He is Himself the greatest curse that could be imposed on His own creation.

A god so heartless and so arbitrary cannot be the God who so loved the *world* that He gave up His only begotten Son to exile, sorrow, suffering, shame, and death. He cannot be the God who cries with sorrowing heart and infinite compassion, "Look unto me and be ye saved, all the ends of the earth, for I am God, and there is none other" (Isa. 45:22). He cannot be the God whose grace has appeared for the salvation of all men (Titus 2:11 RSV). Such an arbitrary god is not the God we worship and adore, the God in whom we trust.

Calvinists often deny that the doctrine of unconditional particular election represents God as arbitrary. Berkouwer asserts that

Where there is eschatological perspective, arbitrariness is ruled out.

. . . .

God's election has nothing to do with sinister arbitrariness . . . this election is not an arbitrariness in which no meaning can be discerned, but the purposeful way in which God's plan is realized in history.[27]

But the question of arbitrariness does not hinge on whether "meaning can be discerned" or whether God has a plan and purpose which He is working out in history. The question rather is whether God offers grace to all, or only to some . . . whether it really is true that "the grace of God has appeared for the salvation of all men," as Paul asserted, or whether, quite to the contrary, Calvin was correct: "We say, then, that Scripture clearly proves this much, that God by his eternal and immutable counsel determined once for all those whom it was his pleasure one day to admit to salvation, and those whom, on the other hand, it was his pleasure to doom to destruction" (3:21:7).

It is beyond question that God, as a sovereign Creator, has the right to be completely arbitrary in His dealings with men without thereby becoming answerable to man, and this is precisely what Paul affirms in Romans 9:6-29. But that is not the whole of the truth. In the remaining portion of Romans 9-11, as we have observed, Paul shows that God does not exercise His right to be arbitrary, but instead is governed in all His dealings with men—both Jews and Gentiles—by something of much more concern to Him than His sovereign right to be arbitrary: His gracious purpose to have mercy on all. Because of His purpose to have mercy on all, the election of grace, as we have observed, embraces all men potentially. Therefore the call to repentance and faith, the call to God's gracious salvation, is to all men. Calvin, however, asserts

Paul teaches that God wills all to be saved (I Tim. 2:4). Hence, it follows that God is not master of His promises, or that all men without exception must be saved. If he should reply that God, so far as He is concerned, wills all to be saved, in that salvation is offered to the freewill of each individual, then I ask why God did not will the Gospel to be preached to all indiscriminately from the beginning of the world. Why did He allow so many people for so many centuries to wander in the darkness of death?

_____
[27]*Ibid.*, pp. 66-68.

For the context goes on to say that God willed all to come to the knowledge of the truth. (E.P. 9:5).

But Calvin overlooks the import of the fact that through all generations God "left not himself without witness" to all nations (Acts 14:17), a witness sufficient to enable men to act affirmatively toward Him within the limits of the knowledge they possessed (Rom. 1:18–2:16). The witness of God has been given to all men in all generations, both through creation (Psalm 19, Acts 14:17, Rom. 1:18-20) and through the human conscience (Rom. 2:14f.). The witness has been sufficient that men are "without excuse," for it has been sufficient to enable all men to "seek the Lord, if haply they might feel after him and find him" who is "not far from every one of us" (Acts 17:27).

It must always have been true that God is "a rewarder of them that diligently seek him" (Heb. 11:6), acting upon whatever knowledge of Him they have possessed. Although "some have not the knowledge of God" in the fulness of the revelation given to us in Christ (I Cor. 15:34), to the shame of the Church, which has not fully discharged her missionary responsibility, the fact remains that God has given sufficient witness to all men to enable them to seek Him, and He has rewarded every man in every generation who has sought Him. We may reverently assume that the principle declared by James, "draw nigh to God, and he will draw nigh to you" (4:8), is unfailing in its operation, and God always gives more knowledge of Himself and His saving grace to every man who sincerely seeks Him in terms of whatever knowledge he has. Cornelius, a case in point, must be representative of many such men.

"Do not be afraid, but speak and do not be silent, for I am with you, and no man shall attack you to harm you, for I have many people in this city" (Acts 18:10 RSV). Such was the word of the Lord to Paul in Corinth. Who were these "many people" whom God considered His? Obviously they were people as yet unknown to Paul and therefore not among those already won to faith in Christ in Paul's initial labors in Corinth.

We must conclude therefore that they were people who, not having heard and believed the Gospel as yet, already were positively disposed toward God—people in whom the Gospel would find ready acceptance. Peter's words in the house of Cornelius are pertinent at this point: "Truly I perceive that God shows no partiality, but in every nation any one who fears him and does what is right is acceptable to him" (Acts 10:34f. RSV). The point is not that such people do not need the Gospel, but rather that such people are disposed to believe the Gospel even before they hear it because they are positively disposed toward God, a fact of which God takes account, as the Scriptures imply.

In the annals of missions in more recent times are accounts of individuals and groups who never had heard the Gospel but who already were anticipating the coming of the missionaries when first they appeared among them, and of persons whom God providentially led through various circumstances to an encounter with the messengers of the Cross, persons whose hearts were hungry for the knowledge of God and His ways. Is it possible that the man of Macedonia whom Paul saw in his vision (Acts 16:9) was a real person whose heart hungered for more knowledge of God, rather than merely a fantasy representing the general populace of Macedonia or the many who became converts through the missionary labors of Paul and others? In the light of certain affirmations of Scripture, this is possible. In any event, it always has been true that God has given to all men sufficient knowledge of Himself to enable them to act affirmatively toward Him and has rewarded those who sought Him. It was no mockery or pitiless deception when God cried through His servant Isaiah, "Look unto me and be ye saved, all the ends of the earth, for I am God, and there is none other" (45:22). The call is authentic and sincere, and it is addressed to all men in good faith.

Again, Calvin contends that God has deliberately restricted the preaching of the Gospel, implying that the Gospel call is not to all:

What then? Did Paul not know that he was prohibited by the Spirit from preaching the word of Christ in Asia and from crossing over into Bythinia where he was proceeding? (Acts 16:6). (E.P. 8:2)

Here Calvin apparently assumes that the preaching of the Gospel in the first generation of the Church was somehow limited to the labors of Paul. But Paul was not at all the only preacher of the Gospel or the only Apostolic missionary. True, the Holy Spirit forbade Paul to carry out his plan to go into Bythinia and on into Asia and sent him instead into Macedonia and Europe. But the Holy Spirit sent Thomas to Asia and others of the Apostles and first-generation preachers of the Gospel into other parts of the world. The accounts in the Book of Acts, limited largely to the labors of Peter and Paul, present only a representation of the total work of missions accomplished in the first generation of the Church. The broad scope of the missionary endeavors in the Apostolic age is implied in Paul's words to the Romans, "your faith is spoken of throughout the whole world . . . [the mystery now is] made known to all nations, for the obedience of faith" (1:8; 16:26), and in his words to the Colossians, "indeed in the whole world [the gospel] is bearing fruit and growing . . . the gospel which you have heard, which has been preached to every creature under heaven" (1:6,23 RSV). Although Paul's words obviously are hyperbolic, certainly they forbid any such assumption as Calvin's that the preaching of the Gospel was not intended for all nations and all generations of men. Our Lord's commission to His disciples was to preach the Gospel in all the world, to every man. The message is intended for all men, and the call is to all.

Calvinism's assumption that God has limited the effectiveness of the Gospel call to certain individual men arbitrarily and unconditionally chosen to be the heirs of salvation rests in part on the fact that, in numerous Scripture passages, the words "called" and "calling" have reference specifically to believers.[28]

---

[28]Cf. Acts 2:39, Rom. 8:28-30, I Cor. 1:26; 7:17, Eph. 1:18; 4:14, Phil. 3:14, I Thess. 2:12, II Thess. 1:11; 2:14, II Tim. 1:9, Heb. 3:1, I Pet. 5:10, II Pet. 1:10.

Such passages, however, simply reflect the fact that those who respond affirmatively to the universal call become in a particular sense "the called." In like manner, those in whom God's universal purpose of election becomes realized are spoken of as "the elect" in contrast with the rest of mankind.[29] Reference to believers as "the called" and "the elect" does not in any way imply the positive, unconditional reprobation of other men. The corporate election of Israel to temporal privilege did not constitute the reprobation of the rest of the world, for the way always was open for all men to become proselytes and to share in the heritage of Israel. Furthermore, Israel was called to be God's channel of blessing for all mankind. In like manner, the corporate election of the Church does not constitute any reprobation of the rest of mankind. To the contrary, the Church is to be the vehicle of grace and salvation for the world. The Israel of God comprehends all men potentially, and the election of grace may be realized in any man. "Look unto me and be ye saved, all the ends of the earth, for I am God, and there is none other" (Isa. 45:22). The call is to all, and all who respond in faith to God's universal call are "the called according to his purpose" and those

II. Whom He Justified.

Although the Bible affirms that there are men who, never having heard the Gospel, are yet positively disposed toward God, the Gospel of Christ is addressed to men, not on the supposition that men can somehow save themselves and need only a word of encouragement, but rather to men as lost in sin and "without strength"—utterly unable to save themselves by any power or virtue of their own. Although God in a sense "accepts" men positively disposed toward Him (Acts 10:34f.), He does not save any man on the basis of any merit of his own (Titus 3:4-7), but rather by His grace and by the merits of Jesus

---

[29]Cf. Matt. 24:22,24,31, Mk. 13:27, Lk. 18:7, Rom. 8:33; 11:7, Col. 3:12, I Thess. 1:4, II Tim. 2:10, Titus 1:1, I Pet. 1:2; 5:13.

Christ, His Son. All men alike—the "good" and the "bad"—have sinned and come short of the approval of God (Rom. 3:23), and only by the grace of God can any man be saved. The good news of the Gospel is that all men may be "justified freely by his grace through the redemption that is in Christ Jesus, whom God has set forth as a propitiation through faith in his blood . . . that he might be just, and the justifier of him who believes in Jesus" (Rom. 3:24-26).

The Bible clearly affirms that the initiative in salvation rests with God rather than man: "when the fulness of the time was come, God sent forth his Son . . . who verily was foreordained before the foundation of the world . . . whom God set forth as a propitiation . . . for the sins of the whole world" (Gal. 4:4, I Pet. 1:20, Rom. 3:25, I Jn. 2:2). The whole spectrum of the divine initiative in the salvation of men is implied in the words of Jesus, "the Son of man came to seek and to save that which was lost" (Lk. 19:10).

In Jesus Christ, "the grace of God has appeared for the salvation of all men" (Titus 2:11 RSV). Anticipating His death, only a few score hours away, Jesus said, "And I, when I am lifted up from the earth, will draw all men to myself" (Jn. 12:32 RSV). Our Lord's words confront us with one of the most solemn questions we ever shall face: what is my response to this gracious drawing of Christ? The initiative in salvation indeed is God's, implemented in the gracious acts of the Father, the Son, and the Holy Spirit. But there is a secondary initiative which belongs to man, for which he is responsible to God and which God does not violate. That initiative is man's personal response to God's gracious saving purpose in Christ. "It pleased God through the foolishness of preaching to save them that believe" (I Cor. 1:21).

Calvinists, of course, contending for the doctrine of unconditional particular election, reject faith as the condition of election and salvation.[30] For example, Berkouwer asserts that

---

[30]Faith, as the condition of election and salvation, has been considered in Chapter IV. However, a brief consideration of the matter is germane at this point.

the Reformed doctrine of election rightly rejects "every interpretation of the election in Christ in which faith would become the condition of election"[31] and deplores "any correlation which makes the election of God dependent on our act of faith."[32] But elsewhere he concludes that, in the determination of individual election or reprobation, there are no other "causes than those given to us in prayer, faith, and confession of sins."[33] In like manner, Calvin asserts that personal "election is prior to faith" (E.P. 8:6) and rejects the contention that "those only peculiarly belong to the Father who make a voluntary surrender by faith" (3:22:7). But elsewhere he writes that

When Paul speaks of the Scripture, "foreseeing that God would justify the heathen through faith" (Gal. iii. 8), what other meaning can you give it than that God imputes righteousness by faith? Again, when he says "that he (God) might be just, and the justifier of him who believeth in Jesus" (Rom. iii. 26), what can the meaning be, if not that God, in consideration of their faith, frees them from the condemnation which their wickedness deserves?

· ·

you see that [justification] is entirely through the interposition of Christ; you see that it is obtained by faith. (3:11:3)

A man will be *justified by faith* when . . . he by faith lays hold of the righteousness of Christ, and clothed in it appears in the sight of God, not as a sinner, but as righteous. (3:11:2)

The above citations are representative of the obvious inconsistencies of Calvinists who endeavor to retain the unbiblical doctrine of unconditional particular election and at the same to reckon with the many affirmations in the Scriptures of faith as the condition of individual salvation and election. Their difficulty arises from the fact that they continually labor under

---

[31]Berkouwer, *op. cit.*, p. 144.
[32]*Ibid.*, p. 26
[33]*Ibid.*, p. 216.

the unfounded assumption that if salvation is conditioned on faith, it is somehow not of grace. But quite to the contrary, Paul asserts (as we considered in Chapter IV) that "[justification] is of *faith*, that it might be by *grace*" (Rom. 4:16). Far from nullifying grace, faith, as the condition of salvation, actually establishes grace. E. Y. Mullins has well said

Beyond doubt faith is a condition of salvation. The question is whether it is also the ground of salvation. The Scriptures answer this question in the negative.[34]

Certainly, while faith is the *condition* of salvation, the *ground* of salvation is the grace of God. Thiessen writes

[Faith] is the *condition* of our justification, not the meritorious ground of it. "We are not justified on account of our faith, considered as a virtuous or holy act or state of mind . . . Faith is the condition of our justification" (Hodge [Chas. Hodge, *Systematic Theology*] III, 118). It is not "for" faith that we are justified, but "by" faith. Faith is not the price of justification, but the means of appropriating it.[35]

The words of Mullins, Thiessen, and Hodge fall considerably short of Paul's assertion that "Abraham believed God, and it was counted to him for righteousness . . . his faith is counted for righteousness" (Rom. 4:3,5) and of the whole purport of Hebrews 11 and other passages of Scripture, but they do present faith as the condition of salvation, as affirmed in the Scriptures. It is abundantly clear from the Scriptures that it is "by grace, through faith" that men are saved and enter into God's gracious election.

Wonderful is the grace of God—the grace that in Jesus Christ "appeared for the salvation of all men." "In this was manifested the love of God toward us: that God sent his only begotten Son into the world so that we might live through him. Herein is love; not that we loved God, but that he loved us and sent his Son to

---

[34]Edgar Young Mullins, *The Christian Religion in Its Doctrinal Expression*, p. 343.

[35]Henry Clarence Thiessen, *Lectures in Systematic Theology*, p. 366.

be the propitiation for our sins" (I Jn. 4:9f.) As Walter Russell
Bowie has said so well,

[Jesus took] upon himself the consequences of the world's sin. In him the
love of God, even when it seemed most repudiated, was reaching out to
save. "Father, forgive them; for they know not what they do," Jesus had
prayed for those who crucified him. "Today you will be with me in
Paradise," he said to the penitent thief who in his dying turned to him.
And Jesus crucified came back as Jesus risen. "Having loved his own who
were in the world, he loved them to the end"—and beyond the end. As he
had died for them, so now he was alive for them, and they could live in
him. So when he said, "I am the way," that was only the beginning of his
invitation and his promise. He is more than an example; for to think of
him as merely an example could leave us smug and self-satisfied if we
imagined that we could measure up to that example, or despairing if we
thought we were expected to, and knew that we never could. He is more
also than the truth; more than the revelation to us of what we need to
know. "I am the life," he said. That is to say, he can come to us as
forgiveness for what we are, and as the grace by which what we are not
may become what we are meant to be in him.

So—even when we are most conscious of our shortcomings and our
sins—we can be undismayed. We can remember the thankful cry of Martin
Luther: "Lo, to me an unworthy, condemned, and contemptible creature,
altogether without merit, my God of His pure and free mercy has given in
Christ all the riches of righteousness and faith, to that I am no longer in
want of anything except faith to believe this is so." It is not on any
righteousness of our own that we have to depend. It is by the undeserved
gift of the love of God through the risen Christ that we can be lifted to a
life redeemed.[36]

How often and with what good reason do we feel ourselves to
be, in the words of Luther, "an unworthy, condemned, and
contemptible creature, altogether without merit." In the con-
sciousness of the majesty and purity of Christ, have we not
sometimes shared with Peter the overwhelming sense of
unworthiness and shame that drew from his lips the cry,
"Depart from me, for I am a sinful man, O Lord!" Who of us

---

[36]Walter Russell Bowie, *Christ Be With Me: Daily Meditations and Personal
Prayers*, pp. 66f.

does not understand and share the fervent cry of the hymn writer,

> Oh, to be saved from myself, dear Lord;
> Oh, to be lost in Thee![37]

In a real sense we must be saved from ourselves, and by the grace of God in Jesus Christ, we may indeed.

But we cannot be saved from ourselves in the sense of being relieved of all responsibility for personal decision and commitment, for there is an initiative given to man by his Creator which is intrinsic in his being, which God does not violate. This is affirmed and implied throughout the Scriptures, and vividly so in the words of Jesus, "the true worshipers will worship the Father in spirit and in truth, for the Father seeks such to worship him" (Jn. 4:23). God does not compel men to worship Him; indeed He cannot, for it is of the essence of worship, as of friendship, that it can only be voluntary. *Acknowledgement* may be compelled,[38] but not *worship* in its true sense. Therefore the Father *seeks* men who will worship Him. The Gospel is addressed to men as those who must make a decision, and whether the Gospel is a message of "life unto life" or of "death unto death" (II Cor. 2:14-17) depends on the response of those who hear. If the witness of creation and the human conscience is enough to leave men without excuse for not responding affirmatively to God, much more does the preaching of the Gospel—the Spirit's witness to Christ—make men answerable to God. God wills that all men be saved, but men have it within their power to "reject the purpose of God for themselves" (Lk. 7:30). It is an awsome thing to be a human being.

We heartily agree with Berkouwer that man's spiritual "hardening can never be broken by man in his own power" and that "there is no other therapy that can bring about a change

---

[37]From the hymn "Not I, But Christ," with music by A. B. Simpson and words attributed only to A.A.F.

[38]Cf. Phil. 2:10f.

except the divine healing in Christ and the superior power of the Spirit."[39] But while it is not within man's power to do for himself what needs to be done for his salvation, certainly the Scriptures affirm that man has within himself the faculty of choosing whether to allow God to do for him what desperately needs to be done, a faculty which God never ignores or violates and for which man must answer to his Creator. For example, God's gracious promise through Ezekiel is, "And I will give them one heart, and I will put a new spirit within you; and I will take the stony heart out of their flesh and will give them a heart of flesh, that they may walk in my statutes" (11:19f.). But He also admonishes, "make you a new heart and a new spirit: for why will ye die, O house of Israel? For I have no pleasure in the death of him that dies, says the Lord God. Wherefore turn yourselves and live" (Ezek. 18:31f.). Again, God declares, "I will give them a heart to know me" (Jer. 24:7), but He also entreats, "O Jerusalem, wash your heart from wickedness, that you may be saved" (Jer. 4:14). All through the Scriptures may be found two parallel truths equally emphasized: the assurance of God's gracious initiative in salvation, and fervent appeals and exhortations predicated on the initiative of men and the necessity of their deliberate response to the prior initiative of God in the realization of personal, individual salvation. Not one man ever has turned to God for saving grace except on the basis of the prior initiative and enabling grace of God. And not one man ever has sought God and His saving grace without the deliberate exercise of his own initiative in response to God's gracious initiative. Asaph's prayer "Turn us again, O Lord God of hosts; cause thy face to shine, and we shall be saved" (Ps. 80:3,7,19) is the prayer of one who already has turned to God with sincere heart, for no man can pray such a prayer with an impenitent heart.

The many appeals to men to seek God often are dismissed by Calvinists as merely symbolic rather than authentic, on the plea that man's depravity makes it impossible for him to comply

---

[39]Berkouwer, op. cit., p. 252.

with God's commands and appeals. Failure to recognize hyperbole, a frequent device in Biblical literature, has involved many in an erroneous definition of human depravity that makes God's appeals and exhortations ludicrous, if not shamefully insincere. Here is obvious hyperbole: "The wicked are estranged from the womb: they go astray as soon as they be born, speaking lies" (Ps. 58:3). But here, too, is hyperbole: "there is none that seeketh after God" (Rom. 3:11). In Psalm 14, from which Paul quotes in Romans 3, David asserts that none seek after God; but he also speaks of God's people, whom the non-seekers oppress, and of those for whom the Lord is a refuge. It is obvious that non-seeking was not universal in David's day, despite his hyperbolic assertion, and the Scriptures witness that in every generation some have sought God, who always has had His remnant. Certainly the Scriptures teach that "all have sinned and come short of the approval of God" (Rom. 3:23) and that human depravity is real, universal, and tragic. But they also teach that God, Who desires all men to be saved, is "a rewarder of them that diligently seek him" (Heb. 11:6) and that His invitations and exhortations to men are authentic rather than symbolic. "Whosoever will. . . . "

Commenting on John 3:16, Lange asserts that *whosoever believeth* expresses at once the universal offer of salvation and the condition of it."[40] "By grace, through faith . . . but without faith it is impossible to please God . . . [for] it pleased God by the foolishness of preaching to save them that believe" (Eph. 2:8, Heb. 11:6, I Cor. 1:21). God is "just, and the justifier of him who believes in Jesus" (Rom. 3:26). And whom He justified,

III. Them He Also Glorified.

Our consideration of Romans 8:28-30 invites again the question of perseverance, which has been considered in Chapter II. Because it is especially germane at this point, the following material from my work *Life in the Son: A Study of the*

---

[40]John Peter Lange, *Commentary on the Holy Scriptures, ad loc.*

Doctrine of Perseverance is cited herewith, including a portion cited in Chapter II:

*   *   *

[Romans 8:29,30] has often been called "an unbreakable chain"—foreknowledge, predestination, calling, justification, glorification. For the elect, it is indeed an unbreakable chain; and only the elect are comprehended in Paul's affirmation (v. 33). The calling, justification, and glorification constitute the implementation of the predestination (conformity to the image of the Son) which God purposed for the elect. For them, calling and justification will issue in ultimate glorification, in accordance with the eternal purpose of God to "bring many sons unto glory" (Heb. 2:10), the glory of full conformity to the image of His Son. But there is nothing about Paul's affirmation which establishes that election is unconditional or that all who experience calling and justification will inevitably persevere. Certainly it is true that the elect will persevere. But that is only half the truth; for it is equally true that they who persevere are elect. The latter solemn truth is presented in the Holy Scriptures, not as the inevitable outcome of some inexorable divine decree with respect to specific individuals unconditionally, but as a matter for the constant concern and holy endeavor of believers.

The certainty of election and perseverance is with respect, not to particular individual men unconditionally, but rather with respect to the *ekklēsia*, the corporate body of all who, through living faith, are in union with Christ, the true Elect and the Living Covenant between God and all who trust in His righteous Servant (Isa. 42:1-7, 49:1-12, 52:13-53:12; 61:1,2). Consider the following:

God's eternal purpose in grace:

> Eph. 1:4, He chose us in Christ that we should be *hagious kai amōmous* before Him.

> Col. 1:22, He reconciled us to Himself in Christ, through His death, to present us *hagious kai amōmous* before Him.

Fulfillment corporately (certain):
  Eph. 5:27, Christ will present the *ekklēsia* to Himself *hagia kai amōmos.*

Fulfillment individually (contingent):
  Col. 1:23, He will present us *hagious kai amōmous* before Him—if we continue in the faith grounded and settled and be not moved away from the hope of the Gospel.

To assume that eternal glory is the inevitable terminus of "an unbreakable chain" for everyone who once experiences saving grace is to ignore the explicit warnings, not only elsewhere in the Scriptures, but in the very passage before us. Paul warns: "Therefore, brethren, we are debtors, not to the flesh, to live after the flesh. For if ye live after the flesh, ye shall die: but if ye through the Spirit do mortify the deeds of the body, ye shall live. For as many as are led by the Spirit of God, they are sons of God" (Rom. 8:12-14). "And if children, then heirs; heirs of God, and joint-heirs with Christ; if so be that we suffer with him, that we may be also glorified together" (v. 17).

. . . .

"If we endure," writes Paul, "we shall also reign with him: if we deny him, he also will deny us" (II Tim. 2:12 RSV). "He that overcometh," promises the risen Saviour, "the same shall be clothed in white raiment; and I will not blot his name out of the book of life, but I will confess his name before my Father, and before his angels. . . . Be thou faithful unto death, and I will give thee the crown of life. He that hath an ear, let him hear what the Spirit saith unto the churches. He that overcometh shall not be hurt of the second death" (Rev. 3:5; 2:10,11).[41]

*   *   *

As we have earlier observed, with equal truth Paul can assure us that God "has chosen us [corporately] in Christ before the

---

[41] Shank, *Life in the Son,* pp. 365ff.

foundation of the world" (Eph. 1:4) and Peter can admonish us to "give diligence to make your calling and election [individually] sure" (II Pet. 1:10).

We have observed that the Gospel call is to all men alike, and that those who answer affirmatively become in a particular sense "the called." We must also observe that those who "continue in the faith [and are] not moved away from the hope of the gospel" (Col. 1:23) are in the final analysis "the called according to his purpose." Commenting on Romans 8:28, Liddon writes

The Divine *calling* emerges into time and history in the preaching of the Gospel and, in the widest sense of the expression, all are said to be *called* who are reached by it. But of these the many are contrasted by our Lord with the *worthy* (S. Matt. xxii. 8) and with the *chosen* (S. Matt. xx. 16), who are comparatively few. These last are *called* in a narrower sense; they hear and obey. . . . They are the last class described in the Parable of the Sower (S. Luke viii. 8, 15), and thus correspond to the *preserved called* of S. Jude 1, and to the *called according to purpose* of this passage.[42]

To Liddon's comment may be added the observation that those who will share in Christ's ultimate triumph are "called, and chosen, and faithful" (Rev. 17:14). If we would share in the triumph of the coming King of Kings and Lord of Lords, we must give earnest heed to the many exhortations to persevere in the faith, with which the Holy Scriptures abound.

Closely related to the question of perseverance is the question of assurance. For Calvinists, committed to the thesis of unconditional particular election, the question of assurance has been a vexing problem. Berkouwer acknowledges that the Reformed doctrine of election

has acquired an ominous character in the thinking of many people.

•   •   •   •   •   •   •   •   •   •   •   •   •   •   •   •   •   •   •   •

Around the halo of God's mercy always remains the dark edge of the

---

[42]H. P. Liddon, *Explanatory Analysis of St. Paul's Epistle to the Romans,* p. 139, English rendered for Greek (italics).

inscrutable election, of an eternal decision which cannot be altered, the counsel of God's absolute freedom.

. . . .

For many people the divine foreknowledge, the idea of "before the foundation of the world," and His good pleasure have an element of threat and uncertainty rather than of comfort. They see in it the depth, distance, and unknown by which nothing that comes to us in this dispensation is completely free from threat and uncertainty. And once they are on this way, they read into it a sort of metaphysics, an objective state of affairs regarding the relation between eternity and time whereby time represents the known and eternity the unknown, the uncertain, and therefore the threat.[43]

Again, Berkouwer writes

It is surprising that the explicit relation between election and the certainty of salvation has often become the great problem of the doctrine of election, for this tension is nowhere found in Scripture. In Scripture the certainty of salvation is never threatened or cast in shadows because of the fact of election.[44]

We must agree with Berkouwer that no tension is found in the Scripture between the assurance of personal salvation and the fact of election . . . but precisely, however, because Scripture knows nothing of any such election as Calvin's unconditional particular election, which posits an eternal decree of God in which men have no way of deliberately concurring. In the Calvinist definition, man can never act authentically. Instead, in reality he is only *acted upon,* and whatever he "does" is only symbolic. Thus one can only hope that he was included in the election determined before the world began and that any apparent evidences of grace in his personal experience are authentic. Herein arises the tension between the fact of election (in the Calvinist definition) and the experience of personal assurance.

---

[43]Berkouwer, *op. cit.,* pp. 8,12,150.
[44]*Ibid.,* p. 13.

Calvin recognized that his doctrine of unconditional particular election invites much apprehension and loss of assurance:

> Among the temptations with which Satan assaults believers, none is greater or more perilous than, when disquieting them with doubts as to their election, he at the same time stimulates them with a depraved desire of inquiring after it out of the proper way. By inquiring out of the proper way, I mean when puny man endeavours to penetrate to the hidden recesses of the divine wisdom and goes back even to the remotest eternity, in order that he may understand what final determination God has made with regard to him. In this way he plunges headlong into an immense abyss, involves himself in numberless inextricable snares, and buries himself in the thickest darkness. For it is right that the stupidity of the human mind should be punished with fearful destruction whenever it attempts to rise in its own strength to the height of divine wisdom. And this temptation is the more fatal that it is the temptation to which of all others almost all of us are most prone. For there is scarcely a mind in which the thought does not sometimes arise, Whence your salvation but from the election of God? But what proof have you of your election? When once this thought has taken possession of any individual, it keeps him perpetually miserable, subjects him to dire torment, or throws him into a state of complete stupor. (3:24:4)

The question of assurance is a problem with which Calvin struggled at length. The following excerpt from *Life in the Son* is germane at this point:

*   *   *

Although Calvin taught that, for the elect, an important means of assurance is the inner witness of the Spirit, he also taught that the reprobate may receive a similar inner witness, actually experiencing the grace of God to such an extent that they imagine themselves to be of the elect. But since they are not, God (as he believed) has no intention that their experience of His grace shall endure. From the outset, His intention is that they shall wither away and die. "There is nothing strange," he writes, "in [God's] shedding some rays of grace on the reprobate, and afterwards allowing these to be extinguished" (3:2:12). This is accomplished, according to Calvin, through "an inferior operation of the Spirit," the whole purpose of which is "the better to convict them and leave them without excuse" (3:2:11). (To Calvin, this was in perfect accord with " . . . the doctrine which I maintain, that the reprobate are hateful to God, and that with perfect justice, since those destitute of His Spirit cannot produce anything that does not deserve cursing" [3:24:17].)

Contending that the reprobate may respond to the Gospel, exercise faith in Christ and the mercies of God, and actually experience grace to such an extent that they sincerely believe themselves to be of the elect, Calvin wrote (3:2:11,12):

. . . experience shows that the reprobate are sometimes affected in a way so similar to the elect that, even in their own judgment, there is no difference between them. Hence it is not strange that by the Apostle a taste of heavenly gifts, and by Christ himself a temporary faith, is ascribed to them. Not that they truly perceive the power of spiritual grace and the sure light of faith; but the Lord, the better to convict them and leave them without excuse, instils into their minds such a sense of his goodness as can be felt without the Spirit of adoption. . . . Therefore, as God regenerates the elect only for ever by incorruptible seed, as the seed of life once sown in their hearts never perishes, so he effectually seals in them the grace of his adoption, that it may be sure and stedfast. But in this there is nothing to prevent an inferior operation of the Spirit from taking its course in the reprobate. Meanwhile, believers are taught to examine themselves carefully and humbly, lest carnal security creep in and take the place of assurance of faith. We may add that the reprobate never have any other than a confused sense of grace, laying hold of the shadow rather than the substance, because the Spirit properly seals the forgiveness of sins in the elect only, applying it by special faith to their use. Still it is correctly said that the reprobate believe God to be propitious to them, inasmuch as they accept the gift of reconciliation, though confusedly and without due discernment; not that they are partakers of the same faith or regeneration with the children of God; but because, under a covering of hypocrisy, they seem to have a principle of faith in common with them. Nor do I even deny that God illumines their minds to this extent, that they recognize his grace;[2]

_____

[2]But Paul declared that "the natural man receiveth not the things of the Spirit of God: for they are foolishness unto him; neither can he know them, because they are spiritually discerned" (I Cor. 2:14). Jesus taught that men can know the truth of His

but that conviction he distinguishes from the peculiar testimony which he gives to his elect in this respect, that the reprobate never obtain to the full result or to full fruition. When he shows himself propitious to them, it is not as if he had truly rescued them from death and taken them under his protection. He only gives them a manifestation of his present mercy. [Footnote: The French adds, "Comme par une bouffee'—as by fits and starts.] In the elect alone he implants the living root of faith so that they persevere even to the end. Thus we dispose of the objection that if God truly displays his grace, it must endure for ever. There is nothing inconsistent in this with the fact of his enlightening some with a present sense of grace, which afterwards proves evanescent.

Although faith is a knowledge of the divine favour towards us and a full persuasion of its truth, it is not strange that the sense of the divine love, which though akin to faith differs much from it, vanishes in those who are temporarily impressed. The will of God is, I confess, immutable, and his truth is always consistent with itself; but I deny that the reprobate ever advance so far as to penetrate to that secret revelation which Scripture reserves for the elect only. I therefore deny that they either understand his will considered as immutable, or steadily embrace his truth, inasmuch as they rest satisfied with an evanescent impression; just as a tree not planted deep enough may take root, but will in process of time wither away, though it may for several years not only put forth leaves and flowers, but produce fruit. In short, as by the revolt of the first man the image of God could be effaced from his mind and soul, so there is nothing strange in His shedding some rays of grace on the reprobate, and afterwards allowing these to be extinguished.[4]

---

[4]This was Calvin's explanation of the fact that many fall from grace, a fact which he acknowledged. His theology required him to assume that those who fall from grace do so by the express design of God. They believe for a while, only to fall away because they are not of the elect and therefore must perish. God wills that they perish, for such is the sole purpose and destiny for which He created them. Calvin's assumption, essential to the defense of the logic of his theology, is completely contrary to the total affirmation of the Holy Scriptures.

teaching only if they sincerely will to do God's will (John 7:17), which is quite the opposite of Calvin's "covering of hypocrisy." Calvin himself declares (1:6:2) that "... it is impossible for any man to obtain even the minutest portion of right and sound doctrine without being a disciple of Scripture. Hence the first step in true knowledge is taken when we reverently embrace the testimony which God has been pleased therein to give of Himself. For not only does faith, full and perfect faith, but all correct knowledge of God originate in obedience." And obedience, let us add, is far removed from any "covering of hypocrisy."

Calvin recognized that his argument involved him in a serious difficulty. "Should it be objected," he writes, "that believers have no stronger testimony to assure them of their adoption, I answer that though there is a great resemblance and affinity between the elect of God and those who are impressed for a time with a fading faith, yet the elect alone have that full assurance which is extolled by Paul, and by which they are enabled to cry, Abba, Father" (3:2:11).

But Calvin's answer in no way eliminates his difficulty. For if (as he declared) it is impossible for the reprobate Christian to perceive that the inner witness of which he is conscious is not really valid, and if in his own best judgment it is impossible for him to observe any difference between himself and the true elect, and if the reprobate Christian is completely sincere in believing God to have been propitious to him and to have given him the gift of reconciliation and in believing himself to be truly elect, how can one's personal feeling be reliable ground for "full assurance" of salvation? Actually, according to Calvin's argument one cannot know whether his feeling of assurance is warranted, or only vain presumption.

.   .   .   .

It is evident from his writings that Calvin ultimately concluded that, in the last analysis, the only real ground for the assurance of one's election is his deliberate perseverance in faith. Hodge arrived at the same conclusion. In his comments on Romans 8:29,30, he asserts that "Election, calling, justification, and salvation are indissolubly united; and, therefore, he who has clear evidence of his being called has the same evidence of his election and final salvation."[9] But what is the "clear evidence" of one's call? In his concluding remarks at the close of the chapter, Hodge concedes that "The only evidence of election is effectual calling, that is, the production of holiness. And the only evidence of the genuineness of this call and the certainty

---

[9]Charles Hodge, *Commentary on the Epistle to the Romans*, p. 207.

of our perseverance is a patient continuance in well doing."[10]
In other words, the only real evidence of election is perseverance, and our only assurance of the certainty of persevering
is—to persevere!

John Eadie states the same conclusion. In his commentary on
Colossians, his excellent comments on 1:23 include:

While . . . the perseverance of the saints is a prominent doctrine of
Scripture and a perennial source of consolation, it is not inconsistent with
exhortations to permanence of faith and warnings of the sad results of
deviation and apostasy. He who stops short in the race, and does not reach
the goal, cannot obtain the prize. He who abandons the refuge into which
he fled for a season is swept away when the hurricane breaks upon him.
The loss of faith is the knell of hope.

. . . .

For man is not acted on mechanically by the grace of God, but his whole
spiritual nature is excited to earnest prayer and anxious effort. His
continuance in the faith is not the unconscious impress of an irrestible law,
but the result of a diligent use of every means by which belief may be
fostered and deepened. . . . Thus, as rational beings are wrought upon by
motives, so warnings and appeals are addressed to them, and these
appliances form a special feature of God's plan of preserving them. The
apostle thus shows them how much is suspended on their perseverance.[11]

All Calvinist theologians ultimately agree with Hodge, Eadie,
and Calvin that the only unfailing evidence and ground for
assurance that one is elect is deliberate perseverance in faith in
Jesus Christ. Professor John Murray of Westminster Theological
Seminary aptly states the matter:

. . . let us appreciate the doctrine of the perseverance of the saints and
recognize that we may entertain the faith of our security in Christ only as

---

[10]*Ibid.*, p. 212.

[11]John Eadie, *Commentary on the Epistle to the Colossians*, p. 85 f. It is odd
that a Calvinist should speak of "how much is suspended on perseverance." For
according to "tulip" theology's doctrine of unconditional election, *nothing at all* is
suspended on perseverance. Quite to the contrary, perseverance is supposedly
suspended on election. But when men get close to the Scriptures, they often get far
from their theology. Eadie has it right: *much* is suspended on perseverance, according
to the Scriptures—all theology to the contrary notwithstanding.

we persevere in faith and holiness to the end. It was nothing less than the goal of the resurrection to life and glory that Paul had in mind when he wrote, "Brethren, I count not myself to have apprehended: but this one thing I do, forgetting those things which are behind, and reaching forth unto those things which are before, I press toward the mark for the prize of the high calling of God in Christ Jesus" (Phil. 3:13,14).

The perseverance of the saints reminds us very forcefully that only those who persevere to the end are truly saints. We do not attain to the prize of the high calling of God in Christ Jesus automatically. Perseverance means the engagement of our persons in the most intense and concentrated devotion to those means which God has ordained for the achievement of his saving purpose. The scriptural doctrine of perseverance has no affinity with the quietism and antinomianism which are so prevalent in evangelical circles.[12]

. . . .

Let us hear the conclusion of the whole matter: Objectively, the elect will persevere, and they who persevere are elect. Subjectively, the individual is elect *only as he perseveres.* This conclusion is inescapable, regardless of one's definition of election.[45]

* * *

Despite his erroneous definition of election, Calvin was on solid ground in his ultimate conclusion that valid assurance of election and salvation is impossible apart from conscious, deliberate perseverance in faith. Right about many things, he was never more right than in his emphasis on looking to Christ alone for the assurance of election and salvation:

But if we are elected in [Christ], we cannot find the certainty of our election in ourselves, and not even in God the Father if we look at him apart from the Son. Christ, then, is the mirror in which we ought, and in which, without deception, we may contemplate our election. For since it is into his body that the Father has decreed to ingraft those whom from

---

[12]John Murray, *Redemption—Accomplished and Applied*, p. 193.

[45]*Life in the Son*, pp. 289-301. The entire portion offers a fuller résumé of Calvin's treatment of the question of assurance.

eternity he wished to be his, that he may regard as sons all whom he acknowledges to be his members, if we are in communion with Christ, we have proof sufficiently clear and strong that we are written in the Book of Life. (3:24:5)

If Pighius asks how I know I am elect, I answer that Christ is more than a thousand testimonies to me. For when we find ourselves in His body, our salvation rests in a secure and tranquil place, as though already located in heaven. (E.P. 8:7)

Since the certainty of salvation is set forth to us in Christ, it is wrong and injurious to Christ to pass over this proffered fountain of life from which supplies are available, and to toil to draw life out of the hidden recesses of God. Paul testifies indeed that we were chosen before the foundation of the world; but, he adds, in Christ (Eph. 1.4). Let no one then seek confidence in his election elsewhere, unless he wish to obliterate his name from the Book of Life in which it is written.

. . . .

For God is said to give us to the Son so that each may know himself an heir of the heavenly kingdom so long as he abides in Christ, apart from whom death and destruction beset us on every side. (E.P. 8:6)

The above passages, representative of others which might be cited, indicate Calvin's strong emphasis on the necessity of looking to Christ for the certainty of election and salvation. This path alone is the way of assurance, and in this emphasis on looking to Christ alone in abiding faith, Calvinists and non-Calvinists alike must unite.

All men who bear the name of Christ can unite, too, in the recognition that more important than understanding all mysteries and having all knowledge is to have love—love for God and for our fellow men as ourselves; for only faith that works through love avails in Jesus Christ (Gal. 5:6). Love is faith in action, and he who loves not knows not God (I Jn. 4:7-21).

The needs of the Church of Christ on earth today are many. Surely, none is more urgent than the need for a new birth of love. Only love for God and for mankind for whom Christ died can enable the Church to fulfill its mission on earth in this present critical hour: to carry to the world the Gospel of the saving grace of God in Christ, to beseech men on Christ's behalf to be reconciled to God through Him, to shepherd the souls of the faithful and to nurture them in the holy faith, and to recover those who have wandered from the Way.[46]

One word describes so well so large a segment of the Church today: Laodicean (Rev. 3:14-22). Outside the Laodicean church, at the door, stands the risen Lord, the Amen, the faithful and true witness and the beginning of God's creation, with words of stern rebuke and just rejection ... and yet with tender words of gracious invitation:

I counsel you to buy of me gold tried in the fire, that you may be rich; and white raiment, that you may be clothed and that the shame of your nakedness may not appear; and anoint your eyes with eyesalve, that you may see. As many as I love, I rebuke and chasten: be zealous therefore and repent. (v. 18f.)

Regardless of whether the church at large heeds the appeal of Christ, individual men within the church may answer the invitation for themselves and bid the Savior welcome in their hearts once again:

Behold, I stand at the door and knock: if any man hear my voice and open the door, I will come in to him and will dine with him, and he with me. (v. 20)

What grace is this!—that One who once had sought and found the wanderer, only to be shamefully ignored and forgotten, should return and patiently stand at the door and knock and ask to be invited in for the renewal of fellowship in the bond of love!

---

[46]For a consideration of the question of restoration—a ministry so desperately urgent in the churches today—see *Life in the Son*, Chapter XIX, "Is Apostasy Without Remedy?"

When thou wast lost on mountains bleak and wide,
One sought thee sorrowing at eventide.
Now, at thy door with heavy grief opprest,
He gently knocks and prays to be thy guest.
   Dost open wide the door?
Ah, faithless soul! Though thou hast wrought Him ill,
The face, so marred, is smiling on thee still!
Patient He waits, till thou shalt turn and see
The arms of love outstretched to welcome thee,
   The love that never fails.[47]

What grace, what love, what fellowship and feast divine await all who open the door and bid the Savior welcome! Christ is Himself the feast that sustains and satisfies the soul.

Bread of the world, in mercy broken,
   Wine of the soul, in mercy shed,
By whom the words of life were spoken,
   And in whose death our sins are dead,

Look on the heart by sorrow broken,
   Look on the tears of sinners shed,
And be Thy feast to us the token
   That by Thy grace our souls are fed.[48]

Staupitz told Luther to find himself in the wounds of Christ and then predestination would be to him inexpressibly sweet. To the request of a troubled woman, Luther replied, "Hear the Incarnate Son. He offers thee Himself as Predestination."[49]

He who called not to the Father for legions of angels, but went His way from Gethsemane to Golgotha to be lifted up on a cross that He might draw all men to Himself, is Himself the Election, in Whom alone we may make our calling and election sure.

Elect in the Son . . .

---

[47]Emily Huntington Miller.

[48]Reginald Heber.

[49]William Childs Robinson, in "Basic Christian Doctrines: Predestination," *Christianity Today*, April 24, 1961, p. 23.

Appendices

Appendix A

The Question of the Order of the Decrees

From beginning to end, the Holy Scriptures testify to the sovereignty of God and to the fact of divine purpose. The fact of *purpose*—to which creation, human history, and the experience and conscience of every man bear witness—is intrinsic in the very being of a sovereign God. From the fact of the sovereignty and omnipotence of God derives the concept of decrees, a concept both affirmed and illustrated in the Scriptures.

A problem theologians long have pondered is the "order of the decrees" relevant to election. Three principal views have been advocated by Calvinists, differing in the order of the decrees and in the definition of certain decrees:

Supralapsarian	Infralapsarian	Sublapsarian
1. The decree to elect some and reprobate others.	1. The decree to create man.	1. The decree to create man.
2. The decree to create man.	2. The decree to permit the fall.	2. The decree to permit the fall.
3. The decree to secure the fall.	3. The decree to elect some of the fallen.	3. The decree to provide salvation sufficient for all.
4. The decree to provide salvation sufficient for the elect.	4. The decree to provide salvation sufficient for the elect.	4. The decree to elect some of the fallen.

Under supralapsarianism, the election is unconditional and particular and has as its counterpart unconditional particular reprobation. The fall is effected by the directive (some affirm permissive) will of God, the atonement is limited provisionally, being sufficient only for the elect, and grace is irresistible. Supralapsarianism posits monothetism, determinism, and monergism. This view may be established from the writings of Calvin and is the position of hyper-Calvinists.

Under infralapsarianism, the fall was by the permissive will of God. The decree to elect comprehends man as fallen and embraces particular men unconditionally. Reprobation is regarded by some as positive and by others as incidental (the latter position is untenable, for the unconditional election of particular men constitutes per se the unconditional reprobation of all men not chosen, as we have observed). The atonement is limited provisionally, sufficient for only the elect. Except for the permissive fall, infralapsarianism posits monothetism, determinism, and monergism. This view may be established from the writings of Calvin.

Under sublapsarianism, the fall was permissive. The atonement is sufficient for all, but efficient only for the elect, who are unconditionally elect as particular men. Reprobation is regarded by some as positive and by others as incidental. Except for a permissive fall, sublapsarianism posits monothetism, determinism, and monergism. This view may be established from the writings of Calvin.

Discussions and disputings over "the order of the decrees" contributes nothing to a correct understanding of the Biblical doctrine of election. Although the purpose of God is fulfilled in a chronological sequence of events, to conceive of the decrees as sequential is to invite confusion and misconception. All decrees relevant to election—creation, the fall, the atonement, and the election (corporate and objective)—are equally posited by the eternal kingdom purpose of God. Decrees of a sovereign God who "declares the end from the beginning" and says, "My counsel shall stand and I will do all my pleasure," the decrees must be understood as concomitant rather than sequential.

Appendix B

An Examination of the Rationale of Calvinism

Central in the theological system of John Calvin is a complex of five cardinal doctrines: (1) the unconditional election and reprobation of particular men, (2) a limited atonement (limited either in sufficiency or in application by arbitrary decree), (3) total depravity (in the sense of complete inability to respond affirmatively to God without divine assistance specifically granted by arbitrary particular decree), (4) irresistible grace, and (5) the inevitable perseverance of the particular elect. The pivotal thesis is the unconditional election and reprobation of particular men, which doctrine posits the necessity of the other four.

The thesis of unconditional particular election and reprobation is predicated (presumably) on Romans 9:6-29, which passage is regarded as the definitive passage and in essence all that the Bible posits on the question of election:

... that memorable passage from Paul [Romans 9] which alone ought easily to compose all controversy among sober and compliant children of God. (E.P. 5:3)

Paul in the ninth chapter of the Epistle to the Romans first establishes God as the arbiter of life and death ... who has mercy on whom He will have mercy and who hardens whom He will. (E.P. 8:4)

But Calvin's thesis of unconditional particular election and reprobation is predicated on a misapprehension of the import of Romans 9:6-29 which is in radical contradiction of both context (9:30–11:36) and the central thesis of the Epistle to the Romans, "The just shall live by faith" (1:17).

223

From the fatal misapprehension of Romans 9:6-29 is derived the assumption of monothetism-determinism, the concept so apparent in Calvin's definition of election:

Of the Eternal Election, By Which God Has Predestinated Some to Salvation and Others to Destruction. (The title of 3:21)

By predestination we mean the eternal decree of God, by which he determined with himself whatever he wished to happen with regard to every man. All are not created on equal terms, but some are preordained to eternal life, others to eternal damnation; and, accordingly as each has been created for one or the other of these ends, we say that he has been predestinated to life or to death. (3:21:5)

The thesis of monothetism-determinism posited in the above quotations is to be rejected, first, because it is in radical contradiction of the witness of the Scriptures (including the central thesis and total context of the Epistle to the Romans, in which it supposedly is posited), specifically of such *universal* passages as I Tim. 2:4-6, II Pet. 3:9, Titus 2:11, John 3:14-17; 6:33,51; 12:32, I John 2:2, II Cor. 5:19, Rom. 5:18, and many cognates, all of which are categorical. The most objectionable feature of Calvin's theology is the necessity it imposes of resorting, for its defense, to ingenious interpretations of some of the most explicit categorical affirmations in the Scriptures, to wild proof-texting that cares nothing for context, and to irresponsible manipulation of such critical factors as frames of reference. An objective, grammatical, contextual approach to the Holy Scriptures dictates the rejection of Calvin's central complex of theology and the unwarranted assumptions on which it rests.

Calvinism's monothetism-determinism is objectionable also because it posits a strange world view. Quoting Augustine, Calvin writes

Who does not tremble at these judgments with which God works in the hearts of even the wicked whatever He will, rewarding them none the less according to desert? . . . God works in the hearts of men to incline their wills just as He will, whether to good for His mercy's sake or to evil according to their merits. . . . [1]

. . . .

God finds the material cause for exercising His wrath in all except those whom He gratuitously elected. For, he says, the rest of mortal men, who are not of that number, are born of the same human race from which those come and are made vessels of wrath for their benefit. (E.P. 10:11)

Thus the mass of mankind are created with no prospect of salvation, but exist only for the benefit of the arbitrarily and unconditionally elect minority, to provide the milieu within which the purpose of election may be unfolded . . . for which the mass of mankind, having lived and died with no possibility of salvation, receive eternal damnation. Happily, this world view is equally as unbiblical as strange, for which God be praised. Human experience and history are indeed the milieu within which the election of grace is implemented; but that the mass of mankind are arbitrarily and unconditionally proscribed from participation in the election in Christ, who died for all men alike, is an assumption without foundation in the Holy Scriptures.

Calvinism's monothetism-determinism-monergism is objectionable because it posits a strange view of man—a conception

---

[1]Here Calvin posits determinism, attributing to God the evil deeds of men and the inclination of human wills to evil. However, in the same paragraph he earlier had asserted that God is "Himself unable to will evil." Still earlier in the paragraph, however, he had asserted that "it is a quite frivolous refuge to say that God otiosely permits [evils] when Scripture shows Him not only willing, but the author of them." Again, he asserts in E.P. 10:7 that "it must be observed that the will of God is the cause of all things that happen in the world; and yet God is not the author of evil" . . . which stance he then repudiates in the second sentence following: "Whatever things are done wrongly and unjustly by man, these very things are the right and just works of God." A footnote reads, "French has: evil and sin are nothing in themselves but only a disorder or corruption of what ought to be." That anything may be other than "what it ought to be" cannot legitimately be affirmed without totally rejecting the thesis of monthetism-determinism. Calvin's uncertain leaps back and forth between determinism and indeterminism are symptomatic of the frustrations and self-contradictions that attend the path of all advocates of his doctrine of unconditional particular election (with the exception of the hyper-Calvinists, who alone of Calvinists are consistent and logical, though certainly not Biblical).

untenable both because it is unbiblical per se and because it contradicts the nature of God as defined in the Scriptures. "God is love," and love must have an object. God, who "so loved the world," created man in His own image for companionship (Rev. 21:3), and the fulfillment of His purpose requires that man be other than the totally passive automaton predicated by Calvin's theology. The love of God demands a response in kind, if not in degree: "We love him because he first loved us." Plastic figures for a "wax museum" may be made altogether lifelike and, in our technological age, may be animated and programmed to speak, to sing, and to "worship." But in their performance there would be neither companionship nor worship for their creator. Friendship, love, worship—these predicate volition, for they must and only can be voluntary. In a profound sense, the love of God predicated the fall of both angels and men quite as much as it predicated the atonement. In the context of a moral universe, in which alone love and worship can exist, angels fell and man sins. Because man can sin, he also can worship; he can do the latter only because he can do the former. In the circumstance of a moral universe peopled by moral beings, God now *seeks*[2] men who will worship Him . . . men who *can* worship because they have the faculty of choice. Men who worship God in their own free and authentic response to His grace, who love Him because He first loved them, will enjoy His love and be His companions forever in the everlasting Kingdom.

Calvin's doctrine of election and the unwarranted assumptions of monothetism-determinism-monergism on which it is predicated must be rejected. Confounding predestination with election, denying the authentic agency of Christ in election in its full dimension, positing an *in abstractio* election in which the atonement is symbolic and accessory, Calvin's doctrine of election rests on serious misapprehensions and misconstructions of Scripture. "Calvin's exegesis, in a word, is theologically oriented," writes John Murray in his introduction to the

---

[2]The implications of the word *seeks* are profound indeed.

Eerdmans edition of the *Institutes*. This is true–in a sense which Murray did not intend. The pity is that Calvin's theology was not more precisely exegetically oriented. Instead, the Bible has been accommodated to theology.

Both the process of the evolution of the *Institutes* into its final form and the stance assumed by Calvin in his task may be ascertained from a reading of the prefaces of the several editions. In his address to the king of France, prefatory to the first edition (1536), Calvin writes

When I first engaged in this work, nothing was farther from my thoughts than to write what should afterwards be presented to your Majesty. My intention was only to furnish a kind of rudiments by which those who feel some interest in religion might be trained to true godliness.

. . . .

That this was the object which I had in view is apparent from the work itself, which is written in a simple and elementary form adapted for instruction.

Designed for use as a primer in doctrine, the first edition of the *Institutes of the Christian Religion* was a rudimentary syllabus. In the Epistle to the Reader prefacing the second edition (1539) Calvin writes

In the First Edition of the work, having no expectation of the success which God has, in his goodness, been pleased to give it, I had for the greater part performed my office perfunctorily, as is usual in trivial undertakings. But when I perceived that almost all the godly had received it with a favor which I had never dared to wish, far less to hope for, being sincerely conscious that I had received much more than I deserved, I thought I should be very ungrateful if I did not endeavor, at least according to my humble ability, to respond to the great kindness which had been expressed towards me, and which spontaneously urged me to diligence.

Calvin proceeds in his preface to assert that, in the new edition,

I have endeavored to give such a summary of religion in all its parts, and have digested it into such an order as may make it not difficult for anyone who is rightly acquainted with it to ascertain both what he ought principally to look for in Scripture, and also to what head he ought to refer whatever is contained in it. Having thus, as it were, paved the way, I shall not feel it necessary in any Commentaries on Scripture which I may afterwards publish to enter into long discussions of doctrine or dilate on commonplaces, and will therefore always compress them. In this way the pious reader will be saved much trouble and weariness, provided he comes furnished with a knowledge of the present work as an essential prerequisite.

In his preface to the French edition, published at Geneva in 1545, Calvin writes

I dare not bear too strong a testimony in its favor and declare how profitable the reading of it will be, lest I should seem to prize my own work too highly. However, I may promise this much, that it will be a kind of key opening up to all the children of God a right and ready access to the understanding of the sacred volume. Wherefore, should our Lord give me henceforth means and opportunity of composing some Commentaries, I will use the greatest possible brevity, as there will be no occasion to make long digressions, seeing that I have in a manner deduced at length all the articles which pertain to Christianity.

And since we are bound to acknowledge that all truth and sound doctrine proceed from God, I will venture boldly to declare what I think of this work, acknowledging it to be God's work rather than mine. . . . My opinion of the work then is this: I exhort all who reverence the word of the Lord to read it and diligently imprint it on their memory if they would, in the first place, have a summary of Christian doctrine, and in the second place, an introduction to the profitable reading both of the Old and New Testament.

In the Epistle to the Reader prefacing the final edition (1559), Calvin writes

In the first edition of this work, having not the least expectation of the success which God in his boundless goodness has been pleased to give it, I had, for the greater part, performed my task in a perfunctory manner (as is usual in trivial undertakings); but when I understood that it had been received by almost all the pious with a favor which I had never dared to ask, far less to hope for, the more I was sincerely conscious that the reception was beyond my deserts, the greater I thought my [ingratitude] would be if, to the very kind wishes which had been expressed towards me, and which seemed of their own accord to invite me to diligence, I did not endeavor to respond, at least according to my humble ability. This I attempted, not only in the second edition, but in every subsequent one the work has received some improvement. But though I do not regret the labor previously expended, I never felt satisfied until the work was arranged in the order in which it now appears.

. . . .

I may further observe that my object in this work has been so to prepare and train candidates for the sacred office, for the study of the sacred volume, that they may both have an easy introduction to it and be able to prosecute it with unfaltering step; for, if I mistake not, I have given a summary of religion in all its parts, and digested it in an order which will make it easy for anyone who rightly comprehends it to ascertain both what he ought chiefly to look for in Scripture, and also to what head he ought to refer whatever is contained in it. Having thus, as it were, paved the way, as it will be unnecessary in any Commentaries on Scripture which I may afterwards publish to enter into long discussions of doctrinal points and enlarge on commonplaces, I will compress them into narrow compass. In this way much trouble and fatigue will be spared to the pious reader, provided he comes prepared with a knowledge of the present work as an indispensable prerequisite.

The immediate, enthusiastic reception given the *Institutes* by many adherents of the Reformation movement, already well established and gathering momentum, may in part be explained by the fact that it was elementary and didactic, and people desired instruction in the faith. The time was opportune. Furthermore, the work is well documented from the Scriptures, which strongly appealed to adherents of the Reformation movement, a cardinal principle of which was *sola Scriptura,* the outgrowth of the biblicism which in the later Middle Ages had developed more and more at the expense of scholasticism, preparing the way for the Reformation. And finally, the enthusiastic reception given the *Institutes* may in part be explained by the fact that it offered in simple, concise form some well defined polemics with which to controvert portions of the theology and certain aspects of the polity of the Catholic Church. The immediate uncritical popular acceptance of the *Institutes* in toto was unfortunate, though it is understandable.

It is true that the foundation of Calvin's system is found in Augustine, and that Luther, Melanchthon, Zwingli, and others of the Reformers also drew heavily from Augustine. It is also true that Augustine was one of the greatest minds and spirits in Christendom and left a large legacy to the Church (though not of unmixed benefit). Despite the heavy burdens of his ecclesiastical responsibilities, Augustine managed to survey much of the broad spectrum of holy truth found in the Scriptures. But he left unresolved numerous radical inconsistencies in certain areas of his theology, especially in his doctrine of "predestination" (election and reprobation). In the *Institutes,* Calvin systematized a substantial portion of Augustine's theology, including his doctrine of election (and thereby gave it his own name inadvertently). Inheriting the inconsistencies and contradictions in Augustine's doctrine of election, Calvin left them unresolved.

Surprised and gratified by the popular reception accorded the *Institutes,* Calvin was fully confirmed in his persuasion of the validity of all his theological constructions. Thenceforth he had a well defined system of theology which, as he believed, needed only to be expanded and, above all, defended. Subsequent editions of the *Institutes* were only refinements and expansions of the original work, which had its beginning as a rudimentary syllabus published when Calvin (who had spent four of his years studying law rather than theology) was 27 years of age at most. In his lifelong development of the *Institutes,* Calvin never substantially modified any of the basic concepts or assumptions he entertained in his mid-twenties. Sincerely persuaded of the essential validity of all his constructions in the first edition of the *Institutes,* he labored only to substantiate the positions he had assumed.[3]

Calvin's sincere persuasion of the validity of his doctrines as first formulated militated against objectivity in his approach to

---

[3]Although there are marked disparities between portions of his *Commentaries* and the *Institutes,* as many have observed, the fact does not reflect any real process of maturing in Calvin's understanding and thought through the years. For a consideration of this point, see the footnote on page 295 of *Life in the Son.*

the Scriptures. The same persuasion likewise has militated against objectivity among his disciples. He who comes to the Bible already knowing "what he ought chiefly to look for in Scripture, and also to what head he ought to refer whatever is contained in it" will, of course, find what he looks for and will readily fit whatever he finds into the system of doctrine already at hand. Many there are who have been spared "much trouble and fatigue" by approaching the Bible always with the *Institutes* as the "key" and the "indispensable prerequisite," and who have faithfully followed Calvin's rule, First to the *Institutes,* then to the Scriptures. Such is not the path to a correct definition of the faith once delivered to the saints.

In a review of my earlier work *Life in the Son: A Study of the Doctrine of Perseverance,* a theologian whom I admire and from whom I have read with profit objected that the thesis of the book "raises theological problems." This is true only for those committed to the defense of Calvin's system of theology. And as a matter of fact, nothing could be more fraught with theological problems than Calvinism's central complex. In defense of Calvin's doctrine of election and its four essential corollaries, Calvin and his apologists posit both determinism and indeterminism, freedom under necessity, culpability without authentic agency, command without enablement, choice without viable options, compulsion without coercion, fear without anxiety, worship without choice, universal invitation (accompanied by exhortation) proscribed by arbitrary interdiction, and love imposing unconditional reprobation (or, at best, passing by its objects in total unconcern).

It is understandable that in his polemics, laboring as he did under the burden of the many radical contradictions implicit in his theology, Calvin so often was driven to quit the field with such appeals as "Nay, but O man, who art thou that repliest against God? . . . To God belong the secret things. . . For as the heavens are higher than the earth, etc. . . . Oh, the depth—how unsearchable . . . Our God is in the heavens, he hath done whatsoever he hath pleased." Such appeals are regularly made whenever Calvin finds himself boxed-in dialectically, which is often. Quitting the field with some such appeal, Calvin proceeds as if he has made his point—which he never does in the many instances in which he resorts to his well-worn "escape texts" as a means of begging the question.

Calvin's difficulties derived in part from the sheer magnitude of the task of dealing comprehensively with so large a body of truth as the Scriptures afford. A long lifetime is a short time in which to endeavor really to know the Holy Scriptures. To offer the world an *Institutes of the Christian Religion* at age 27 was a venture quite as optimistic as ambitious. Subsequently to regard nothing in the original monograph as tentative was tragic.

But Calvin is rightly to be held in honor and esteem. Not without his faults and failings (what mortal is?), he was a devoted servant of God who, though he might have chosen an easier way, followed a toilsome, difficult path and suffered much for Christ. Despite the fallacy of the central complex of his system of theology, many of his expositions are excellent and he is still to be read with profit. Zealous for holy truth as he understood it, he spent himself without reservation in the service of Christ and the Church, striving ever to be "prompt and sincere in the work of the Lord."

Bibliography, Indexes

BIBLIOGRAPHY

Alford, Henry, *The Greek Testament*. London: Rivingtons, 1868.

Barth, Karl, *Church Dogmatics, Vol. II: The Doctrine of God*. Translated by G. W. Bromiley. Edinburgh: T. & T. Clark, 1957.

Bartlet, J. Vernon, *The New Century Bible: The Acts*. Edited by Walter F. Adeney. Edinburgh: T. C. & E. C. Jack.

Bengel, John Albert, *Gnomon of the New Testament*. 5 vols. Edited by Andrew R. Fausset. Edinburgh: T. & T. Clark, 1860.

Berkouwer, G. C., *Divine Election*. Translated by Hugo Bekker. Grand Rapids: Eerdmans, 1960. Used by permission.

Bloomfield, S. T., *The Greek Testament with English Notes, Critical, Philological, and Exegetical*. Boston: Perkins and Marvin, 1837.

Bowie, Water Russell, *Christ Be With Me: Daily Meditations and Personal Prayers*. Nashville: Abingdon Press, 1958. Used by permission.

Calvin, John, *Commentary on the New Testament*. 15 vols. Translated by Henry Beveridge, John Owen, John Pringle, and William Pringle. Grand Rapids: Eerdmans.

_____, *Concerning the Eternal Predestination of God*. Translated by J. K. S. Reid. London: James Clarke & Co., Ltd., 1961.

_____, *Institutes of the Christian Religion*. 2 vols. Translated by Henry Beveridge. Grand Rapids: Eerdmans.

Cook, F. C., *et al.*, *The Holy Bible, With an Explanatory and Critical Commentary*. 10 vols. New York: Charles Scribner's Sons, 1886.

Delitzsch, Franz, *Biblical Commentary on the Prophecies of Isaiah*, Vol. II. Translated by James Martin. Grand Rapids: Eerdmans, 1949.

Denney, James, *The Christian Doctrine of Reconciliation*. New York: George H. Doran Company, 1918.

_____, *The Death of Christ*. New York: The American Tract Society, 1903.

Eadie, John, *Commentary on the Epistle of Paul to the Colossians*. Grand Rapids: Zondervan.

_____, *Commentary on the Epistle of Paul to the Ephesians*. Grand Rapids: Zondervan.

Fairbairn, Patrick, *Commentary on the Pastoral Epistles.* Grand Rapids: Zondervan.

Godet, Frederick Louis, *Commentary on the Epistle to the Romans.* Translated by A. Cusin. Grand Rapids: Zondervan.

———, *Commentary on the First Epistle to the Corinthians.* 2 vols. Translated by A. Cusin. Grand Rapids: Zondervan.

———, *Commentary on the Gospel of John.* 2 vols. Translated by Timothy Dwight. Grand Rapids: Zondervan.

Huther, Joh. Ed., *Critical and Exegetical Handbook to the Epistles to Timothy and Titus* (Meyer's *Commentary*). Translated by Maurice J. Evans. New York: Funk & Wagnalls, 1885.

———, *Critical and Exegetical Handbook to the General Epistles of James, Peter, John, and Jude* (Meyer's *Commentary*). Translated by Paton J. Gloag, D. B. Croom, and Clarke H. Irwin. New York: Funk & Wagnals, 1887.

Lange, John Peter, *Commentary on the Holy Scriptures: Ephesians.* Translated by Philip Schaff. Grand Rapids: Zondervan.

———, *Commentary on the Holy Scriptures: Romans.* Translated by Philip Schaff. Grand Rapids: Zondervan.

Liddon, H. P., *Explanatory Analysis of St. Paul's Epistle to the Romans.* London: Longmans, Green, and Company, 1893.

Lightfoot, J. B., *Notes on the Epistles of St. Paul.* Grand Rapids: Zondervan.

Meyer, H. A. W., *Critical and Exegetical Handbook to the Acts of the Apostles.* Translated by Paton J. Gloag. New York: Funk & Wagnalls, 1886.

———, *Critical and Exegetical Handbook to the Epistles to the Corinthians.* Translated by D. Douglas Bannerman. New York: Funk & Wagnalls, 1884.

———, *Critical and Exegetical Handbook to the Epistle to the Romans.* Translated by John C. Moore and Edwin Johnson. New York: Funk & Wagnalls, 1884.

Mullins, Edgar Young, *The Christian Religion in Its Doctrinal Expression.* Philadelphia: The Judson Press, 1917.

Murray, John, *Redemption–Accomplished and Applied.* Grand Rapids: Eerdmans, 1955. Used by permission.

Robertson, A. T., *Word Pictures in the New Testament.* 6 vols. New York: Harper & Brothers, 1930.

Rotherham, Joseph Bryant, *The Emphasized New Testament.* Cincinnati: The Standard Publishing Company, 1897.

Shank, Robert, *Life in the Son: A Study of the Doctrine of Perseverance.* Springfield: Westcott Publishers, 1960.

Strong, Augustus H., *Systematic Theology.* Philadelphia: The Judson Press, 1907.

Thayer, Joseph Henry, *A Greek-English Lexicon of the New Testament.* Edinburgh: T. & T. Clark, 1901.

Thiessen, Henry C., *Introductory Lectures in Systematic Theology.* Grand Rapids: Eerdmans, 1949. Used by permission.

Tillich, Paul, *A History of Christian Thought.* New York: Harper & Row, Publishers, 1968.

Westcott, B. F., *The Gospel According to St. John.* London: John Murray, 1903.

_____, *Saint Paul's Epistle to the Ephesians: The Greek Text with Notes and Addenda.* Grand Rapids: Eerdmans, 1952.

INDEX

INDEX OF SCRIPTURE REFERENCES

NOTES

NOTES

NOTES

NOTES

NOTES

NOTES

NOTES

NOTES

NOTES

NOTES

NOTES

NOTES

NOTES

23719196R00144

Made in the USA
Middletown, DE
01 September 2015